# Democracy, Economics, and the Public Good

# Democracy, Economics, and the Public Good

## Informational Failures and Potential

John M. Budd

palgrave
macmillan

DEMOCRACY, ECONOMICS, AND THE PUBLIC GOOD



First published in 2015 by PALGRAVE MACMILLAN® in the United States—a division of St. Martin's Press LLC, 175 Fifth Avenue, New York, NY 10010.

Where this book is distributed in the UK, Europe and the rest of the world, this is by Palgrave Macmillan, a division of Macmillan Publishers Limited, registered in England, company number 785998, of Houndmills, Basingstoke, Hampshire RG21 6XS.

Palgrave Macmillan is the global academic imprint of the above companies and has companies and representatives throughout the world.

Palgrave® and Macmillan® are registered trademarks in the United States, the United Kingdom, Europe and other countries.

ISBN: 978-1-137-44815-6

Library of Congress Cataloging-in-Publication Data is available from the Library of Congress.

A catalogue record of the book is available from the British Library.

Design by Scribe Inc.

First edition: February 2015

10 9 8 7 6 5 4 3 2 1

Transferred to Digital Printing in 2015

# Contents

# Acknowledgments

I would like to express my thanks to Graham Higgs and Twyla Gibson for the many conversations on topics related to this book. Their wisdom has been invaluable to the composition of the work. Any errors are, of course, mine.

# Introduction

There wouldn't be a book here if I didn't believe (and didn't intend to demonstrate) that there are many reasons not only why people should be fully informed that these phenomena occur but also *how* and *why* they are important. The belief that business should be the model for government misses an essential point that will be discussed at some length in the pages to follow. I'll be making some assumptions that are definitely not intended to insult readers. The matters that inform the heart of the book are complex and are interconnected in sometimes mysterious ways. Democracy in the United States, for example, has been likened to (or even dependent upon) capitalism since before the Union was created. I should note the following: when the word "economy" is used throughout this work, it will signal the breadth of social, cultural, and political—as well as more general—economic phenomena. The three critical elements of the triad will be treated as ineluctably connected. The unified approach is not limited to the practical aspects and outcomes of daily life; it incorporates theory as well (understanding that some theorists also adopt a unified approach, even as others segregate the phenomena as though they have no impact on one another). The conceptualizations of the three key elements—important as they are—will be prolegomena to the more complete examination of how people in the United States are, and may be, informed about the essential matters that affect their political, cultural, intellectual, and economic lives and values. How we think and act must depend on what we *know*, not merely what we are told by some groups or individuals. Do these informing sources serve us well? Do they do us a disservice? As we will see, there is some of the former and a considerable amount of the latter. There are books available that complain about specific putative informing sources; this work is intended to be a thorough, critical analysis of the totality of what we face each day.

Who does not support fostering the public good? This is not a rhetorical question; it is meant to be taken seriously, and it provides something of a theme for this work. Perhaps no one would admit to being opposed to the public good, and almost no one would subvert the public good intentionally or openly. In fact, it may be that just about anyone asked would express a desire to work *for* the public good and would agree that the citizenry, the state, and the government should have the enhancement of the public good as a fundamental objective. Anyone against this objective would also oppose mom, apple pie, and puppies, right? But hold on a moment—what *is* the public good? Is it something that all people can agree on? Is it tangible, material, and manifest as some sort of welfare? Is "public" constitutive of all citizens (or vice versa)? Can we limit public to citizens, or should it include all residents? These are just some questions to be tackled en route to the informational examination to come. Moreover, the extent to which capitalism and democracy support or impinge upon the public good is an open question. A premise on which this book is based is that the three key elements—capitalism, democracy, and the public good—are inextricably connected at this time in US history. While the premise may not have held just a few decades ago (or, at the very least, it would have been manifest in different ways), politics, economics, and what people consider "good" have changed over time. Another matter that cannot be ignored is that many people claim that rights are the essential element rather than goods.

The premise may require some elaboration. It is not trivial to recognize that there are variant (perhaps widely variant) conceptions of the key elements. To build upon what was just said, as an exemplar of challenges faced, the public good is a contested idea. Since the public good may be thought of in different ways (and may even be rejected in favor of some other conceptions), the means by which it can be realized could also be conceived of in different ways. One can say the same about capitalism and democracy. It is in the differences that the informational aspect comes into play. The majority of what is presented here is not theoretical (although background theories of capitalism, democracy, and the public good will be presented briefly). The theoretical provides a framework, a situatedness, within which the three key elements can be examined. What *will* be covered in detail are the actions and statements of beliefs within the three realms. The central ideas of capitalism, democracy, and the public good will have to be inferred from the statements and claims and from the reports of actions that are taken. For instance, a sound bite from a candidate for political office may require interpretation for the development of a stance regarding the public good. The candidate's words may include claims about aspects of the economy and how they relate to democratic values. The relationship might be expressed in terms of rights, obligations, opportunities, or some other foundation. In addition to what is said, there will be an examination of the important matters of access to what is said (the context and locus of reportage, for example), analysis of statements and claims (for accuracy, as well as for meaning), inclusion of contexts for what is said, and (at times) exclusions from statements (which might be manifest as conflicts of interest).

There are assumptions that many in our society consider comfortable and safe. A purpose of this book is to call many of these assumptions into question. Is this radical? Yes. Will it be discomfiting to many readers? I hope so. That said, I would expect that some readers of the present book may also mischaracterize it as a polemic. Any serious analysis of political, social, economic, or discursive matters carry, of necessity, an accountability that requires eschewing neutrality in favor of a reasoned and principled theoretical and action-oriented stance. Critical adoption of a theory is an act of will and rationality. The examination of important social factors is thus bound by a responsibility to weigh merits of theories, the ethical implications of choices, and the intellectual defense of actions. In this way, I will attempt to follow Mary Midgely in making decisions grounded in moral obligation—not shying away from potentially calamitous crossroads. In fact, we now face a crossroads; the United States can continue to allow the deterioration of civil political discourse, or it can shun those who would befoul the polity with untruths, innuendoes, and misprisions.

Theory is a place to begin, but the reasoned choice of theory must be contextualized by clear and complete definitions of fundamental ideas. The title of this book presents several ideas that have been explicated and problematized in various ways for a number of years. The words themselves carry weight that sometimes forces discussions to waver and collapse. Democracy, for example, is generally accepted as an almost unequivocally desirable state. Its requirement for establishment, maintenance, and development is less frequently examined, except in certain instrumental ways. Facile adoption of words that are intended to stand in for ideas is never adequate. Far too often, and in too many potentially serious contexts, the words are reduced to slogans that may have little more than propagandistic value. Standing on a stage to tout democracy is not substantive. The sloganeering is officious and is an offense to people who need and desire meaning in their public and private lives. If ideas are complex (and important ideas are undoubtedly going to be complex), those who espouse the ideas owe it to people to define the ideas and to describe precisely how they are to be applied.

It would seem apparent to readers that the theoretical approach here is fundamentally political. There are numerous political approaches; a melding of a few will shape this inquiry. At the risk of turning off some readers, Marx will not be ignored. His diagnostic writings will especially feature here. It should be mentioned that Marx's work is suffused with ethical considerations. The informational responses with which this book will culminate will likewise have an ethical theoretical base. Political theories of democracy that include those of Robert Dahl, Michael Walzer, Michael Sandel, Carl Schmidt, Will Kymlika, Chantal Mouffe, Ernesto Laclau, Richard Posner, Ronald Dworkin, and several others will be investigated. The broad-ranging thinking of John Rawls, Jürgen Habermas, and so on is also useful. It would be foolish to hold obstinately to the thought of any single theorist; the aforementioned individuals have articulated varied, sometimes not entirely consistent, ideas over the courses of their careers. Elements of their work, however, can be informative. Additionally, original ideas of the discursive practices, relative to individual and collective action, will be presented.

I have set stringent criteria for myself. The conceptions of capitalism, democracy, and the public good—as well as information—must be explored in depth and with clarity (a seemingly gargantuan task for an academic). What will follow is an investigation of how these ideas have been conceived and used. Potentially contradictory statements about them, as well as counteractive practices, will be analyzed. It is well to mention here that people have intended many things by the uses of the words, including deliberately obfuscatory language designed to hide motives. The contradictions and counteractions are numerous and constitute a daunting but inescapable challenge. So it is necessary that a work of this sort be as accessible as possible to all readers; academics who come from many specializations may constitute a portion of the audience, but the larger target is the group of intelligent readers who seek an open and critical examination of some of the issues that challenge us today.

Ultimately, my purpose here is to study the putative informational structures that are employed to convey the discourse of the ideas. A starting point will have to be a definition of information, in the same way that capitalism, democracy, and the public good require definitions. The study will include discernible motivations, including variations in the content of the discourse. Existence of internal consistency will be sought, and ramifications of inconsistency will be examined. Variances may (indeed will) occur over time, location, and speaker. The variances carry importance for the genuine meaning of each idea. There is no beginning premise regarding capitalism, democracy, or the public good as a concept since there *will* be variance in discourses. According to this premise, for example, capitalism is not taken to be beneficial or corrupting a priori. Only theoretical and practical examination can yield a conclusion. So a determination is not possible without complete investigation into the words and actions that constitute a phenomenon like capitalism. Ideals of capitalism, democracy, and the public good will certainly be noted, though.

The first chapter of this book will address the theoretical matters concerning democracy. This chapter concentrates primarily on the political as a means to contextualize how Americans conceive of themselves and the government's relation to them. A question asked is this: How do people articulate the desired condition of the relationship? An answer to such a question is entwined in the roles of capitalism and the public good (along with the dialectic of the public good and rights). Some of the articulations are typified by statements from organizations, such as the Tea Party and Occupy movements. Others emanate from traditional party political sources. Still others come from individuals who attempt to offer notions of dissent against conventional discourse. Political campaigns present expressions of ideas that can be examined. One thing that must be addressed here is the imposed need for candidates today to communicate briefly. It is difficult for anyone to capture the electorate's attention and retain it for more than a few minutes at a time. Even in presidential debates, the candidates may be limited to ninety seconds per response. News outlets—conventional and alternative—frequently select even more compressed versions of the expressions of the candidates; there could be important context lost in the reporting.

Political speech is transformed today by several phenomena that range from Supreme Court decisions, such as that of *Citizens United v. Federal Election Commission*, and other factors, including "Super-PACs," and so on. More than ever before, money influences elections at just about all levels, even local ones. More money can result in more advertising—the impact of which tends to support the advertiser, especially the one who has more money. The matter of campaign financing might be made to seem simplistic, though, particularly as it is reflective of speech. The tools of capitalism are not separated from campaigning. An industry, even a particular company, is likely to support a candidate it believes will treat it favorably. What lies behind the confidence in favorable treatment may be complex and far-reaching. To what extent are the influences determining support reported? More to the point, how easy is it for inquisitive citizens to discover who (including what corporations or other entities) is supporting which candidates and to what extent? This question is not intended to connote a direct correspondence between sources of support and the stances of candidates. It does, on the other hand, point to a potential informational challenge faced by the diligent citizen. The money spent on a campaign is used to a considerable extent on delineating differences between candidates' positions on what is considered to be the good. Social and moral issues (or what may be presumed to be social and moral issues) are also exploited in politics and not just at election time. Sources of what is said, who says it, how it is said, how the speech is presented, and how accessible it is are topics for consideration.

The goal of this work is to alert readers to complex dynamic interrelationships among things that are said about capitalism, democracy, and the public good. Along with this is the goal of comparisons to actions—policy, economics, legislation, advocacy, and other actions—that affirm the discourse, confuse those who read and hear the discourse, or deliberately deceive. The dynamics of discourse and action are sufficiently complex that they require a *new* analysis. What is different about this work is the informational examination. There has been underlying failures on the parts of all informational outlets and agencies—failures of analysis, failures in reporting or transmitting, and failures of ethical responsibility. This is an admittedly damning accusation. The only possible solution to the dilemmas related to capitalism, democracy, and the public good is a reformed informational response to the dilemmas.

Chapter 2 will address economic issues more specifically. Building on theories of capitalism, the chapter will include an investigation of the workings of business, industry, and finance. Particular attention will be paid to the extensiveness of the reach of markets and the degree to which they are "free." The markets are connected to government, as the flow of regulation and deregulation over the past few decades demonstrates. The deregulation advocates frequently cite the possibility of greater market efficiency as a reason to accelerate the process. The definition of "efficiency" is elusive, though, as can be the identification of who benefits from certain efficiencies. Where, for instance, does efficiency enter when it comes to mundane things like gasoline prices? Some matters that impinge upon the three key elements discussed here clearly require explication. Rising levels of poverty in the United States have been reported, but public awareness of the magnitude of the problem is an open question. To what extent are people informed about these kinds of matters? Income, homelessness, hunger, and other related phenomena carry political and social implications. Voting rates, federal food and housing subsidies, and crime are just some things that people need to comprehend if they are to participate in a democratic society. Such issues are complex, and there are not likely to be simple, market-based solutions to them. Seemingly insurmountable difficulties extend to environmental considerations, provision of clean potable water in the future, and sustainable and safe food supplies. Ideological efforts—and the Tea Party and Occupy movements are two examples—may obfuscate more than clarify the nature of the challenges and possibility of solutions. Charitable giving is a more tenuously related issue, but it also is a largely separate thing from markets and governments and cannot be relied on to solve intractable problems.

The extension of capitalism into places where it was once foreign is a concern for those along the political spectrum. Again, some people may concentrate on efficiency and on the adjustment of markets to provide high-demand commodities by cost-beneficial means. One of the areas into which capitalism has entered is research. At a point in the past, many companies supported large in-house research and development operations. Many of the largest companies continue to maintain these kinds of operations, but others find it more efficient to finance research on university campuses. The US federal government is still the largest funder of research, but industry financing is growing. In itself, there is nothing to cause concern when corporations fund research endeavors in higher education. On the other hand, if a company stands to gain most when research results are favorable to the product, the possibility of intrusion into the conduct of inquiry and the reporting of findings grows. When the research deals with such things as the food supply or pharmaceuticals, the stakes are immediately raised. The issue at hand becomes one of control, which is related to the safety and welfare of the populace. Companies may exert control over the publication of the research findings, creating a serious informational gap. In the extreme, there could be ignorance regarding the efficacy of a drug, even as it makes its way onto the market. Research into vital matters of health, food, and other matters aside, there is the possibility for faculty at colleges and universities to influence public policy. To offer just one example, a number of professors of economics and business have sat, and continue to sit, on corporate boards. The boards of directors of many financial institutions include academics. There need not be conflicts of interest, but the potential exists. Whether or not there is conflict may not be apparent; public awareness of the behavior of the academics could lead to skeptical responses to their proclamations *as* academics.

Chapter 3 will bring the public good explicitly to the fore. It is present throughout the book, but it receives special attention here. At the heart of the discussion at this point will be a detailed examination of the distinction between good and rights. All the foregoing analysis and argument will have to be boiled down to the manifestation of the public good within a political and economic system. The word "system" is used here both deliberately and pragmatically. (The pragmatism spoken of here refers to the earlier stages of American pragmatism rather than latter-day neopragmatism and its antirealist bent.) Since democracy, capitalism, and the public good are inextricably related in contemporary American society (at least rhetorically), there is a tacit notion that the elements operate in some synchronic, if not cooperative, manner. The extent to which there is systemic operation is a matter for informational investigation. In particular, meaning must be sought in what is said and written and in what might be missing from common reportage. Questions are raised by any idea of systemic operation, however. Do democracy and capitalism effect the public good (i.e., does their very existence contribute to, lead to, the public good)? Are there obligations on the parts of democracy and capitalism to enhance the public good? If democracy and capitalism are material entities, is the public good likewise material? Can one gauge the success or effectiveness of democracy and capitalism, in part, by measures of public good? An analysis of the state of politics and economics today could, contrary to the systemic view, reveal that the public good is, at present, in a diminished state. A result of the analysis could be the conclusion that the present forms of democracy and capitalism are antithetical to the development of the public good. Even a less extreme conclusion may be that the present forms do little to support the public good.

Chapter 4 will undertake the informational analysis (detailing the failures of communication media to present a rich and complete body of information that can be subjected to interpretation) but also will propose ways to create a vital informational environment. The facile axiom that applied democratic practice relies on an informed citizenry is put to the test throughout the book. This analysis does not necessarily imply that the political and economic action of the recent past and the present is a consequence of the existing informational practices. The interrelations of capitalism, democracy, and the public good are far too dynamic to suggest a simplistic set of causal links. As was hinted at earlier, the examination presented in this book could result in the identification of an exceedingly complex dialectic. If this is the case, the current informational environment cannot possibly eliminate the dialectic; it must be designed to revise the dialectic. The investigation, and its results, is most likely to demonstrate that the assumptions that have defined political, economic, and social behavior over the last several decades should no longer hold.

The last chapter prescribes a new way of operation for a new way of informing the people, of giving shape to the polis. What is proposed is both a revised ethos for informing—by those in the popular media, people engaged in virtual communication (including blogs and the like) and formal institutions such as libraries—and an altered sense of purpose. That purpose concentrates on accuracy, meaning, and truth. I hasten to add that "truth," as is the case with knowledge, is fallible and corrigible. People can make errors, but it is incumbent on everyone to acknowledge and seek to correct errors when they are made. The ultimate intended end is a public that can more genuinely be *informed*. The thought—and action (in keeping with Marx's dictum)—of people should be given shape by accurate, meaningful, and truthful information. The proposal should help achieve this end and should help foster a much greater degree of trust in informing practices, whatever and wherever they may be.

# 1

# Democracy

## Ideals and Practicalities

Of course, scholars and commentators have thought seriously about what democracy should be, how capitalism should work *effectively* as well as efficiently, and what constitutes its relationship to the public good. Some who might call themselves realists have sought to explain how beneficial compromise might be achieved so that the ideals do not have to be entirely forsaken, but the conceits of the world may not upset the intentions too much. What, in the United States in which we live, is democracy? People frequently refer to the US Constitution as the hallmark of democracy, but if the Constitution is the sine qua non of our democratic state, why are there thousands of statutes at all governance levels? Why are there countless lawsuits, many of which challenge laws and even the constitutionality of people's actions? The Constitution and the existing laws actually do not provide *answers* in the sense of dispute-ending final words. Many lengthy books have been written about these questions; this brief chapter cannot even summarize all the opinions and scholarship. What will be presented is a selection of some influential—even controversial—operational ideas about the central topics of this book, beginning with democracy, so that we can examine the efficacy of informing forces of media and other entities. In short, democracy, capitalism, and the public good are so complex and are in such dispute (and are each subject to ideology) that the provision of informing substance to people is problematic in the extreme while simultaneously being among the most vitally important to the future of the body politic.

To the disappointment of some (and I hope to disappoint, as well as to meet the approval of individuals), I will say now that the hopes and aspirations for the human goals advocated here must avoid a trap—institutional fetishism. There is no single institution, not even a set of institutions, that can (by virtue of their existence) be the salvation of hopes and dreams of American citizens. On the contrary, too often the institutions themselves are the seats of frustration and oppression. This notion has its origins in Marx's critique of commodity fetishism. In capitalist societies, including (perhaps especially) democratic ones, commodities become a central focus of the entire economy. In actuality, pertaining to commodities, as Marx (1976) points out, "The product becomes increasingly one-sided and *massive in nature . . . The commodity* is a transfiguration of capital that has valorized itself, and its sale must now be organized on the scale and in the *quantities* necessary to realize the old capital value and the old surplus-value it has created" (pp. 953, 954). Moreover, though, Georg Lukács (1971) built on Marx's commodity fetishism to extend the point to a result of the reification of humanity and society:

> The commodity can only be understood in its undistorted essence when it becomes the universal category of society as a whole. Only in this context does the reification produced by commodity relations assume decisive importance both for the objective evolution of society and for the stance adopted by men towards it. Only then does the commodity become crucial for the subjugation of men's consciousness to the form in which this reification finds expression and for their attempts to comprehend the process or to rebel against the disastrous effects and liberate themselves from servitude to the "second nature" so created. (p. 86)

The words of Marx and Lukács set the tone for this chapter and then next.

It is possible—no, it is probable—that some readers will wish that some particular sources would have been used here. Also, some readers may well wish that some sources would have been omitted. The selection of background works is undertaken in attempts to demonstrate the most influential scholarship and popular work. Occasionally, controversial, even prejudiced, works will be mentioned to demonstrate the breadth of writing and thought that exist. In all cases, the sources will be subject to a critical eye. There will be times when departures from the ideals will generate anger and frustration, in me as well as in readers. The excitement of response is deliberate—otherwise, the premise of failings of informing entities would be false and empty. In many instances, it will be the eschewing of the ideals that will generate the anger, especially when the neglect of the ideals rests at the feet of the people and bodies that should be speaking out. Now some detail is required to provide the background for analysis.

## Liberty

Democracy, perhaps especially American democracy, sees itself as the cradle of liberty. That, of course, is primarily a rhetorical claim; as such, it requires examination on several fronts. The first issue to investigate is the definition and practice of "liberty." Momentarily, we will study classical liberalism; here we take a more grand and general look at liberty. First of all, there is a challenge awaiting that relates to setting the parameters of a discussion of liberty. While one might extend the limits and talk about liberty as it may apply to the areas of life that include leisure, venal acquisition of goods and property, and so on, the discourse here will concentrate on the broad political that affects everyone's lives in some way. The US Constitution, as well as many political theorists, couches some expressions of liberty in the syntax of "freedom from" as well as "freedom to" or "freedom for." The First Amendment articulates some freedom from interference or freedom from obstruction. An example is that Congress shall pass no laws abridging freedom of religious practice, speech, the press, assembly, or redress of grievances. In a similar form, the Fourteenth Amendment prohibits restricting citizens' pursuit of life, liberty, and property without due process of law. Some commentators are of the opinion that the Fourteenth is the most important amendment at this time in the nation's history. There may be a more important and necessary distinction to be made between negative and positive liberty. Putterman (2006) suggests that the foundation of negative freedom is power, while the foundation of positive freedom is moral. There is merit in his claim; the difference will be upheld here.

The foregoing examples focus primarily on public action, and legal actions have tended to address claims of restriction or abridgments of the rights. While there is not sufficient time and space here to provide evidence of the tendency, there are resources that provide cases dealing with elements of free speech or expression. It must be added that there are also works by scholars who believe that there *should* be restrictions on some speech, including hate speech, that is intended to do palpable harm to individuals or groups (see, for example, Waldron, 2012). The point to be taken away here is that, even with a text as authoritative as the US Constitution, there will be interpretations—and variant interpretations at that. Liberty is bound to be an object of conflict and tension and probably always will be so. When one accounts for the many, many federal and state laws, the tension is of a high magnitude. Another realization is necessary here. While "liberty" and "freedom" are oftentimes equated, we should follow Dworkin's (2006) admonition that "liberty is not just freedom. No one has the right to live precisely as he wishes; no one has a right to a life dedicated to violence, theft, cruelty, or murder" (p. 69). The laws that exist attempt, for the most part, to minimize the harms that people can do—or at least to punish those who would perpetrate the harms.

Claims by learned people illustrate the enormity and the nature of the tension. Berlin (2002) speaks to the difficulty of the matter:

> The assumption that men need protection against each other and against the government is something which has never been fully accepted in any part of the world, and what I have called the ancient Greek or classical point of view comes back in the form of arguments such as this: "You say that an individual has the right to choose the kind of life he prefers. But does that apply to everyone? If the individual is ignorant, immature, uneducated, mentally crippled, denied adequate opportunities of health and development, he will not know how to choose." (p. 284)

These kinds of concerns have not gone away; people ponder them seriously at all times in history. Any astute reader will recognize immediately that the issue is not simply the capacities of individuals but *who makes determinations about those capacities*. Not one of the detriments to judgment that Berlin mentions has one single objective measure that can assure the citizenry of just application for the benefit of the body politic. This is not merely a question for science; it is a matter of deliberation for all people. Moreover, the decision processes rely on informational structures that can—literally—give shape to thoughts, arguments, and decisions. At the present time (and, it can be safely said, at no time in human history), we lack the informational apparatus that would justify abridging liberty and freedom, *and participation*, in political discourse and its outcomes.

There are some commentators who offer responses to concerns raised by Berlin's ideas. For example, Lukacs (2005) suggests, "Freedom means the capacity to know something about oneself, and the consequent practice or at least the desire to live according to limits imposed on oneself rather than by external powers" (p. 222). Self-knowledge is an extreme challenge for every human being. It requires not only maturity but also wisdom to set limits for oneself. Where would this knowledge come from? Is it to be entirely of internal discovery, or can there be external sources that can be absorbed? These cannot be unanswerable questions, or Lukacs's goal will never be realized. In actuality, we learn about ourselves, to a great extent, by living *with* others (the *with* in this sentence is intended to be significantly richer than simple living *among* others). Our awareness and acumen must reach levels that enable each of us to discern the right and the true. The good life—if we can so refer to this—presumes more than living; it necessarily requires living *for ourselves and others*. Lukacs is cognizant of the added complexity; he speaks of the meaning of life as well as the means according to which we should live. Further, Lukacs aptly marks the distinction between patriotism (the love of one's land and traditions) and nationalism (the selfish love of a political ideology): "Nationalism is both self-centered and selfish—because human love is not the love of oneself; it is the lover of *another*" (emphasis in original; p. 73). That may be the most important lesson to take away.

Berlin may be making a point for discussion; it is not necessarily his belief. Raz (1986) makes his own stance explicit: "Cannot one simply state that freedom is intrinsically valuable? I will call this the simple principle. If it is valid then it follows that there is a reason against every restriction of freedom. Hence every political act restricting anyone's freedom requires a justification which overcomes that reason against such acts" (pp. 12–13). It must be remembered that neither Berlin nor Raz (two eminent theorists on liberty) are stating positions that are based on human action aimed at producing good for the individual in question and also producing no harm for any other individual. Thus a person investing wisely in the stock market and building his or her wealth is not harming anyone else, primarily because any other individual could engage in like behavior and realize personal benefit. On the other hand, if the first individual had inside information about a company, then that person could benefit by harm done to others who lack that knowledge. Informational action always carries ethical import and responsibility; that maxim cannot be either understated or forgotten.

As might be expected, politicians have also written on liberty. Recently, US presidential candidate Ron Paul wrote a book titled *Liberty Defined* (2011). His point of view may be evident from the dedication—to Ludwig von Mises and F. A. Hayek, among others. Paul has categorized himself as a libertarian (libertarianism will be discussed in the section following "Liberalism"). In the introduction to his book, Paul (2011) writes, "Liberty means to exercise human rights in any manner a person chooses so long as it does not interfere with the exercise of the rights of others. *This means, above all else, keeping government out of our lives*" (emphasis added; p. xi). In the book, Paul lists fifty issues and takes stances on each one of them. For example, he argues against abortion but also against bipartisanship. Reception of the book has varied; Akers (2011) writes, "Ron Paul's latest book, *Liberty Defined*, is a gem of political wisdom. It covers topics deeply enough to interest political wonks, yet so clearly that the novice can enjoy it" (p. 33). On the other hand, Doherty (2011) says, "But while *Liberty Defined* has a leftish tinge, Paul is not afraid to send the typical liberal reader screaming for the exits by expressing skepticism about global warming, advocating the Second Amendment as a defense against tyranny, and insisting that there is no right to medical care. Paul believes a free market produces so much wealth that we need not choose between freedom and the amelioration of poverty. But he says he would be for freedom anyway" (p. 85).

Ron Paul is not a political philosopher, so it should not be a surprise that his positions on the various topics lack absolute clarity and consistency. That said, it could be telling that politicians lack the clarity and consistency that the country and the world require for genuine contributions to the public good. Also, while Paul's book is something of a polemic, it has received little attention in the mainstream press, even though it became a bestseller. Here is someone who ran a serious campaign for the presidency, but there is precious little to inform people about what the candidate himself has to say about his beliefs (unless a person reads Paul's own words). People who would be inclined to learn more about Paul could be interested in discovering that he thinks all schooling should be in the hands of local school boards so as to avoid the potential tyranny of federal requirements (pp. 78–82). He does *not* consider that the localization of schooling does not equal liberty. In fact, it could result in localized repression—repression that leads to illiberal and partisan education for a great number of America's young people. Yes, people could read his book, but his opinions could also be fodder for reportage on a large scale. In fact, given that he was a presidential aspirant, there *should* have been serious, and informing, reportage.

By no means does everyone agree with Paul—or with libertarianism more generally. Walzer (2004), for one, believes that there is reason to think that government is efficacious in promoting liberty and in helping people realize freedom: "Civil society cannot become a home for either freedom or pluralism without state action" (Walzer, 2004, p. 73). The concept of pluralism is now introduced, but what does it mean? In short, pluralism is the case for an open forum for all voices and freedom for people from all walks of life. People of all political and ideological stripes ought to have the freedom to express their opinions and beliefs, even if (especially if?) the majority disagrees with them. The sources of difference may include racial, gender, ethnic, age, geographic, socioeconomic, cultural, religious, linguistic, and associational elements as well as politics. Most frequently, the differences embody complex combinations of factors. A poor, working, white, lesser-educated male from, say, Appalachia will have little in common with a well-to-do, highly educated, white-collar Latina from California. Nonetheless, the pluralism Walzer (2004) speaks of is problematic in today's United States. He expresses the challenge, "Especially in traditionalist religious and ethnic communities, the freedom and mobility of subordinate members, women most importantly, are radically curtailed. The state could act on behalf of these subordinate members, but most of the time it supports the dominant elites. When that happens, civil society is not the realm of freedom" (p. 75).

## Justice

To return to democracy more directly, if we actually want to begin with a question for the definition, we might turn to John Rawls first. One reason to start with him is his overwhelming influence on the topic. That is certainly not to say that everyone agrees with him; in fact, about as many people disagree with him as agree with him. He does, though, articulate one framework for democratic action and behavior to which people can react. In a nutshell, his program is an effort to discover the most efficacious source of justice for everyone. Continuing to reduce his program, justice is whatever results in the greatest degree of fairness for everyone. Of course, these are oversimplifications, but his principles do hold closely to these points. He (1999) begins by stating, "Justice is the first virtue of social institutions, as truth is of systems of thought" (p. 3). Justice, while both a first principle and a primary objective, is a social phenomenon that can be present or absent in law, contracts, institutional behavior, and just about all human settings. In particular, Rawls concerns himself with what is required to create a just and fair society in which no one, and no group, is privileged by law; that is, he desires that all in society are treated fairly. A primary means by which fairness occurs is the application of what Rawls (1999) calls the "veil of ignorance" (pp. 118–23). The application of this principle requires that the social position—including wealth, social status, employment, and so on—of any person is unknown. Behind that veil, everyone can be treated equally, since each individual should presume that it is he or she behind the veil *as well as* that it is he or she *not* behind the veil. If these presumptions obtain, fairness should be the outcome.

One concept runs throughout Rawls's work: The state should be neutral regarding the definition and determination of the good life. One might consider this something of a libertarian ideal, but it is not. While Rawls is not explicit about describing what constitutes the good life, he does expound upon that manner by which individuals decide the constitution of the good life for themselves. That decision process includes the means by which people impose the burden of fairness upon everyone as an essential component of the process. Joseph Raz (1986) presents an explication of Rawls's stance: "Since in the original position no one knows his own moral ideals, his own conception of the good, Rawls concludes that no perfectionist standards will be adopted in it" (p. 124). The importance of Raz's statement to the thesis of the present book cannot be overstated.

While we will not review the entirety of thought on democracy here, we must note that Rawls's is not the last word on liberty, justice, or good. For Gutmann and Thompson (2004), deliberation is essential; in their conception, the citizenry is not merely some mass of objects to be governed. Individuals are to be able to act as agents with voices that can be heard; the processes and products of governance are to be reasoned and accessible to people; there is a binding element to deliberation so that the product is not an amalgamation of empty words; and the process is dynamic (i.e., it is not seasonal or occasional; pp. 3–6). Is their conception difficult to achieve? Decidedly! A reason for the difficulty is, perhaps, inherent in the politics of the West (and maybe everywhere). Individuals in power—the representatives elected by the people—seek to hold their power dear. Transparency could be deemed a threat to power; any misstep by politicians could be used to unseat them. The nature of political speech is such that incivility is all too often the prevalent form of discursive practice. Furthermore, governance in many Western countries (certainly the United States) also includes unelected officials who wield substantial power. The extent to which they are answerable to the people varies, and the benefit of their independence is an open question. Some may say that the absence of election allows the officials to avoid being beholden to special interest groups and donors. That actuality does not eliminate outside influence, however.

The very idea of deliberation signifies a group effort. Each individual should have a mind open to reasonable argument and should not dig in his or her heels on the basis of indignant or oppressive stubbornness. Deliberation, as does Rawls's idea of justice, necessitates an acceptance of the equality of all citizens and must be open, to some extent, to his "veil of ignorance." In straightforward terms, deliberation requires listening as well as speaking (in fact, the former might well be superior to the latter). Gutmann and Thompson (2004) add to principles that are also necessary for deliberative democracy: "The principle of publicity requires that reason-giving be public in order that it be mutually justifiable. The principle of accountability specifies that officials who make decisions on behalf of other people, whether or not they are electoral constituents, should be accountable to those people" (p. 135). Both principles are extremely important; in fact, democracy is all but impossible without the presence of both. They must also be taken very seriously—it may be a simple matter to fake them. Empty speech, for example, may be assumed by the speakers to be adhering to the principle of publicity. A central message of this book is that, without checking, without verifying claims, the publicity principle is empty and meaningless. The discussion on informing and becoming informed (in a later chapter) will make this assertion clear. The foregoing image of deliberation articulated by Gutmann and Thompson is undeniably an ideal. To bring us back to reality, Shapiro (2003) reminds us that "it is doubtful, first, that government can ever really insist that people deliberate. Government can try to structure things so as to make deliberation more or less likely, but ultimately deliberation depends on individual commitment . . . Second, my suggestion is that by strengthening the hand of the weaker party in the types of circumstance discussed, government can increase the likelihood that insiders will deploy their wisdom to search for the deliberative solutions that may be waiting to be discovered" (p. 49).

The ideal of Gutmann's and Thompson's is not very different in kind from Habermas's discourse ethics. Habermas (1994) expresses his ideal succinctly: "Anyone who seriously engages in argumentation must presuppose that the context of discussion guarantees in principle freedom of access, equal rights to participate, truthfulness on the part of participants, absence of coercion in adopting positions, and so on" (p. 31). While straightforwardly stated, these ideals are fragile and all too easily corrupted. As we have seen with applications of ideology to language, minorities may well be prevented from having a voice. Truthfulness, additionally, is not something one can take for granted, but what are the consequences for breaches of this ideal? If there is no corrective—no demonstration of falsehood, fabrication, or equivocation—with what is the population left? More to the point, who has the responsibility to call attention to falsehood? Individuals who recognize it ought to call it out; that is a function of discourse ethics. Further, falsehood should be reported as widely as is the original statement. If the president of the United States lies and if the lie can be found out and the truth located, then there must be a record of the recognition—and communication—of the lie and its contrary, truth. The failure to so record the truth is an informational failure. It is failure insofar as a false shape is given to what is said, and that false shape is *intended* to be adopted and believed by people.

Deliberation (in and of itself as a positive quality) or discourse ethics (as an ideal process for deliberation) depend on some key features for them to work. First, citizens must contemplate the issues at hand earnestly and with resistance to ideological intrusion. Second, the people must converse in a civil manner so as to be able to weigh strengths and weaknesses of evidence and arguments. Third, citizens must be informed; they not only must have access to informing acts and objects but also must avail themselves of those opportunities. These are, without question, burdens that are weighty upon people who would wish to be able to deliberate on political issues. A primary responsibility in this system, ideal though it may be, is to become fully informed and to have sound opinions on the matters that are of political importance. Geuss (2010) points out a challenge, though: "Forming and holding opinions and engaging in discussion of those opinions are, of course, important parts of human life, but (a) opinion formation and discussion are not all there is to politics, and (b) even the formation and evaluation of opinions is comprehensible only in one or another of a number of different wider historical and institutional contexts" (p. 3). What is then needed is action, and taking action involves much more than tacit contemplation.

How do we take action, and what action is to be taken? We have seen the Rawlsian and deliberative responses to the questions, but there are other possibilities. Sen (2009) suggests that asking what is required for a just society is not an efficacious beginning; he posits some particular considerations as a starting point:

1. dealing with comparative assessment and not merely identifying a transcendental solution;
2. taking note of social realizations and not only the demands of institutions and rules;
3. all incompleteness in social assessment, but still providing guidance in important problems of social justice, including the urgency of removing manifest cases of injustice; and
4. taking note of voices beyond the membership of the contractarian group, either to take note of their interests, or to avoid being trapped in local parochialism. (p. 70)

As is evident, Sen's fundamental approach is unique. Institutions do not hold primacy; it is not the existence of a group of a collective that necessitates justice or just action. Further, reaching a contract among participants is not optimal since the agreement may well be founded upon limited features and responsibilities (and other responsibilities might be excluded).

The actions related to justice, particularly when it comes to rights and duties, have a strong moral component (see Sandel, 2009). In fact, Sandel (2009) is able to derive specific categories to which we should pay close attention:

**Three Categories of Moral Responsibility**

1. Natural duties: universal; don't require consent
2. Voluntary obligations: particular; require consent
3. Obligations of solidarity: particular; don't require consent (p. 225)

It is obvious that the categories are social. Our rights and duties involve others; we are not alone in our decisions or actions. As Sandel (2009) wisely says, "With belonging comes responsibility" (p. 235). When it comes to justice as a practical matter, there are some merits and demerits to various positions. While utilitarianism is held to be efficacious by many, Sandel (2009)—again, wisely—notes some shortcomings: "The utilitarian approach has two defects: First, it makes justice and rights a matter of calculation, not principle. Second, by trying to translate all human goods into a single, uniform measure of value, it flattens them, and takes no account of the qualitative differences among them" (p. 260). The social imperative of justice (along with rights and duties) once more comes to the fore.

Michael Walzer (1983) raises some concerns that are somewhat similar to those of Sen. When it comes to certain capabilities (do note that this is not the same as *abilities*), there are citizens who are disadvantaged by poverty. Those in the middle and upper classes have resources that the poor may never have. An individual may have musical or artistic talent, for example, but the parents of the person might not have the wherewithal to help the individual develop those talents and to sell those talents as products in a marketplace. Similarly, a young person could have the makings of becoming a proficient manager. If that person is not able to attend college (perhaps even the *right* college), he or she may not have an opportunity to become a manager. That person may not have the opportunity even if he or she excels in, say, sales in an organization. A requirement for a managerial position could be a bachelor's degree, so he or she is out of luck. Given these shortcomings of a realizable world, Walzer (1983) defends a position: "Every political community must attend to the needs of its members as they collectively understand those needs; that the goods that are distributed must be distributed in proportion to need; and that the distribution must recognize and uphold the underlying equality of membership" (p. 84). The key word in his statement is "equality." If each citizen is a member of society, then there is some obligation on the part of society to meet each person's legitimate needs (such as life, liberty, and the pursuit of happiness). Failing the provision for needs, the society does not achieve justice, and some members of society are denied equality.

Walzer (1983) adds some specific points about justice and the distribution of goods that should be mentioned here (his words apply not only here but also to the discussion of economics and finance):

1. All the goods with which distributive justice is concerned are social goods. They are not and cannot be idiosyncratically valued.
2. Men and women take on concrete identities because of the way they conceive and create, and then possess and employ social goods.
3. There is no single set of primary or basic goods conceivable across all moral and material worlds—or, any such set would have to be conceived so abstract that they would be of little use in thinking about particular distributions.
4. But it is the meaning of goods that determines their movement.

5. Social meanings are historical in character; and so distributions, and just and unjust distributions, change over time. (pp. 7–9)

Not everyone agrees with Walzer (although I do), so there must be some attitudes toward justice that are submerged within other political conceptualizations.

## Liberalism

It might be expected that this chapter would begin with a treatment of liberty, but liberalism both underlies and is antagonistic to the ideas that many people hold of democracy. So (as was mentioned earlier) let us begin with the tradition that could be called "classical liberalism." This is a starting point because the history of liberalism would probably surprise a great many Americans. To understand the classical variety, we will have to travel back as far as Thomas Hobbes, but certainly we would have to pay very close attention to John Locke, Adam Smith, Thomas Malthus, James Mill, and (perhaps especially) John Stuart Mill. A few typicalities can define classical liberalism—civil liberty, political freedom, property rights, limited government, and a free market. We begin here because the labels "liberal" and "conservative" are now what in semiotics should be called empty (or floating) signifiers. The meanings (if one can even say that the words have meaning at all) of the two labels are highly variable and individualized. Depending on who is using the words, they may be spoken of with pride or may be used as invectives. In other words, they stand for all that is good and/or all that is wrong with politics, morals, and so on but signify little of consequence.

It may be that the most recognizable voice of political liberalism is, once again, John Rawls's. In his lectures on the subject, he asks two "fundamental" questions: "What is the most appropriate conception of justice for specifying the fair terms of social cooperation between citizens regarded as free and equal, and as fully cooperating members of society over a complete life, from one generation to the next? . . . What are the grounds of toleration so understood and given the fact that of reasonable pluralism as the inevitable outcome of free institutions?" (pp. 3, 4). With these seemingly simple questions, Rawls establishes a ground for the essential character of liberalism, with the social at the heart of all thought and action. People are to be not merely allowed but facilitated in the process and actions of exploring what constitutes a good life. The good life is not just freedom from want but also freedom *to* explore and realize what can make a person happy. Moreover, the freedom is such that it does not end with the life of one person but accumulates and is a consequent of family; the material and nonmaterial elements of freedom continue on past the life of an individual. Toleration within a pluralistic environment is also an institutional hallmark.

An institution that may leap to mind initially is the legal system. "Justice for all" is supposed to be ensured for citizens regardless of foundational beliefs and disagreement with institutional powers (within reason). That initial response is definitely correct; the legal system is supposed to be sensitive to the pluralism that is historically valued (at least rhetorically) in the United States. Let me suggest another institution where tolerance and pluralism are mainstays—the public library. At its optimal functioning, public libraries are open to everyone, are in favor of free speech and association by means of standing policy, and provide access to the broadest and most complete variety of ideas and opinions possible. If, as we shall shortly see, libraries adhere to Mill's conception of openness, the true and the false are to be present so that individuals will be able to weigh the merits of all propositions and arguments, deciding ultimately in favor of those ideas on the bases of their force and merit. It is time to suggest a difference between the library and the open discussions of the potentially contentious concerns in what amounts to public forums. In 2003, the US Supreme Court ruled that public libraries are *limited* public forums (not as open as streets, sidewalks, parks, and some other public spaces). Mill did not use the language, but he appeared to have the open public spaces in mind. As Gathegi (2005) says, the designated, or limited, character of libraries is a severely limiting feature. He (2005) writes, "Once created, designated public forums afford the same level of protection from regulation of speech as the public forums do. As in the public forums, valid time, place, and manner regulations are allowed. To be valid, however, the regulations must (1) be content neutral, (2) be designed to serve significant government interests, including public health and safety, and (3) leave ample alternative channels for expressive activity" (p. 7).

This is, however, Gathegi's own opinion and is not based in either statute or case law. In most instances, public libraries act precisely according to the previously stated guidelines. That said, there are restrictions against citizens simply speaking aloud in the public space of the library or the library becoming as open as a sidewalk with respect to unfettered speech. The principal reason is that the public library is a government-funded institution and, as such, is subject to the limitations of not merely the content of speech but the forms of expression that may disrupt other policy- and regulation-based action. Libraries may, however, have meeting rooms that are open to citizen groups for speech within the confines of the space. It is customarily held that the collections and access to information may be as open as possible, constrained only by laws prohibiting obscenity and selected other content (such as child pornography). Even that openness might be questioned, though, given that the space is not one of public debate and exchange of ideas so that people may choose based on the merits of the speech. Ideology, in the most severely pejorative sense, might sway readers who are not privy to alternative ideas.

There is, of course, dissent regarding liberalism. In the coming sections, alternative conceptions and ideologies will be examined. At the present time, one dissenting voice should be mentioned, primarily because this voice is both powerful and enduring. Approximately two centuries ago, Hegel was investigating classical liberalism and adopted a skeptical attitude, especially of a rights-based construction. A challenge, as Hegel envisioned it, was that modernity (and the Enlightenment) predated what would become a more or less orthodox liberalism in the nineteenth century. The modernity of the seventeenth century included the possibility of mastery over the natural world (at least as far as Descartes and Bacon might conceive it). The mastery could then be envisioned to extent to control over the social world by means of a systematic social structure in which the rights of individuals could be placed in an ascendant position. It should be remembered that even this notion had some Enlightenment origins, especially in the form of Locke's philosophy. Within the historical context, it would appear that Hegel and his dialectic is out of place. If Smith (1989) is correct, though, Hegel's place in liberalism should be recognized: "Hegel's emphasis on authority, order, sovereignty, and law have seemed to many to conceal a conservative, if not a reactionary, intent. If I am right, however, Hegel's chief accomplishment has been to show that the state and the community are not just a precondition for, but a dimension of, freedom" (p. 233).

For the time being, let us concentrate on the articulation of what classical liberalism stands for. Numerous books have been written on classical liberalism; for the present purposes, attention to Mill's *On Liberty* (2007 [1869]; quotations and paraphrases will be made to this edition) will provide an adequate setting from which the chapter can proceed. It is extremely vital to note that Mill's background includes a great amount of work in logic and in utilitarianism. While the work on liberty is largely independent, the influence of logic and (especially) utilitarianism is unmistakable. Throughout his treatise, Mill emphasizes that liberty is a social dynamic and is founded on the extent to which society or the state can impose or infringe on what the individual is able to do. The emphasis is so reasonable that just about all succeeding thinkers and writers about liberty share the foundation. In short, liberty is most decidedly *not* license; individuals cannot do anything they please. Mill, and all who followed him, struggled to strike a harmonious balance between freedom and authority; both were (and are) deemed necessary to the management of a civil society. One of the hallmarks of Mill's thesis is that "first, by obtaining a recognition of certain immunities, called political liberties or rights, which it was to be regarded as a breach of duty in the ruler to infringe, and which, if he did infringe, specific resistance or general rebellion was held to be justifiable" (p. 64). The requirement is a powerful one and holds the governing body strictly accountable.

There is a kind of simplicity to Mill's position: "That the only purpose for which power can be rightfully exercised over any member of a civilized community, against his will, is to prevent harm to others" (p. 70). The individual, other than the aforementioned restriction, is to be safe from the impositions of both the ruler (or state) *and* the majority—if the majority intends to exercise limitations on the individual's liberty. Simplicity is deceptive, though; the accomplishment of the goals of liberty requires structure that will be upheld strictly and uniformly. One of Mill's claims is that freedom of speech be strictly unabridged. It is by placing every idea and thought and expression into circulation that each free person can weigh alternative, even contradictory, stances and decide for himself or herself which is the most compelling proposition or argument. This is a position that many contemporary commentators disagree with. To mention just a couple of problematic instances, the matters of pornography and hate speech are disputed (sometimes quite heatedly) today. To side with Mill at this time, if certain types or subjects of speech are potentially abridged, is there a possibility—even a probability—that any other type or subject of speech could be challenged? That is to say, is there the possibility of a slippery slope that could endanger liberty?

A summation can be made by adding a rather lengthy passage from *On Liberty*. The four points add up to a synopsis of Mill's fundamental argument and suits the discussion here very well:

> First, if any opinion is compelled to silence, that opinion may, for aught we can certainly know, be true. To deny this is to assume our own infallibility.
>
> Secondly, though the silenced opinion be an error, it may, and very commonly does, contain a portion of truth; and since the general or prevailing opinion on any subject is rarely or never the whole truth, it is only by the collision of adverse opinions that the remainder of the truth has any chance of being supplied.
>
> Thirdly, even if the received opinion be not only true, but the whole truth; unless it is suffered to be, and actually is, vigorously and earnestly contested, it will, by most of those who receive it, be held in the manner of a prejudice, with little comprehension or feeling of its rational grounds. And not only this, but, fourthly, the meaning of the doctrine itself will be in danger of being lost, or enfeebled, and deprived of its vital effect on the character

> and conduct: the dogma becoming a mere formal profession, inefficacious for good, but cumbering the ground, and preventing the growth of any real and heartfelt conviction, from reason or personal experience. (pp. 108–9)

It appears appropriate to conclude the matter of Mill and classical liberalism with Skorupski's (2006) assessment "that the utility [of Mill's] must be utility 'in the largest sense, grounded on the permanent interests of man as a progressive being' . . . Yet [Mill] also thinks that societies in which universal free self-culture becomes truly possible comes about only through a long historical development" (p. 25).

Liberalism is, of course, more varied (and inconsistent) today, and, of course, there are many interpretations of (and prescriptions for) what liberalism should be today. One major theorist, Kymlicka (1989), addresses what he believes to be essential characteristics of liberalism: "Individuals must therefore have the resources and liberties needed to live their lives in accordance with their beliefs about value, without being imprisoned or penalized for unorthodox religious or sexual practices, etc. . . . And individuals must have the cultural conditions conducive to acquiring an awareness of different views about the good life, and to acquiring an ability to intelligently examine and re-examine these views" (p. 13).

In keeping with classical liberalism, at least according to some of Mill's views, difference is to be accepted as a premise with which to begin. In keeping with most ideas of liberty, difference is to be accommodated as long as it holds the potential for individual good while not presenting harm to others. That difference is not the end of liberalism, though. Hobhouse (1964), commenting on Mill, says, "The Liberal does not meet opinions which he conceives to be false with toleration . . . He meets them with justice . . . Let error have free play, and one of two things will happen. Either as it develops, as its implications and consequences become clear, some elements of truth will appear within it . . . Or, in the alternative, no element of truth will appear" (p. 63).

There are other conceptions of liberalism (not surprisingly) that compose a complex critique of what is frequently an entangled political state of being. If we begin with the premise that no political stance is pure, we can, perhaps, more readily grasp the challenges presented by liberalism. In some conceits, liberalism is explicitly and ineluctably connected to material prosperity; liberalism as a system is not possible in the absence of, say, capitalism (see, for example, von Mises, 2005). Geuss (2001) expresses some of the conundrums that arise:

> First of all, liberalism is committed to some version of a principle of toleration, that is to the view that absence of systematic persecution of

> non-violently deviant modes of living is one of the cardinal virtues of a human society, and especially of the political order of society. A second complex of characteristically liberal views revolves around a certain conception of the nature and social role of freedom . . . The third feature is two headed: it emphasises on the one hand individualism and on the other hand autonomy, that is, it holds that the agents in the society should decide what they want to do as much as possible for themselves even if this goes against existing social expectations and patterns of thought, preference, and behaviour. (p. 73)

Beyond the individualism that Geuss speaks of, there is a collective responsibility that is manifestly evident in liberalism. The lessons of the past (including the recent past) enforce that responsibility. As Raskin (2004) says, "The crucial test for liberal democracies is to prove that they have the proper instruments to effect empathy, caring, and freedom for transforming social, political, and economic institutions" (p. 245). Can a democratic society have a foundation in individualism? Liberalism, for the most part, suggests that it not only can but also must. That is a claim worthy of further attention.

## Libertarianism

The first question to address is whether libertarianism is a genus unto itself or a species of liberalism. The quick and simple answer is that it is a genus, distinct from liberalism and conservatism. Libertarianism, over the last decades, has developed its own platforms and at least some degree of consistency in political positions. As is true of other labels, it is not easy to pin down precisely what a typical libertarian's beliefs are; there is a range, albeit constrained, of opinions, stances, and beliefs. It may be that the opinions of one professed libertarian emphasize fiscal matters and the need for all government bodies to reduce their spending to such matters as the protection of the populace and maintenance of an effective infrastructure. Another may stress social issues and state that laws such as those prohibiting same-sex marriage or consensual living arrangements between any adults are illegitimate. A keystone of libertarian ideology is placing limits on governments and their extension into the lives of citizens. This is frequently connected to particular ideas of civil rights; these rights are based in what is seen to be constitutional freedoms from governments' interference into people's activities. These hallmarks are, according to some commentators such as Boaz (1997), like the principal tenets of classical liberalism of the nineteenth century (although Boaz and others claim that those ideals of liberalism have atrophied throughout the twentieth century and beyond).

Boaz (1997) concludes his book with what may be a controversial idea: "One difference between libertarianism and socialism is that a socialist society can't tolerate groups of people practicing freedom, but a libertarian society can comfortably allow people to choose voluntary socialism" (p. 288). It may be that not all libertarians will agree with Boaz's distinction between libertarianism and socialism.

Some of the opinions of Ron Paul (2011) are mentioned previously, but his ideas extend to such matters as the Central Intelligence Agency (which he criticizes for having a failed intelligence record), global warming skepticism (in the face of overwhelming scientific evidence), and opposition to hate crime legislation. The last of the items is of particular note with respect to a libertarian point of view. A hallmark of the political ideology (not intended to be taken as pejorative) is freedom/liberty. The concept of freedom should include all people, and that means members of minority groups. Waldron (2012), who makes a forceful case in favor of special consideration for the commission of hate crimes, says that these kinds of crimes do not merely damage individuals (in the way that a crime directed against any individual diminishes the individual). Waldron argues that crimes against minorities (including heinous crimes like cross burnings at the homes of African American families or maiming or murdering people *just* because of their sexual orientation) have intensely deleterious effects for *all* members of those groups. One outcome is that a crime directed against someone from a minority group strikes fear into all members of the group simply *because they are members of the group*. Opposition to laws that are aimed to prevent such acts is morally and intellectually bankrupt, if for no other reason than that it is a betrayal of the very values one purportedly espouses.

At times, it may seem difficult to distinguish libertarianism from liberalism, but there are indeed distinctions to be made. Many of the distinctions are rooted in economics and so will be addressed in the next chapter. Suffice it to say at this point, freedom for libertarians has a decidedly property- and wealth-based character. Those elements are most favorably treated in a system that creates and allows the workings of unfettered markets in which justice is most likely to flourish. This fundamental conception is deeply flawed, but, again, the analysis will wait until the next chapter. For now, suffice it to refer to Tomasi (2012), who maintains, "Libertarians employ foundationalist or 'naturalistic' forms of argument. Their political recommendations can be grounded on a variety of bedrock ideas, including various conceptions of natural liberty. In its paradigmatic formulation, libertarianism is founded on an ideal of persons as *self-owners*" (emphasis in original; pp. 53–54). Perhaps the best example of a foundationalist approach to politics (especially libertarianism) is the writings of

Robert Nozick. He (1974) gets to the crux of the matter in one of his major works: "The fundamental question of political philosophy, one that precedes questions about how the state should be organized, is whether there should be any state at all . . . More to the point, especially for deciding what goals one should try to achieve, would be to focus upon a nonstate situation in which people generally satisfy moral constraints and generally act as they ought" (pp. 4, 5). His idea of utopia consists in a minimal state that can enable communities to offer people the wherewithal to succeed as individuals and within groups. In short, people are capable of exerting control within a structure and system of their own making, without the imposition of statist domination. Nozick is the philosophical voice of libertarianism, and he speaks through the employment of reason. It is through reason that his thought must be accepted or rejected.

A bone of contention with libertarian followers is taxation. The opinions range from elimination of all taxes to retention of those taxes that provide for national security and a safe infrastructure. In general, most libertarians are opposed to a welfare state and what is sometimes referred to as antipoverty legislation (see, for example, Miron, 2010, pp. 17–19). Sometimes the argument is a utilitarian one against such programs: "Whatever the ex-ante merits of anti-poverty programs, and however large their unintended consequences, anti-poverty programs have obviously not reduced poverty" (Miron, 2010, p. 19). There may be more specific issues related to poverty that capture the attention of libertarians. One of these issues is the minimum wage (state or federal). Miron (2010) speaks to this phenomenon as well: "Standard economics explains that a minimum wage reduces efficiency by artificially raising the price of low-skill labor. The only possible justification for a minimum wage, therefore, is to raise the income of low-wage workers" (p. 115). Minimum wage discussions only infrequently make news. Very recently, it arose in conjunction to a Washington, DC City Council vote on the Large Retailer Accountability Act of 2013, which would raise the minimum wage for workers at companies such Walmart to $12.50 an hour. Alex Barron, of Walmart, wrote, "From day one, we have said this legislation is arbitrary, discriminatory, and discourages investment in D.C. We have gone to great lengths to have thoughtful conversations with Council members about why LRAA will result in fewer jobs, higher prices and a smaller number of total retail options. It means most shopping dollars will stay in the suburbs, unemployment will remain in the double-digits in some neighborhoods and underserved communities will continue to have disproportionate access to affordable groceries" (Berfield, 2013). The threat of fewer jobs is an ideological one; evidence to suggest that companies would suffer if minimum wages were to rise is scant. The choice by companies, if applied as purely business decisions (with, perhaps, a public good conscience added), might be as successful in DC as anywhere.

Duncan and Machan (2005) argue that other mechanisms assist the poorest Americans more effectively than the minimum wage. They cite the federal Earned Income Tax Credit (EITC) as one tool that has lifted millions of people out of poverty (p. 114). A flaw in their argument is that the tax credit works optimally for people who have children; it is a bit less effective for single individuals and couples. Further, it places a burden on low-income people to make the best use of the credit by comprehending precisely how to file to receive it (or by paying someone to assist with tax filing). In either case, employers would be off the hook if it were not for a minimum wage. In fact, employers might pay *below* the minimum wage were it not for state and federal laws. Duncan and Machan, as well as others who discuss the matter, tend to concentrate on workers who are paid official minimum wages. Where those amounts tend not to apply, including the pay for foreign laborers (especially undocumented ones), the pay issue is considerably more complex, regardless of one's political leanings. Some who work in particular farm sectors may earn in the neighborhood of $300 a week, sometimes for more than 12 hours of work per day (Black, 2011). On the other hand, according to Plumer (2013), there is a shortage of workers for US farms (many of whom had been undocumented workers, but those numbers are shrinking). Plumer (2013) also observes that 23 percent of farm worker families live below the poverty level.

The preceding matters address only some libertarian positions (along with critiques). There is, of course, much more to libertarianism. Machan (2006) defines libertarianism as thus: "Libertarianism is to a considerable extent a theoretical extension of crucial concepts found in the American political tradition—e.g., liberty, consent, rights, equality, due process—so the position is not a radical challenge to the American tradition" (p. 103). Following Machan, libertarianism is not ideologically very different from liberalism. Not all will agree with Machan, though; some who lean toward conservatism claim that libertarians emphasize "freedom from" rather than "freedom to." Questions arise—such as *whose* right, *whose* liberty, and so on. Further, it is clearly apparent that libertarianism has concerns with the present economic state of the United States and the world; perhaps it is economics that draws many people to the idea and the political party. As will be demonstrated in the next chapter, libertarianism has a particular affinity for the Austrian economic tradition represented by Ludwig von Mises and Friedrich von Hayek.

## Conservatism

Conservatism has a long history, perhaps even longer than liberalism. Many colonial and early US individuals who were opposed to the Federalist movement were of a conservative bent. Rebelling against British rule did not necessarily signal a liberal ideology. It must be mentioned here as well that many people who identify themselves as conservatives would also claim to be on the center-right of the political spectrum. "Conservative" does not equal far right; it need not even equal "Republican." There are, however, some shared beliefs that identified conservatives have. One of those shared beliefs is that there should be a limited role for government. This marks a similarity with libertarians, but most conservatives would not limit government's duties and responsibilities to the extent that libertarians would. Many conservatives would not eliminate government's role in such matters as the economy and the regulation of some industries. In particular, the government has the duty to see to it that the people are not subject to excesses and that a moderate approach to regulating industries that affect public safety is wise.

The moderation model is, in fact, a part of the history of conservatism. Honderich (2005) asserts, "Conservatism has never been in favour of the alteration, involving unfamiliarity, that is *change*" (emphasis in original; p. 10). Honderich refers to Edmund Burke (1960) to bring home his point: "Change is novelty, and whether it is to operate any one of the effects of reformation at all, or whether it may not contradict the very principle upon which reformation is desired, cannot be certainly known beforehand" (p. 16). Burke—and Honderich—demonstrate skepticism with respect to radical change that, they say, will run the risk of tossing out any positive and worthwhile elements of a society. Revolution is to be viewed with such skepticism since the risk involved is that the good might be subsumed under the desire to change *everything*. The Russian Revolution of the early twentieth century could be viewed as such a dangerous change mechanism. A further caution is that while many may express the desire for (and may fight for) revolution, they may regret the magnitude of change at the end of the day. Whether this concern is a signifying reality of conservatism is an open question, though. In a vein similar to Honderich's perspective, Sullivan (2006) avers, "While not denying that the truth exists, the conservative is content to say merely that his grasp on it is always provisional. He may be wrong. He begins with an assumption that the human mind is fallible, that it can delude itself, make mistakes, or see only so far ahead" (p. 173). Again, it is not entirely clear how these qualities distinguish conservatives from those whose beliefs are otherwise ideological.

With the foregoing as a kind of conceptual background, there are less philosophical and more action-oriented practices that may be said to characterize some versions of conservatism. For some followers, emphasis could be on fiscal policy and action. A fiscal conservative may be in favor of very limited taxation (only enough to fund the essential work of governments). Even this belief is inconsistent among conservatives, as it tends to be among followers of almost all ideologies (except, perhaps, libertarians, who may oppose all taxes). A principal point of contention is the matter of determining which government programs and expenditures are essential. For example, a younger person may be opposed to the entirety of the Social Security and Medicare programs. An older individual, who has paid into the programs throughout a working life, may defend them on the grounds of recouping the payment as some version of an investment (with emphasis on being *vested* in the programs). Are both of these people conservative? The answer may well be yes, since conservatism, as is the case with liberalism and libertarianism, is a house with many mansions.

There are many people who identify themselves as conservatives because of the root meaning of the word. They find much that they believe to be worth conserving; those things may be the fiscal resources of governments, the wealth of individuals, the institutions that have been social mainstays (including churches and other religious institutions, social organizations, community associations, etc.), certain sets of personal and putative community values, and other things. In short, there is a notion that change of some kind is not desirable; traditions are more comforting and, supposedly, superior to alternatives. Sullivan (2006) points out, though, that even the most seemingly steadfast of institutions have been subject to change, especially in recent years. He uses the Catholic Church as an example and mentions alterations to the liturgy, the language of the Mass, and relations with communities (p. 13). No institution or party is immune to change, and the change can have external, as well as internal, sources.

Throughout his book, Sullivan (2006) suggests that conservatism (which he sometimes refers to as the "political right") has experienced resurgence and growth over the last few decades, in part, because of the disarray of the political left. His case is partly convincing, primarily because there does not appear to be a strong and coherent political left at this time. The political right, on the other hand, has been able to coalesce around fairly consistent messages, even if the messages do not capture essences of beliefs. Observers such as Lee Edwards (1999) are also correct in noticing that the climb of the political right did not have a single beginning; the rise emerged from an already quite conservative America in the 1950s (conservative in large measure because World War II was fresh in people's consciousnesses). The political right of the likes of Eisenhower, though, was more centrist (it was he, after all, who could speak of a military-industrial complex). Yes, Barry Goldwater was thrashed in the 1964 election by Johnson, but Goldwater provided a new and different voice for a much more strident conservatism that would brook nor tolerate any antiwar movement or anything but the tightest fiscal restraint. Only four years after his defeat, the way was paved for Nixon's election (and subsequent reelection) to the presidency. Nixon's anti-Left rhetoric was fairly strong, but it paled in comparison to that of his vice president, Spiro Agnew (and his dismissal of "nattering nabobs of negativism"). Even today, many observers claim that Nixon's henchmen's break-in at the Watergate Hotel might have been forgiven by the people if it had not been covered up. The claim is an absurd one because the cover-up followed the break-in immediately. Also, the break-in was, itself, an egregious malfeasance.

Edwards (1999) and others note that the Reagan years probably did more to revitalize a particular kind (primarily fiscal) of conservatism in the United States than anything else. It is almost impossible to disagree with the observation, but the Reagan years were certainly problematic in many ways. Specific events, such as the firing of air traffic controllers, drew praise by some, but the action was possibly more successful as an anti–organized labor action than anything since the Great Depression. His presidency began on a questionable mark with the release of American hostages in Iran upon his inauguration. The coincidental timing, according to some historians, had much to do with Iran's hatred of Carter; his ouster provided an excuse for the release of the hostages and an end to both a public affairs and internal policy (in Iran) nightmare. That reasoning has not been discussed widely—in 1981 or in more recent times. If these historians are correct, Reagan was not the hero of the day. Little is written or said today about the arms trading with Iran, which was, in fact, a constitutional crisis for the Reagan administration. At the time, media coverage was at a saturation point, with hearings televised every day. Reasoned explanation of the nature of the legal crisis was less well covered, however, than the almost staged testimony of many of the principals in the action, including Oliver North and John Dean (not to mention Fawn Hall).

To sum up this brief treatment, conservatism, for many, is marked by a consistency of policy, action, and public life that resists alteration to what is believed to be tried and true. A great deal is assumed by such belief. One is the tried and true itself and the stance that it can be perpetual. Resistance to change may be a human reaction that is both common and comprehensible; it is difficult, even threatening, to face and accept change. The resistance may not always be logical and reasonable, though. Kekes (1998), in making his argument for political conservatism, makes just these sorts of points to present the case for conservatism. In a sense, he can be correct;

if the good lives of citizens are threatened by some kinds of changes, the status quo should be protected. The good life is not static, however, and can at times require changes in order to be preserved. Resisting change in such instances is not reasonable, and protection of the status quo can actually damage the good life. Kekes (1998) turns to Michael Oakeshott (1991) to support his position: "To be conservative, then, is to prefer the familiar to the unknown, to prefer the tried to the untried, fact to mystery, the actual to the possible, the limited to the unbounded, the near to the distant, the sufficient to the superabundant, the convenient to the perfect, present laughter to utopian bliss" (p. 408). Oakeshott's own language betrays him in portions of his claim. The possible may be superior to the actual; the untried may offer a better life than does the tried. His language also, at times, signals manipulation; the convenient may be inferior not to the perfect but to the *inconvenient* (as has been the case previously, his dictum begs the question, *for whom*?). The convenient should, perhaps, give way to the *potential*. Present laughter may not present what *possible joy* can offer. This brand of conservatism is not necessarily the preservation of the good life but the preservation of the presently comfortable existence. Does reason dictate such a choice?

A species of conservatism is neoconservatism. Little will be said here about neoconservatism except to mention that the intellectual heritage of the ideology begins with Leo Strauss (see Murray, 2006, pp. 2–23). In particular, Strauss's idea of natural rights is attractive to neoconservatives. Strauss's principal influence in recent years had to do with George W. Bush's foreign policy. Followers of Strauss, such as Paul Wolfowitz, incorporated Straussian thinking into practice, which included an examination of surface phenomena and not delving into what Strauss would categorize as an unknown (see Smith, 2006, pp. 178–85). That notion of Strauss's is, perhaps, most prominent in his *Natural Right and History* (1953):

> Since the natural understanding is the presupposition of the scientific understanding, the analysis of science and of the world of science presupposes the analysis of natural understanding, the natural world, or the world of common sense. The natural world, the world in which we live and act, is not the object or the product of a theoretical attitude; it is a world not of mere objects at which we detachedly look but of "things" or "affairs" which we handle. Yet as long as we identify the natural or prescientific world with the world in which we live, we are dealing with an abstraction. (p. 79)

Given Strauss's definition, it seems clear that his thought would be attractive to members of the Bush administration. Even though the likes of Paul Wolfowitz find some of Strauss's works attractive, Norton (2004) observes that the blueprint for failure is also in Strauss's works. He says that Westerners tend to adopt a narrow historicity; if what is seen does not fit what is known about the West, it is not relevant. Foreign policy is threatened by such parochialism.

## Tea Party and Occupy Movements

To begin this section, it should be mentioned that while "Tea Party" includes the word "party," it does not resemble, and is not intended to resemble, any recognizable political party. The published *Tea Party Manifesto* of the movement, written by Dick Armey and Matt Kibbe (2010), states, "This is a movement stirred into action not out of partisan bitterness but as a reaction to what [the members] view as a government that has grown too large, spends too much money, and is interfering with their freedoms" (p. 66). This statement is laden with interpretive challenges, especially in light of other claims and member complaints and of affiliations with other organizations. "Bipartisan" may be intended as a separation from Republican and Democrat identification—as a curse on both houses. At least some of the invocations, however, are explicitly capitalistic; Rick Santelli's impassioned statements on CNBC (see Sullivan, 2009) are taken by many as a hallmark moment in the beginning of the movement, a stance for capitalists: "We're thinking of having a Chicago Tea Party in July [2009], all you capitalists. I'm organizing" (quoted in Armey and Kibbe, 2010, p. 20). Perhaps of particular note is that the Tea Party movement is supported by the organization FreedomWorks, which expresses rhetorical and informational dynamics of its own. One interpretive challenge is to determine the extent to which informational expressions of FreedomWorks and the Tea Party intersect. FreedomWorks got its official start as a 501(c)3, 501(c)4, 527 organization in 2004 with funding provided David Koch of Koch Industries. It is currently chaired by Dick Armey and Matt Kibbey. The names are mentioned because they can be the sources of statements that are intended to influence people identified with the Tea Party.

One Tea Party issue, noted previously, is the perceived government war on affordable energy and coal. The statements emanating from Tea Party supporters tend not to include information about subsidies that, for example, oil companies receive, although there are some conservative and libertarian voices speaking out against the subsidies. There are conflicting voices, including some that point out the costs of oil subsidies (see, for example, Taylor and Van Doren [2011]); Tea Party claims that government interference in free markets should disappear are in conflict with any support for large-scale government subsidies for any industry and, particularly, for individual companies. Elimination of subsidies of all sorts, so goes the claim, would allow markets to reach equilibrium (charging prices that accurately reflect costs). That may lead to higher consumer costs for many goods, but the (truth-based) rhetoric surrounding energy and consumption would have to be reconciled. This example illustrates a problem that affects many analyses of informational content and effect; people are frequently disposed to accept claims that are in agreement with their already held beliefs, even in the face of contradictory evidence.

A much more complex issue is religion, especially as it may be connected to politics. There are numerous statements linking Christianity to the tenets of Tea Party political positions and support for candidates for offices. The statements come from grassroots and national sources. Skocpol and Williamson (2012) report on interviews that reveal that many Tea Party supporters identify themselves as affiliated with evangelical Christian churches. Many also look to the Bible for guidance in political life and as inspiration for, among other things, the US Constitution. A book that is mentioned rather frequently is Cleon Skousen's *The Five Thousand Year Leap* (2009 [1981]), a book that was largely forgotten but was mentioned very favorably by Glenn Beck on numerous occasions. The book attempts to deny the Enlightenment origins of the Constitution and provides links between the Bible and the Constitution. It should be mentioned that Skousen's church, the Church of Jesus Christ of Latter-Day Saints, distanced itself from him and his writings before he died. Even within the numbers of Tea Party supporters, though, there is some dispute about fundamental purpose that extends to the kinds of informational messages that should be communicated internally among the group and beyond to larger audiences. This discursive practice demonstrates a particular disagreement over the extensiveness of "freedom's" meaning.

The discursive practice of the Tea Party sometimes employs sarcasm as a means of persuading its audience of its position. For example, the *Tea Party Manifesto* (2010) holds, "Under the health care legislation passed in 2010, the government mandated that all individuals must buy government-approved health insurance, whether they want it or not. The government should be concerned with protecting my liberty, not my liver" (p. 67). Affordance of life can be interpreted to include the provision of basic health to all individuals, especially those who most need it. The practice also includes some strange conspiratorial claims that have gained substantial acceptance. Theda Skocpol and Vanessa Williamson (2012) have recently published an extensive examination of the Tea Party's influence on party politics in the United States. They reported that a plan for improvements to the electrical grid, known as the "Smart Grid," would result in the control of citizens' home thermostats to the government (p. 202).

The stated populism of the Tea Party movement can be examined in two ways. One is the internal ideology that has been articulated by the voices of the movement. Confrontation between "ordinary" people and elites bears out a populist bent; there is an expression of antagonism on the part of many Tea Party supporters. The majority, and its desires, is being stymied by a minority of perceived rulers who do not have the interests of the people in mind. This political populism is of a particular sort; it finds its expression in predominately negative terms (in the sense of identifying opponents and stating that the movement is against what they stand for). The primary positive message of the Tea Party's internal populism is freedom—even though the freedom is usually *from* something, such as taxation, spending, and government interference in matters that include health care. A search for an external populism, a source that would affirm membership and support for the Tea Party, yields little substance. Claims of bipartisanship, for example, can be problematic in informational and interpretive terms; 57 percent of Tea Party supporters polled had a positive opinion of George W. Bush as he left office, as opposed to 27 percent of the general public (Ashbee, 2011, p. 158).

The Occupy movement, like the Tea Party, is (in many ways) populist in nature. The impetus behind its beginning and organization was the vast discrepancy in wealth among US citizens. The claim of representing the 99 percent is indicative of the discrepancy, with the wealthiest 1 percent of the population separated by so much from the remaining 99 percent. The first marches and protests did indeed target Wall Street and the emblematic physical locus of wealth. Protesters literally occupied Zuccotti Park, near Wall Street, from September 17 to November 15, 2011. The sentiment expressed in Zuccotti Park spread quickly, and protests were organized in cities large and small in a very short time. The protesting of wealth distribution enlarged to include the practices of many banks relating to the housing bubble and other lending practices.

In a short book, which supports the movement, editors argue for the extension of the movement beyond the specific wealth-building and banking practices to embrace the treatment of people in a capitalist society. Van Gelder and the editors of *YES! Magazine* (2012) enumerate ways in which the movement brought forth a wide-ranging and encompassing set of changes:

1. It names the source of the crisis.
2. It provides a clear vision for the world we want.
3. It sets a new standard for public debate.
4. It presents a new narrative.
5. It creates a big tent.
6. It offers everyone a chance to create change.

7. It is a movement, not a list of demands.
8. It combines the local and the global.
9. It offers an ethic and practice of deep democracy and community.
10. We have reclaimed our power. (p. 13)

Not all the points have been successful, perhaps especially number ten. Also, as opposed to the Tea Party movement, Occupy did not develop legislative action or a plan to get sympathetic candidates elected. That is, in all probability, the biggest (and may be the longest lasting) difference between the two movements.

## Democracy

So much has been written about democracy (favorably, unfavorably, questioning, etc.) that it is a mighty challenge to pretend that a cogent summary can be presented here. Well, authors frequently embrace folly and attempt the impossible. Actually, I do not believe a summary is impossible, so here is a beginning. As one can expect, there are liberal (Leftist), conservative (rightist), skeptical (socialist, libertarian, anarchist) viewpoints on American government and politics. There are also idealist and pragmatic (both with and without the capital "P") stances. To some extent, all these positions must be mentioned and evaluated here. What follows is in large part descriptive, but it is also somewhat normative; value judgments will be made in order that media and informational assessments can eventually be made. I will note here that conservative claims will not be dismissed out of hand, and liberal ones will not be accepted uncritically. It would be the height of irresponsibility to make decisions based on any one person's fundamental political leanings. This is not to say that everyone's claims will be accepted as equal; the critical acumen of the speaker and the reasonableness of the utterances will be the determining factors here and throughout the book.

Some foundational matters should begin the discussion here. One—probably the most important—is the definition of democracy. As might be expected, there is no absolute consensus on what democracy is and on how (or even it) it is manifest in the United States. In fact, the United States does not have, and never has had, a pure democracy. The governing structure may be referred to as a representative democracy, with elected officials acting and speaking on behalf of the people who elected them. Or it may be called a federal republic with a division of power between states and a central government. If the Latin root is considered—res publica, or in no way the province of private governance—then the United States is indeed a federal republic. The actual governance of the United States is really very complicated, since the Constitution is a mix of multiple governance structures and ideals. The Tenth Amendment to the US Constitution reads, "The powers not delegated to the United States by the Constitution, nor prohibited by it to the States, are reserved to the States respectively, or to the people." Many of the amendments to the Constitution are problematic, and the Tenth Amendment qualifies as one of these that can throw a monkey wrench into governance. If the text reads that rights are reserved to the states, there would be a clarity that could allow for decisions in matters of law and/or dispute. The addition of "or to the people" can confuse the rights of states and the extent of federal government reach. For example, Jensen and Entin (1998) point to specific cases in order to illustrate the difficulties the judiciary has in attempting to interpret what was intended by the amendment within the overall context of a federal republican structure. The confusion remains more than two hundred years after the ratification of the amendment.

As is noted previously, consideration of democracy necessitates accounting for the ideal and the pragmatic. The accounting also necessitates looking seriously at theory. As has also been discussed previously, people have very different ideas about the role of government in democracy, ranging from an active formative one to near absence. Where is the place of informing in the consideration of theory? We return here to deliberation. Goodin (2003) expresses the challenge as well as anyone: "Aggregation is fine for facts, but deliberation is required when values come into play . . . Votes are good, reasons better" (p. 227). I do not think that I could agree more with Goodin . . . with one exception. Deliberation, reason, and reflection are all essential to the full workings of democracy. However, those elements rely on something even more fundamental. The words "informed citizenry" have been mentioned by many commentators (all favorably). There must be a presentation of facts, places for citizens to turn to receive the facts—and even opinions—regarding the happenings of the locality, the nation, and the world. Without informing sources, deliberation and reflection are not fully possible. Of course, the informing sources include the press and broadcast media, but more is needed. People actually do need blogs, citizen journalism, free and well-supported (and accessible) public libraries, and other resources.

Some specific aspects of life and association most effectively characterize democracy, but there are limits to the aspects that should be noted. For example, a democratic society should embrace pluralism inasmuch as the diverse elements of many cultures, ethnicities, languages, and so on should be accepted into the warp and woof of the nation. Mouffe (2000), though, warns that pluralism could contribute to what she calls "incommensurability," or a kind of incomprehensibility among groups (or, as she says, "valorization of all differences"; p. 20). She further warns that overemphasis on pluralism could lead to permanence of conflict and antagonism. The antagonism could operate in (at least) two directions. Those in a majority or plurality could aim to dominate the minority; those in the minority could come to resent the majority. Avoidance of the problem requires appreciation of "others" on their own merits and—more important—efforts to understand others on their own terms. Examples would be learning about various cultures and traditions, understanding of languages, and so on.

In keeping with Mouffe's analysis, let us assume that democracy in the United States is not perfect (that it is fallible but corrigible). The assumption requires making explicit what the shortcomings of American democracy might be. We can turn to Shapiro (2003) for one element: "the failure of both major parties in the United States to offer practices that benefit the poor [hearken back to the section on Justice] compounds their political alienation, which in turn strengthens politicians' incentives to ignore them" (pp. 105–6). If equity is not foremost in the minds of politicians—at all levels of government—there *will* be inequity. This phenomenon will be discussed in much greater detail in the next chapter on capitalism, but there are fundamental considerations of justice, as we have seen, that must guide both principle and practice. As Shapiro (2003) further states, "No conception of democracy as geared toward reducing domination can ignore the relations between the political system and the distribution of income and wealth" (p. 104). Shapiro is explicitly addressing the theory of democracy, but the matters of which he speaks ought to be ingrained in every citizen's training in civics; these ideas should be introduced to people no later than early secondary schooling.

The issues raised by Mouffe, Shapiro, and others too numerous to mention here have been anticipated by those of previous generations, such as John Dewey. Dewey (1954 [1927]) offers an observation so basic that we may tend to forget it today: "A public articulated and operating through representative officers is the state; there is no state without a government, but also there is none without the public" (p. 67). The primacy of the public is a common theme across ideologies and theories dealing with democracy. Regardless of the conception of democracy, its ideals, and its practices, the reality of the public is a constant. Also (and this is something Shapiro [2003] helps us comprehend), regardless of the form of government or the political ideology that might dominate, government cannot force citizens to deliberate (p. 49). If individuals choose to let others, probably politicians and officials, establish and execute policy, then those in whose hands the power rests will exercise the power. We must remember that, when it comes to most state and local elections, well under half of registered voters go to the polls. We should also recall that many citizens who *could* register to vote do not. So we cannot say that in the United States we have a true deliberative democracy or even a true representative democracy. As Dewey (1954 [1927]) has said, "The democratic public is still largely inchoate and unorganized." (p. 109). It is an open question whether democracy can actually exist given such a state of affairs. One additional word related to Dewey can be added here (and expanded upon in Chapter 3). Democracy and education are inextricably linked. As Dewey (1916) points out, education is not limited to schooling, but education adds to individuals' experiences, which can enable them to learn, discover, and grow.

### More General Democratic Discussion

A starting place can almost be determined by the toss of a coin, but let's begin with some thoughts articulated by Russell Kirk, a prominent conservative intellectual who passed away about two decades ago. In a short work, published posthumously, Kirk forcefully stated some of his most dearly held ideas about what America is and what forces endanger it. Among other things, Kirk defines a particular strain of ideology that, he believed, was threatening the integrity of what the United States stood for historically and presented a danger to contemporary national strength. For example, he (2002) said, "The word ideology means political fanaticism, a body of beliefs alleged to point the way to a perfect society . . . Fanatic ideologues in our time have drawn their strength from faith in their ideas, evil though most of their ideas have been" (pp. 2, 3). On the face of it, one could readily agree with what he has to say, except that he has a particular group of people in mind when he speaks of ideologues. In short, those people do not agree with what he considers the reasoned stance of conservatism; therefore, those people are painted with the brush of ideology, a very narrow and negative term. "Ideology" is, for most of us, much more general in meaning. Other scholars, such as Terry Eagleton and John Thompson (on the political Left—and that word is used here only because it has a common interpretation), come up with different definitions of ideology. Even though their politics are Leftist, their definitions of "ideology" are not close to being as one-sided and biased as the implications with which Kirk leaves a reader. For example, Thompson (1990) says, "*Ideology, on this account, is a theoretical doctrine and activity which erroneously regards ideas as autonomous and efficacious and which fails to grasp the real conditions and characteristics of social-historical life*" (italics in original; pp. 34–35).

In the minds of many people, "ideology" is equated with falsehood or deception (or, sometimes, propaganda). This need not be the prevailing view of "ideology," but governments, agencies, corporations, and even individuals *do* employ these kinds of ideological tactics for their own gain. The word "ideology" has been used throughout this chapter, so we should turn to Eagleton (1991), who reminds us of the several common meaning of "ideology":

> The most general of all meanings of ideology stresses the social determination of thought, thus providing a valuable antidote to idealism . . . A second, slightly less general meaning of ideology turns of ideas and beliefs (whether true or false) which symbolize the conditions and life-experiences of a specific, socially significant group or class . . . A third definition of the term . . . attends to the *promotion* and *legitimation* of the interests of social groups in the face of opposing interests . . . A fourth meaning of ideology would retain this emphasis on the promotion and legitimation of sectoral interests, but confine it to the activities of a dominant social power . . . A fifth definition [holds that] ideology signifies ideas and beliefs which help to legitimate the interests of a ruling group or class specifically by distortion and dissimulation . . . There is, finally, the possibility of a sixth meaning of ideology, which retains an emphasis on false or deceptive beliefs but regards such beliefs as arising not from the interests of a dominant class but from the material structure of society as a whole. (pp. 28–30)

According to the previous set of definitions, ideology is scarcely avoidable (and need not be avoided) in Western society today. Since Eagleton enumerated the definitions, the fourth and fifth meanings may have become the most pernicious in political life, although the first two meanings best describe the usage throughout this discussion of democracy. Eagleton (1991) also notes that discursive practice in public relations is fraught with one or more of the uses of ideology.

An examination of the six definitions reveals a couple extremely important elements for the present investigation. Even if we allow for McLellan's (1995) claim that ideology is what the *other* person/group says and believes, there is a powerful force exerted by ideology. In order to attribute ideological stances to someone else, we would have to able to see completely through the ideological claim at hand. Once that occurs, there are options open: (1) ignore the ideological position as illegitimate, as having to political or social pertinence to our lives, or (2) resist the position actively and counter it (by means of dissident propaganda *or* statements of truth claims). Ignoring ideological discourse is not likely to advance one's position; the claims of the dominant group may continue unabated. Countering the dissimulation with accuracy and truth, grounded in meaningful discourse, is likely to be more effective as a countermeasure. What we do have is a complex informing moment; the proponents of false, but legitimated, discourse may well be able to assume a position of ascendency. The claims, for example, of Iraq having weapons of mass destruction convinced hundreds of millions of people around the world. The truth of the statements was questioned by some individuals at the time of the invasion in 2003, but the determination of beliefs—by Americans and others—was successful. Those who might have been able to reverse the determinate force were weak and feeble and exerted almost no effort at providing genuinely informing discourse.

Even the foregoing may be an oversimplification of ideology. Žižek (1989)—one of the most challenging thinkers to interpret—says, "Ideology is not simply a 'false consciousness,' an illusory representation of reality, it is rather this reality which is already conceived as 'ideological'" (p. 21). Rather than merely being a distortion of reality, ideology is a creation of reality, and that creation subsumes other conceptions within it; ideology represents reality. That is not an easy idea to grasp much less to accept. If serious thought entails representation and if ideology is itself representation, then how can one think clearly about any political matter without becoming drawn into falsity (and more)? Freeden (1996) explicates the dilemma: conceptualization of the political necessitates the expression of ideas. We can only express them by means of words, and words are contested and appropriated. What one individual says about, say, democracy could be turned by another individual who uses most of the same words as the first individual (pp. 48–54). Where does meaning reside? I do not accept that discernment of meaning (or creation of meaning) is impossible, but it exists on the landscape of a battleground. The battle can translate "estate taxes" into "death taxes," for example. A major challenge for the creation of meaning is that the creation requires complex language, while distortion (ideology in a pejorative sense) can be accomplished with linguistic economy. Meaning is, not infrequently, a matter of the structure of language and categories. The ordering of things, events, and ideas can be a powerful force that exerts strong influence over beliefs and opinions: "A classification system constrains thought, giving a basic unity to everything expressed within in, whatever its content, and making alternative systems of classification seem incommensurable . . . Repression of minority cultures similarly acts through suppression of their language" (Hodge and Kress, 1993, p. 64).

How is ideology—as distortion, or even as false consciousness—to be combatted? Herein lies an informing challenge. It is tempting to say that distortion is much easier to accomplish than clarity. According to the Internal Revenue Service (IRS), the 2013 exemption rate on inheritance is $5,250,000 (http://www.irs.gov/Businesses/Small-Businesses-&-Self-Employed/Estate-Tax). An ideologue of the Kirk type may ignore the rates and stress "death tax." A truth claim about estate taxes would emphasize the rates and also the reality that only a minute portion of the American populace would be affected by an inheritance exceeding that amount. A question at the heart of this language (and this is merely one example) is what communicates democratic values. The estate tax is one of the most democratic elements of taxation in the United States; almost all citizens are exempt from paying any of these kinds of taxes. Only the wealthiest inheritors pay, and that payment is for any amount *in excess* of $5,250,000. Another way to look at this fact is that the estate tax is one of the most *antidemocratic* of taxes since the wealthy Americans may pay little or nothing. According to the IRS, as late as 2008 the exemption was $3,500,000. The beneficiaries in recent years are an ever-decreasing percentage of the population. Democracy should have justice as an essential component, but not all aspects of our society include justice for all. Also, the majority of the people are ill informed about this and other important matters.

## A Short Summary

We have seen some differences among some existing political ideologies, but, in anticipation of the discussion of capitalism, it is necessary to revisit "liberalism" and examine what may best describe it today. Again, Dewey (1954 [1927]) provides an international perspective and a reminder of the basis of liberalism as it has developed over the twentieth century: "The 'liberal' party is that which represents established and vested commercial and financial interests in protest against governmental regulations. The irony of history of nowhere more evident than in the reversal of the practical meaning of the term 'liberalism;' in spite of a literal continuity of theory" (p. 134). As we have seen here, "liberalism" can be appropriated by people of just about all ideological stripes. This is so, in part, because liberalism has evolved over roughly a century and a half. What we see as classical liberalism fits today's conservatives—even many moderate libertarians—quite well. What is today used as "liberal" does not closely resemble classical liberalism, except that it usually refers to an extension (sometimes logical, sometimes not) of what the likes of Mill suggested. The transmogrification of liberalism has created a new ideal (something distinct from classical liberalism). Unfortunately, the new liberalism does not have a sound and agreed-upon philosophical framework. That absence, as we will see, renders a cogent, coherent, and consistent response to capitalism quite challenging since there tends not to be a sound foundation upon which to build a response. We will also see that conceptions of the public good lack consistency as well, in part because some ideological positions have a well-developed but incorrect point of view. Others, however, lack consistency, and that foundering makes consistent response very difficult.

# 2

# Economics and Finance

## Where Has Theory Come From and What Do We Face Today?

### Preamble

The first thing that must be said here is that capitalism, as a form of production and of political economy, is not inherently bad or evil. That said, Piketty's (2014) warning is worth heeding: "Indeed, the distribution of wealth is too important an issue to be left to economists, sociologists, historians, and philosophers. It is of interest to everyone, and that is a good thing" (p. 2). There are flaws in capitalism, but there are flaws in all political economies. We should remember, "In 1942, Joseph Schumpeter believed that socialism would inevitably triumph over capitalism. In 1970, when Paul Samuelson published the eighth edition of his famous textbook, he was still predicting that the GDP of the Soviet Union might outstrip that of the United States sometime between 1990 and 2000" (Piketty, 2014, p. 137). It is apparent that socialism can be subjected to venality and corruption—as both a political structure and an economic system. Capitalism is not perfect, but care must be taken to analyze whether the system in place—and its operation in particular—actually *is* capitalism. Few commentators ask that question.

### Introduction

What happened? What went so terribly wrong over the last several years to create so much upheaval and loss of confidence? Perhaps the place to begin an answer to these questions is the recognition that the problem is not as "new" as some claim and has been with us for a long time. In his memoir, Alan Greenspan (2013) writes, "I would argue that [herd behavior] accounts for the long-term stability we see in household spending and saving patterns from one generation to the next" (p. 24). Greenspan may well be correct; there could be behavioral reasons for the actions of individuals and families, and these reasons may have held for generations. A behavioral explanation may be unsatisfying, though, since circumstance contributes to the manners in which people behave. If the circumstances have, perhaps, been created (instead of being spawned by, say, evolutionary forces), then the explanation could be found wanting.

As is true of the first chapter, this is no economics history lesson. The background that is provided exists in order to make the contemporary state of affairs as clear as possible. We can be sure that capitalism is not new; it has a long and complex past, and Joyce Appleby (2010) offers an extensive and excellent recap of that past. She details a lengthy history of markets, commerce, and trade, even as she issues a vital warning that everyone must heed: "It is important to break with [the] cast of mind [that capitalism was inevitable] if we are to understand that capitalism is not a predestined chapter in human history, but rather a startling departure from the norms that had prevailed for four thousand years" (p. 12). Perhaps most importantly, throughout her book, she relates that the "system" of capitalism is human, social, and political. No analysis of the finances of the most recent times would be served well by mechanical models that omit the human element. She concludes her study by noting, "The origins of capitalism's flaws can be detected in its history, when things commercial moved from the periphery in premodern aristocratic societies to form the center of modern ones" (p. 417).

One of the things we will see is the disagreements about the present state of economics, economic theory, and resultant financial practice. On one hand is Stephen Marglin (2008), who plainly states that "over the past four hundred years, the ideology of economics has fostered both the self-interested individual and the market system, and has undermined and continues to undermine, the community" (p. 1). Marglin makes his stance clear at the very beginning of his critique of economics, but that stance is by no means shared by the universe of economists. On the other hand, we find Alan Greenspan and Henry Paulson, who are apologists for the theory and practice that resulted in the most recent recession, which began in 2007. Both these policymakers demonstrate ample analytical ability and are able to explain much of what went wrong, but they continue to see through a neoclassical economic lens.

## Background

Commerce, as Appleby points out, is not a modern phenomenon. The late medieval milieu of western Europe was one of manufacture (in a premodern sense) and trade. Agricultural products were grown for purposes beyond subsistence, and markets allowed for (primarily) the barter of goods for other goods and products. Compared with modern commerce, medieval life was somewhat primitive, but it was based, in part, on markets. The markets were not at all free in a modern sense. (We will see that the very idea of free markets at any time in history is a questionable one; but that argument can wait until later.) The markets, though, flourished as people traded willingly and regularly. The goods and products were quite expansive as well; finished products—including clothing, tools, and other items—led to the emergence of artisans and guilds that provided mechanisms for cooperation and even market control. There were, for example, scribes who worked in university cities and who provided students and institutions with needed texts. Their labor could be traded for money.

There was even nascent technology used by medieval farmers, builders, and manufacturers. Granted, some of the technology was applied to warfare, but given the instability of European territory into the Renaissance, the application is not surprising. With the spread of Renaissance developments from south to north, there were more capitalistic manifestations arising. One of the most noteworthy was printing; by the year 1500, there were printers in every city and many towns in Europe. As many as eight million printed works were produced by that year (see Eisenstein, 1979). Into the sixteenth century, the trade in books was substantial, and, since there was a monetary exchange for the product, something resembling a modern market was being created. Moreover, some printers were able to exert some control (even from the earliest days, such as Aldus Manutius in Venice in the late fifteenth century) over markets. Nearly four hundred years ago, there was sufficient concern about market control that laws were enacted: "The 1624 Statute of Monopolies stabled that patents for new devices would be granted for fourteen years, striking a balance between the inventor's reward and the public's access to useful devices" (Appleby, 2010, p. 47).

The reward, Appleby writes, was material indeed; the inventor held control over a product and reaped the financial benefit of the legitimate use of it. It is noteworthy also, however, that the state was also concerned with the provision of goods for public use. That concern with public use enabled English agriculture to be the most efficient in Europe up to the mid-nineteenth century. Appleby also argues that the developments of markets, the spread of the ability to earn, and the fostering of effective use of technologies (among other things) had consequences for society and social structure. She (2010) states, "Traditional society is structured around statuses, permanent places in the social structure like that of a nobleman or commoner. Social classes came with capitalism and refer to groups distinguished by their wealth or lack of it and their relation to the economy" (p. 88). It is of more than passing import that "economy" can be spoken of by the seventeenth century. Of course, the rise of classes and status is a complicated phenomenon, affected by climate, disease (especially the Black Death), the rise of humanism, concerns with science and law, and other factors. Nevertheless, the impact was profound.

There are numerous works that describe, and these are merely convenient examples, the scientific revolution, the Dutch tulip trade, the seventeenth-century market schemes (such as the Dutch East India Company), and other instances. These represent events that depict the alterations to life that were occurring over an extended period of time.

## Where Did Theory Come From?

### *Smith*

Here we will be rather simplistic. Many economic experts have written reviews on the history of theory development, but an extremely brief overview will suffice here. It makes sense to begin with Adam Smith's *Wealth of Nations* (1991 [1776]). The implication of that publication date is rather fraught, but it will not be addressed here. One of the pieces of discourse that is quite notable in Smith's work is the fact that he can simply presume all readers will follow his analysis of labor. "Labor," as a specified human activity, was a rather recent development. Be that as it may, he (1991) can write that "the improvement of the dexterity of the workman necessarily increases the quantity of the work he can perform; and the division of labour, by reducing every man's business to some one simple operation, and by making this operation the sole employment of his life, necessarily increases very much the dexterity of the workman" (p. 13). Smith is stating, nearly 240 years ago, that something like a division of labor is both possible and desirable. While his topic in the writing is "labor," he is really expressing a preferred mode of production, which, of course, should have the preferred outcome of increased productivity of that labor. His concern with productivity is evident also when he writes that "every body must be sensible how much labour is facilitated and abridged by the application of proper machinery . . . Men are much more likely to discover easier and readier methods of attaining any object, when the whole attention of their minds is directed towards that single object, than when it is dissipated among a great variety of things" (p. 14).

Money is also a topic of interest for Smith, although the roll of money during his time is somewhat different from its place in society today. In part, he (1991) expresses the state of affairs in terms of prices: "The price of the greater part of commodities resolves itself into three parts, of which one pays the wages of the labour, another the profits of the stock, and a third the rent of the land which has been employed in producing and bringing them to market" (p. 233). "Rent," to Smith and others of his time, is a broad conception that actually includes the costs of production that includes land, equipment, and other implements of production. In fact, distribution should also be included here since goods must be taken to market. One thing that is missing from Smith's list, but is vital today, is marketing and merchandising (including such things as advertising, which is a substantial expense). Profit, for Smith, is the money that composes a surplus left after meeting the other costs of production and distribution. As is the case today, businessmen would attempt to minimize the other costs so that profit could be maximized.

Being a pragmatist at heart, Smith equals the profit—the money that one has in reserve after necessary expenditures—to the purchasing power that money has: "But when we say that a man is worth fifty or a hundred pounds a year, we mean commonly to express not only the amount of meta pieces which are annually paid to him, but the value of goods which he can annually purchase or consume. We mean commonly to ascertain what is or ought to be his way of living" (Smith, 1991 [1776], p. 238). Herein is one of the major differences of Smith's idea of money, capital, and wealth from what obtains today. For most of the American population, Smith's observation still holds—but only to a point. When we turn attention to the housing bubble, we can see a difference, but some other alterations exist today. It is not that debt did not exist more than two hundred years ago, but it did not extend to the majority of the population, as it now does. In addition to subsistence, to living within one's means as it were, many households have debt of various sources. Mortgages and rent payments are common, and these are commonly added to the ability of people to equate income with expenditures. But there is also credit card debt, which is an indicator of consumption outpacing income. In a number of instances, such debt can be a substantial portion of an individual's or a household's income. Another debt will be discussed in further detail: student loans, the debt incurred so that one can obtain a postsecondary education degree. When added together, it is possible that debt can exceed income.

Smith also makes many observations about capital—both individual and governmental. In particular, Smith advocated frugality over profligacy so that capital would increase and not be wasted. He (1991) said, "This frugality and good conduct . . . is upon most occasions, it appears from experience, sufficient to compensate, not only the private prodigality and misconduct of individuals, but the public extravagance of government" (p. 283). Moreover, the wealth of nations progresses under frugality and accrues over time. A nation that attends to capital and to the production that contributes to capital thrives—even when there are some individuals, or some times in the government, when there is waste and/or misconduct (Smith, 1991 [1776], p. 284). That said, there can be times when the productivity of a nation can be damaged, such as during periods of war. Smith (1991 [1776]) writes, "In the course of the four French wars, the nation [England] has contracted more than one hundred and forty-five millions of debt, over and above the other extraordinary annual expense which they occasioned" (p. 286). Of special note here (and something that will be emphasized presently), Smith praises those individuals who expend parts of their fortunes on liberality and generosity because those expenditures benefit others and not merely themselves: "The latter species of expense, therefore, especially when directed towards frivolous objects, the little ornaments of dress or furniture, jewels, trinkets, gewgaws, frequently indicates, not only a trifling, but a base and selfish disposition" (Smith, 1991 [1776], p. 290).

Smith also addresses what might be called "capital in action." He primarily refers to lending and its nature and outcomes. His observation holds today:

> But what the borrower really wants, and what the lender really supplies him with, is not the money, but the money's worth, or the goods which it can purchase. If he wants it as stock for immediate consumption, it is those goods only which he can place in that stock. If he wants it as a capital for employing industry, it is from those goods only that the industrious can be furnished with the tools, materials, and maintenance, necessary for carrying on their work. (p. 292)

### *Marx*

It would be irresponsible to ignore Marx in this discussion, but this chapter is not necessarily an extended paean to him. As is true of Smith, Marx has a keen historical sense and relates the nature of labor economics as it had come to be manifest in the early to mid-nineteenth century. His stance toward labor is decidedly different from that of Smith, primarily in his idea that labor has its own value and that value is frequently underrated by capital. Marx did, however, build to a considerable extent upon the ideas of inequality (if not in the same way) of David Ricardo. Marx developed his concepts of use value and exchange value by assessing the writings of both Smith and Ricardo and elaborating on both to make distinctions between kinds and applications of value in political economy. Ricardo's (2004) examination of value has a utilitarian bent: "Utility then is not the measure of exchangeable value, although it is absolutely essential to it. If a commodity were in no way useful . . . it would be destitute of exchangeable value, however scarce it might be, or whatever quantity of labour might be necessary to procure it" (p. 5).

What may be unique in Marx among his contemporaries is his analysis of commodities, which are closely related—analytically—to labor. (Successors of Marx have picked up on his analysis and extended it.) That is, there would be no commodities without labor, and commodities would not have the value (and prices) they have if it were not for the value of the labor that comes into the creation of them. He (1976) writes,

> Commodities come into the world in the form of use-values [the value lies in the actual use to which the commodity can be put in the life of the purchaser or owner of them] or material goods . . . However, they are only commodities because they have a dual nature, because they are at the same time objects of utility and bearers of value. Therefore they only appear as commodities, or have the form of commodities, in so far as they possess a double form, i.e., natural form and value form. (p. 138)

Marx's analysis is extremely important, even today, as material goods can be examined as part of their "value form." In his conception, a coat (as an example) has both a natural form (the materials that compose it) and a value form (the materials *and* the labor that went into making the coat). A coat of inexpensive wool and minimal construction has a low value form; one of expensive cashmere and intensive construction has a higher value form. There is, as Marx notes, a social construction of value that cannot be ignored, and the construction is one that exists not merely among goods such as coats but among commodities as a whole. The comfort and durability contribute to the value form. Later we will examine what comprises both commodity and commodification today.

Marx (1976) observes that earlier theorists miss the point he makes with respect to commodities and value: "Even [classical political economy's] best representative, Adam Smith and Ricardo, treat the form of value as something of indifference, something external to the nature of the commodity itself" (p. 174). At the heart of the theory is the nature and use of money to purchase commodities (plus the existence of money itself). In the twentieth century, Georg Lukács (1971) elaborated on Marx's thoughts on commodification: "The essence of commodity-structure has often been pointed out. Its basis is that a relation between people takes on the character of a thing and thus acquires a 'phantom objectivity,' an autonomy that seems so strictly rational and all-embracing as to conceal every trace of its fundamental nature: the relation between people" (p. 83). The themes of objectivity and autonomy will recur here, as will the idea of commodity rationalism—the suggestion that the fetishism for commodities makes complete sense and is not merely capitalistically normal but individually and socially normal. Lukács (1971) provides a further analysis that is particularly pertinent here: "Consumer articles no longer appear as the products of an organic process within a community (as, for example, in a village community). They now appear, on the one hand, as abstract members of a species identical by definition with its other members and, on the other hand, as isolated objects the possession or non-possession of which depends on rational calculations" (p. 91).

There have been scores of commentators on Marx (too many to credit here); I want to offer some observations by Robert Albritton, since his are especially pertinent. For one thing, he (2007) notes that Marx demonstrates, "pure capitalism rests first of all upon the full commodification of the means of production, which, as a result becomes exclusively owned by the capitalist class, and secondly upon labour power's full commodification that requires each worker be excluded from ownership of any means of production" (p. 8). This is not a trivial matter or observation. Shortly, we will see how the ownership of means of production extends increasingly to higher education. Meanwhile, it is clear that a worker—in construction, automobile assembly, stock trading, and so on—has no ownership over the means of production. Labor is, essentially, a rent agreement. Ownership pays workers for the work done and nothing more; there is no payment for "potential" labor. Owners wield the power over labor and can exercise that power in any of a number of ways. For example, stock ownership in a publicly traded company benefits when costs are cut by the business (and that cost cutting frequently entails reducing the labor force).

Albritton (2007) emphasizes some points made previously by Marx and Lukács about the reification of capital and commodities: "Reification assumes a certain reversal of subject and object. Where commodification is complete the motion of commodities and money in the form of capital takes on some characteristics of subjectivity, while persons who fill certain economic subject positions are objectified" (p. 53). Each of us tends to think subjectively; we imagine ourselves as individuals with volition and some influence over our fates. I will not deny our agency entirely; each of does have some power to exercise over our lives. That said, there are limitations to our powers; as consumers, we tend to be treated as capitalized objects. We have money to spend on products that can range from breakfast cereal to automobiles. In this role, our lives are objectified, but we are told that we have many choices in the open marketplace. The marketplace, though, is less open than we may think. A few players control commodities that are accessible to us, by and large. And advertising plays an influential role in guiding our purchases in particular directions. To what extent does an individual recognize the reification? That is an open question. Albritton (2007) explains the dynamic: "The tendency for the circuits of capital to become more capitalistic through their own motion can be called self-reification. Or in other words, self-reification is the tendency for the commodity form to both spread and deepen by its own dynamic, and it is a tendency that picks up enormous momentum after the industrial revolution" (p. 72).

The most perceptive comments on Marx are offered by David Harvey. Among other points he makes, he stresses that Marx revolutionized the very idea of dialectic. Harvey states that Marx removes synthesis from the traditional dialectical model of Hegel; essentially, there is no final resolution to the interplay of the dynamics (including commodity, labor, exchange value, use value, value in general, and money). For example, Harvey (2010a) writes that "exchange relations, far from being epiphenomena expressive of the deep value structure, exist in a dialectical relation with values such that the latter depend on the former as much as the former depend on the latter" (p. 33). Harvey notes that Marx's dialectic is expansionary; there is no finitude to the components that interact continuously and in complex ways. This new version of dialectic may be one of Marx's most important, and most enduring, contributions.

The reification of capital is related to a phenomenon that Marx observed and is related to the state of labor in capitalism. As he (1976) says, "This fetishism of the world of commodities arises from the peculiar social character of labour which produces them. Objects of utility become commodities only because they are the products of the labour of private individuals who work independently of each other. The sum total of the labour of all these private individuals forms the aggregate labour of society" (p. 165). Lukács (1971) elaborates on Marx's point:

> Consumer articles no longer appear as the products of an organic process within a community (as for example in a village community). They now appear, on the one hand, as abstract members of a species identical by definition with its other members and, on the other hand, as isolated objects the possession or non-possession of which depends on rational calculations. Only when the whole life of society is thus fragmented into the isolated acts

> of commodity exchange can the "free" worker come into being; at the same time his fate becomes the typical fate of the whole society. (p. 91)

## More Recent Theory

### *Rand*

It may be that the thinking of Ayn Rand has never held such sway as it has over the last several years, even though her writings date back a number of decades. One of her first principles of capitalism is that one must consider not the group or the entirety of humankind but the individual. Along these lines, she mentions that, in the past, there may have been de facto property ownership and rights but no de jure rights. Further, it is individuals who both create and manage capital, and individuals do so through the exercise of rationality. (This observation of Rand is extremely important; it is a lesson learned by many of her adherents and their students. For example, rationality is a hallmark of the thinking of the likes of Milton Friedman and Alan Greenspan and subsequently many economists affiliated with the Chicago school of economics—the "Chicago School.") In making the connection between rationality and the political-economic standard of her thought, she (1967) says, "The social recognition of man's rational nature—of the connection between his survival and his use of reason—is the concept of *individual rights*" (emphasis in original; p. 9). It must be noted that, in most of her work, Rand eschews the collective in favor of the individual.

Building upon the previous principles, Rand (1967) defines capitalism: "*Capitalism is a social system based on the recognition of individual rights, including property rights, in which all property is privately owned*" (emphasis in original; p. 10). The concept of individual rights is not a particular extreme or radical idea, but the limitation of property ownership to private hands is not universally held. Rand is obviously at odds with socialism in general and Marx in particular. For Rand, anything but a completely individualistic political-economic structure is irrational—opposed to fact and reality. Altruism is included in the irrational since it removes capital/ownership from the holding individual and awards it to one who has done nothing to earn the ownership. Moreover, she (1967) maintains, "In any collaboration between two men [sic] (or groups) who hold different principles, it is the more evil or irrational one who wins" (p. 161). (Note that irrationality, according to her reckoning, equates to evil.) A hallmark of her conception of capitalism is self-interest, articulated most clearly in her book *The Virtue of Selfishness* (1974). Merrill (2013) explicates the role of self-interest in her model of capitalism:

> Without justifying the individual's right to live for his own sake, no amount of economic superiority, of ability to produce the goods for the most people, will morally validate capitalism because of its roots in self-interest. Any time self-interest is seen as being at odds with the "needs" of "society," it can be forcibly curtailed. In this ethical view, self-interest will always be seen as unfair because it doesn't serve "other people." Today we very often see this collectivist criticism in the complaint that capitalism doesn't distribute wealth evenly—the way the Left thinks is "fair." (p. 35)

The scare quotes used by Merrill demonstrate the contempt he has for anything that smacks of what Rand and her followers call collectivism (including altruism).

One particular fallacy of Rand's philosophical stance must be pointed out. She claims to have developed objectivism. Objectivity depends on concept formation, with epistemological concepts having primacy over others, and a logical determination, with epistemological concepts attaining hierarchical order (Rand, 1990, pp. 211–15). Peikoff (2012) states, "In Rand's theory . . . concepts are neither intrinsic nor subjective, but objective; they are only human devices, and thus nothing apart from man, but devices with a factual, mathematical base" (pp. 31–32). The primary difficulty with Peikoff, and Rand, is that mathematics hardly enters into her work—moreover, neither, in any real or genuine sense, does nature. In fact, man is situated above nature, and the actual application of her theory depends largely upon subjectivism. Much has been written about Rand; this brief excursus suffices here, save to offer one perspective that counters selfishness as a virtue:

> There is nobody in this country who got rich on his own. Nobody. You built a factory out there? Good for you. But I want to be clear: You moved your goods to market on the roads the rest of us paid for. You hired workers the rest of us paid to educate. You were safe in your factory because of police forces and fire forces that the rest of us paid for . . . Now look, you built a factory and it turned into something terrific, or a great idea? . . . Keep a big chunk of it, But part of the underlying social contract is you take a hunk of that and pay forward for the next kid who comes along. (Warren, 2014, p. 215)

### *Chicago*

From roughly the middle of the twentieth century to the present, economists affiliated with the University of Chicago have been enormously influential. Theorists tend to agree with, or react to, the thinking and writings of this group, which has been dubbed the "Chicago School." We will not delve deeply into the Chicago School here (for a complete history and description, see van Overtveldt, 2007). One of the "godfathers" of the Chicago School is Milton Friedman, whose free market and monetarist ideas are still followed by many economists and policymakers today. Friedman himself read closely the works of Ludwig von Mises and Friedrich Hayek, among others. These works helped shape the particular kind of conservatism that Friedman espoused. He (1962) expressed his premise succinctly: "Exchange can therefore bring about co-ordination without coercion. A working model of a society organized through voluntary exchange is a *free private enterprise exchange economy*—what we have been calling competitive capitalism" (emphasis in original; p. 13). The influence of Rand on Friedman also becomes clear in his (1962) writing: "In [a free economy], there is one and only one social responsibility of business—to use its resources and engage in activities designed to increase profits so long as it stays within the rules of the game" (p. 133). There is no place for the likes of altruism in business.

One of the most heeded Chicago School economists over the most recent decades has been Gary Becker (Nobel Laureate in economics), whose most famous book is *Human Capital.* Becker applies rational choice theory, which holds that individuals not only are capable of but also do weigh options and apply rationality to the decisions they make in all aspects of everyday life. The choice model, according to Becker, is employed when people make just about all the major life decisions they face, including educational choices, marriage, having children, selecting employment, and so on. To justify his model, he (1993) writes, "[Job opportunity] can be seen from the fact that women progressed most rapidly under the Reagan administration, which was opposed to affirmative action and did not have a Civil Rights Commission" (p. 19). This particular claim can be used to critique Becker's stance and his logic. It was in the Reagan administration, as we will see, that the economic middle class began to shrink. Interest rates were also very high in the 1980s, so there was pressure for households to include two earners. If women entered the work force under such conditions, it may not strictly have been by choice, save the choice to remain solvent (which was becoming an increasingly difficult task with one income). Becker ignores the plight of minorities without an active affirmative action plan at that time.

A feature of rational choice theory is the possession of information regarding alternatives so that the individual is able to weigh possibilities and make the decision that will be most advantageous. There are some apparent flaws to the theory: (1) it is extremely rare that anyone possesses complete information related to choice events; (2) individuals are by no means always rational agents (it may be more likely that people do *not* behave rationally); and (3) people may make many of their choices according to a social agenda rather than strictly as autonomous individuals. These flaws are actually quite damning; Ian Shapiro and Donald Green (1996) provide a thoroughgoing analysis of rational choice theory and its shortcomings. Their examination focuses on the economic failures, and they do mention Gary Becker as part of their investigation.

### *Contemporary Work*

For the purposes that follow from here, I will borrow the fiat offered by George Akerlof and Robert Shiller (2009): "In our view economic theory should be derived not from the minimal deviations from the system of Adam Smith but rather from the deviations that actually do occur and that can be observed. Insofar as animal spirits exist in the everyday economy, a description of how the economy actually works must consider those animal spirits" (p. 5). There are those, we will see, who concentrate on how the economy *should* work, according to assumptions and subsequent theorizations. Such an attitude not only is intellectually incorrect but also helps bring about some of the most egregious actions and foolish responses to challenges. Obviously, Akerlof and Shiller are drawing from Keynes and are emphasizing that human psychology is a driving force in economic behavior and its outcomes. Their position is in keeping with that of Appleby as well; we cannot ignore the multifarious nature of human and social psychology and how the sometimes less-than-rational behaviors of individuals and societies affect markets of all kinds and the flow of capital.

Unlike many economists, Akerlof and Shiller (2009) do not believe that markets alone can handle the complexities of macroeconomics: "It is our belief—echoing Keynes's view of the role of macro policy—that if there is a macroeconomic void the government must fill it" (p. 90). Their observation could be taken a step further; markets cannot exist with government involvement. Assuming that corporations are responsible, to a substantial extent, for the existence, shape, and operation of markets today, then government already has an essential role. Corporations are creations of government action; they are chartered and work according to an existing set of government rules, regulations, and laws. That said, a market like stock trading, while regulated, is an almost independently operating entity that follows its own rationality (and is treated by many outside of the inner circle of traders as a metonymy—as a separate and distinct *being* with its own consciousness). That conception places the everyday traders and holders of instruments like mutual funds at a disadvantage: "To pretend that stock prices reflect people's use of information about those future payoffs is like hiring a weather forecaster who has gone berserk" (Akerlof and Shiller, 2009, p. 132). While government is involved in markets in a structural sense, the various markets seem to operate autonomously in a real sense.

Some other theorists are more blunt in their assessment of the current condition. Boggs (2000) says that large corporations "are able to dominate virtually every phase of economic, political, and cultural life; they set the agenda for nearly every dimension of cultural life" (pp. 70–71). One way the corporations manage to achieve the domination is by helping to create a consumer society. People make purchases not merely on the basis of need but on the basis of desire for what they perceive as necessary to their lives, what is deemed to be the prevailing fashion, and what others have purchased. Clothing, automobiles, and home accessories are desired not because of functionality but because of a complex social psychological dynamic that marketers can tap into. The purchases made by people may even be less than conscious at times, if the marketers do their jobs well. As Alperovitz (2005) comments,

> The large corporation regularly
>
> 1. Influences legislation and agenda setting through lobbying
> 2. Influences regulatory behavior through direct and indirect pressure
> 3. Influences elections via large-scale campaign contributions
> 4. Influences public attitudes through massive media campaigns (p. 53)

Some contemporary theorists directly address the present state of economic thought and practice. Marglin (2008) says this about the method of today's economics: "My negative claim is that algorithm is not the only legitimate way of justifying belief and arriving at truth, that algorithmic knowledge does not provide a uniquely acceptable basis for justified true belief. I regard the idea that algorithm is the only way to justify belief as essentially ideological in nature, ideological in the sense that it rests on unproven (and possibly unprovable) assumptions about how we can know" (p. 128). In other words, Marglin is drawing a tacit comparison between much of economic theory and the kinds of theoretical constructs that exist in fields like physics. There may be no empirical modeling that can be created to test the theory, but that does not stop the theorists from presenting their ideas as true and applicable. As a corrective, he (2008) presents counterideas:

> My argument consists of three propositions: first, that knowledge and action are everywhere and at all times based on a combination, a synthesis of at least two knowledge systems, algorithmic and experiential knowledge . . . second, notwithstanding the symbiosis in practice, Western culture has elevated algorithmic knowledge to a superior position, sometimes to the point that experiential knowledge is regarded not simply as inferior knowledge, but as no knowledge at all . . . The third proposition is that the ideological hierarchy of knowledge has a powerful influence on the way algorithmic and experiential knowledge has had powerful influence on the way algorithmic and experiential knowledge interact in practice, rendering experiential knowledge illegitimate and even invisible. (p. 129)

There are some particular examples of what Marglin comments on. Quantitative econometric analysis has replaced Keynesian economics (among the thinking of other economists who have followed him). The use of complex mathematics has resulted in tools that include derivatives, credit default swaps, and other arcane instruments that have assumed ascendency in the sphere of economic influence. One difficulty with this trend is that the "human science" of economics—the methods of study that attempt to add actual human decision making and the factors that influence that action—becomes relegated to a world of obsolescence. As Marglin notes, in the absence of completely objective data, ideology enters the mix. With the ascendency of the method comes the ascendency of the ideology.

## Where Have We Gotten To?

### *Beginning*

Before we can examine the most recent recession, we have to pay some attention to the problems of the late 1990s and very early 2000s. Prior to that time, the economy was swimming along, creating quite a lot of wealth for ordinary investors. The years represent early years of Internet-based companies that seemed to hold an enormous amount for the future. Many of the companies (witness Amazon) are still around and are very profitable. Others soared for a short time before descending with a resounding thud. Venture capitalists appeared to be quite happy to give money to almost anyone who had an idea to use the Internet as a platform for his or her business. Speculation was a major driving force behind this new e-commerce. The bubble, in other words, seemed as though it wouldn't burst (but that may be because so many people refused to—or were unable to—see it as a bubble). Blinder (2014) defines "bubble" as "a *large* and *long-lasting* deviation of the price of some asset—such as a stock, a bond, or a house—from its *fundamental* value" (emphasis in original; p. 29). In many instances, the prices of the stocks of dot-com companies were high, even though the companies had little or no profit.

One result of the bubble was a sharp rise in stock indices. The Standard and Poor's index came close to doubling in a short period of time. Were one able to be prescient and foresee the bursting of the bubble, one's personal wealth would have spiked ("Here's Why the Dot Com Bubble," 2010). On March 10, 2000, the NASDAQ average reached 5,408.60. Things seemed to be all well with American business and the stock market. The portfolios of many individuals were looking very good at that time; the market was riding on the tails of what appeared to be a technology boom. The rise in the market seemed to be propelled by new businesses whose success was all but assured. However, many of those stocks declined precipitously in the coming days and weeks. The highly touted Pets.com business failed completely. There had been billions of dollars pumped into new technology businesses by venture capitalists who were certain that there would be prolonged and sustained growth. The growth cycle appeared to be so assured that the Federal Reserve raised interest rates six times in 1999 and 2000. A mere ten days after the NASDAQ peak, Jack Willoughby (2000) asked, "When will the Internet Bubble burst?"

The most thorough examination of this recession is John Cassidy's *Dot. con* (2002). Cassidy investigates when and how the dot-com bubble began, why it lifted stock indices for a few years, and why the bubble burst. He (2002) writes, "The promise of the Internet wasn't just technological: it was also ideological. Once digital networks had liberated [businesses] from the confines of tradition and physical location, human beings would come together and transcend ancient divisions: tribal, religious, racial, and economic" (p. 313). The ideology he speaks of was not limited to business; the utopian overlay on Internet culture held that the totality of society would be freed and differences would be banished. Individuals would be able to communicate with one another behind a veil of unity; equality would be the rule rather than the exception. That ideology shifted within a short time, and the Internet culture became one that could revel in difference and break the bonds of sameness. This ideal could be achieved through the creation of innumerable communities where all inhabitants would share personal and distinct experiences—experiences that set people apart even as they brought people together. In business, the ideological shift would lead to sometimes diversified rather than necessarily unified markets. In short, one size would not fit all.

*What Then?*

The theoretical stances and models discussed have led us to a particular place in our economic world. The monetarism and other positions of the 1970s and 1980s helped create a certain macroeconomic outlook that Jonathan Schlefer (2012) calls "the Great Moderation." This outlook contributed to the deregulation that typified many fields, including the financial sector. It also contributed to the development of derivatives in 2000. A favorable definition of financial derivatives holds, "The first, and most important [factor], is the natural need that the products fulfill. Any organization or individual with sizeable assets is exposed to moves in the world markets. Manufacturers are susceptible to moves in commodity prices; multinationals are exposed to moves in exchange rates; pension funds are exposed to high inflation rates and low inflation rates. Financial derivatives are products which allow all these entities to reduce their exposure to market moves which are beyond their control" (Hunt and Kennedy, 2004, p. xvii). In short, derivatives are supposed to help organizations and individuals manage risk. However, derivatives are themselves risky instruments in that they allow institutions such as banks to maintain less cash so as to manage credit default. *The Washington Post* quotes Warren Buffett as saying in 2002, "We view them as time bombs, both for the parties that deal in them and the economic system" (O'Harrow, 2010). Instead of managing risk, derivatives actually move risk around within the system, thus making it extremely difficult to know where the risk is and when it will materialize. Derivatives heighten risk within the entire structure.

One has to know how to look for the political origins of financial derivatives; many of the explanations of their operation say little or nothing about their genesis. The act that enabled derivatives was signed by Bill Clinton very shortly before he left office in 2001. Senator Phil Gramm and his wife were the creators of the instruments. Gramm is still an unrepentant deregulator years after leaving public office. He maintains that tools like subprime mortgages are mechanisms for financial freedom. Lipton and Labaton (2008) pull no punches though:

> He led the effort to block measures curtailing deceptive or predatory lending, which was just beginning to result in a jump in home foreclosures that would undermine the financial markets. He advanced legislation that fractured oversight of Wall Street while knocking down Depression-era barriers that restricted the rise and reach of financial conglomerates. And he pushed through a provision that ensured virtually no regulation of the complex financial instruments known as derivatives, including credit swaps, contracts

> that would encourage risky investment practices at Wall Street's most venerable institutions and spread the risks, like a virus, around the world.

The irony of the timing and situation at the time Gramm spoke appears to have escaped him. The downturn was well under way, and the housing bubble was bursting.

Derivatives are complex mathematical financial instruments; the complexity of the math has been both attractive (to those who are enraptured by the employment of the mathematics) and repellent (to those for whom the overly complex underpinnings represent a kind of smoke screen hiding clarity of financial transactions). The mathematical foundations of derivatives could, if so applied, result in the effective manipulation of risk within complicated markets. A simplified description holds, "Their trade value is tied to the value of other assets, historically bulk commodities but also corporate shares and currencies. The most familiar derivative contracts are futures contracts, forward contracts and option contracts. A simple options contract, for example, is a contract to sell a commodity at the market price at the moment of the contract's origination within a specified time period in the future" (Maurer, 2002, p. 15). However, the complexity of the foundations tends to obscure the enhanced risks that derivatives bring to market transactions. At the end of the day, the instruments lead to risks that are not well understood by most traders who are not highly trained in the mathematical basis of them. In addition to the technical difficulties of derivatives, other challenges accompany them: The separation of stochastic from epistemological probability—like the separation of facts from interpretations, things from signs, history from memory—is a moral problematic (Maurer, 2002, p. 30).

## What Happened?

In the preface to his new book, Alan Blinder (2014) explains why there is yet another book about the financial crisis: "One reason is simply that *the American people still don't quite know what hit them*, how and why it happened, or what the authorities did about it—especially why government officials took so many unusual and controversial actions" (emphasis in original; p. xvi). To reiterate Alan Greenspan's observation, his awareness of coming catastrophe began on March 16, 2008. In beginning his explanation of the recession, he (2013) writes, "My most worrisome concern is our broken political system" (p. 2). Interestingly, he does not refer to a broken financial system, which demonstrated signs of fracture nearly a decade before with the bursting of the dot-com bubble (even though

Greenspan had referred to "irrational exuberance" in 1996). In fact, and as several reviewers of his book point out, his discussion of the causes of the recession cover barely more than a brief chapter. Much of the book is a lecture on macroeconomics. Robert Solow (2013) is open in his criticism of Greenspan:

> An unregulated financial system, no matter how many smart people have megabucks in the game, can easily become over-leveraged and then fatally underestimate or ignore the amount of risk that financial institutions have taken on and the depth to which their risky balance sheets contaminate each other in hidden ways. When the edifice starts to collapse, central bankers and other policymakers may be left with the choice between bailing out the very people and institutions whose behavior created the crisis and letting the edifice collapse, doing even more harm to millions of people who played no active part in the disaster. The point is that this was not just a bad hair day, or one of those cases where nature presents nothing but bad options. It was a case of bad ideas coming home to roost. Greenspan was a prominent opponent of financial regulation, and it cost him (and us).

Solow (1987 Nobel laureate in economics) hits the nail on the head with his critique of deregulation. But to what extent have the American people been informed of the problem Solow describes? Is a Nobel Prize required to comprehend what's happened?

Greenspan is fond of quoting himself in his analysis. At times what we might call Greenspan 1.0 is undeniably perspicuous in his commentary; in the earlier 2000s, he said, "Megabanks being formed by growth and consolidation are increasingly complex entities that create the potential for unusually large systemic risks in the national and international economy should they fail" (Greenspan, 2013, p. 42). Clearly, he comprehended the potential consequences should banks and other financial institutions fail, which they began to do in 2007. Greenspan 3.0 (the author of the memoir) understands that behavioral economics hold substantial promise in gaining a purchase on the complexities of financial life in the twenty-first century (post-dot-com bubble, postderivative, and postinstitutional merger days). It seems, though, that Greenspan (2013) can write the following without a hint of irony: "Even with the breakdown of our sophisticated risk management models and the failures of credit-rating agencies, the financial system would likely have held together had the third bulwark against crisis—our regulatory system—functioned effectively . . . I have since regretted that we regulators never pursued the issue of capital adequacy in a timely manner" (pp. 46, 47). The second-guessing continues with Greenspan speculating on letting Bear Stearns simply fail. He wonders if Lehman Brothers might have heeded the warning. It is just such thinking that someone like Alan Greenspan, the Federal Reserve governors, and the president's Council of Economic Advisers (and others) are responsible for. Asking "why" at this time, though, is more than a curiosity; it strikes at the matter of accountability for those whose job it was/is to be sagacious.

Greenspan's self-examination requires some context. In his younger days, he was a student of Ayn Rand and an adherent of her conception of objectivism. He (Rand, 1967) wrote—again, without a hint of irony—in the 1960s, "But it is precisely the 'greed' of the businessman or, more appropriately, his profit-seeking, which is the unexcelled protector of the consumer. What collectivists refuse to recognize is that it is in the self-interest of every businessman to have a reputation for honest dealings and a quality product" (p. 126). At that time, he was adamantly opposed to the federal regulation of businesses, and it is just such an absence or inadequacy of regulation that led to the recent recession. In fact, he (Rand, 1967) said, "Regulation—which is based on force and fear—undermines the moral base of business dealings" (p. 129). Regulation, based indeed on force but not necessarily on fear, is needed when businesses fail morally. The examples are far too numerous to relate here, but one is the maximum legal fine of $35 million levied against GM: "The federal government struck a $35 million settlement with General Motors after the company failed to act for 10 years on an ignition switch defect that led to the death of at least 13 people and recall of approximately 2.6 million vehicles" (Rogers, 2014). GM apparently sought to hide a problem and engage in the systematic deception of consumers. Greenspan's idea (and, to the extent to which she agreed with it, Rand) is based solely on opinion (or even wishful thinking) and not empirical evidence.

Where was Henry Paulson at this time? He states, "I came to the Treasury Department in 2006 concerned about the size and increasing complexity of America's biggest banks. During the crisis, lacking other options, we turned to the big banks to help us rescue some of their ailing brethren. In the process they became even bigger. So, in stemming the crisis, we added to an already significant problem" (p. xix). The size of the financial institutions is a phenomenon unlike the potential monopolistic sizes of commodity producers, like soft drinks. If a soft drink company loses customers and, perhaps, eventually fails, it is likely that the cause for the failure will be loss of market share; other companies would probably benefit. If a huge financial institution is threatened with failure, other institutions are also going to be affected, given the interconnectedness of the business. As was the case in the recession, the very similar behaviors of the big banks rendered them all vulnerable (to widely varying degrees) and prompted the need for the $700 billion Troubled Asset Recovery Program (TARP).

Could the problems have been foreseen? Yes, and there were warning signs during the downturn of 2000.

David Stockman (2013), no flaming liberal economist, takes Paulson and others to task over the bailout and its rationale:

> A handful of panic-stricken top officials, led by treasury secretary Hank Paulson and Fed chairman Ben Bernanke, proclaimed that the financial system has been stricken by a deadly "contagion" that had come out of nowhere and threatened a chain reaction of financial failures what would end in cataclysm. That proposition was completely false, but it gave rise to a fateful injunction—namely, that all the normal rules of free market capitalism and fiscal prudence needed to be suspended so that unprecedented and unlimited public resources could be poured into the rescue of Wall Street's floundering behemoths. (p. 5)

Paulson's successor at the Treasury, Timothy Geithner, has also written a book about personal experiences during the recession. Early on, Geithner (2014) recounts telling President Obama that there were five "financial bombs" yet to be defused: "Fannie Mae, Freddie Mac, AIG, Citigroup, and Bank of America . . . not to protect them from the consequences of their mistakes, but to prevent another messy failure from ravaging the rest of the economy" (p. 4). He also admits that there are institutions that are too big to fail (a concept that Stockman [2013] calls "fundamentally anti-capitalist" [p. 3]). Geithner certainly has his detractors; Baker (2014) says,

> Geithner's discussion of the housing bubble and its collapse is sufficiently naïve that one hopes he is not being honest. He recounts research from the New York Fed from the period in which he was its president that concluded there was no bubble in house prices. This research rested largely on the premise that real house prices actually were not rising because conventional measures were not picking up quality improvements. This claim was laughable at the time since we had data showing that spending on quality improvements had actually fallen relative to the value the housing stock. A decade later Geithner really wants to hold this up as the basis for his failure to see the bubble?

Other reviewers note that, while Geithner was not the architect of TARP, he is, without question, an apologist for it. One can question if Paulson and Geithner, as financial insiders, "get it." The banks, many of which were largely responsible for the housing bubble and the foreclosure fiasco, were substantively rewarded for bad behavior. Perhaps even more telling and damning is the fact that, with the TARP funds—taxpayer-supplied funds—the banks have done little or nothing to stimulate the American economy.

Relatively little money has been loaned, either to individuals who are sound risks or to small businesses who may have the wherewithal to affect unemployment and gross domestic product (GDP). As a result, recovery is anemic; the first quarter of 2014 saw negative "growth." Without fundamental and sweeping reforms (which are not spoken of very much in mainstream media), there could be a risk of another recession. The nation, at present, is ill equipped to grow economically, and no one appears to have suggestions for genuine and long-term recovery.

One additional set of empirical data must be mentioned. At the depths of the recession, about a third of US capital equipment was idle; at the same time, 17 percent of the work force was unemployed or underemployed (for the most part in low-paying service jobs) when the occupants of those jobs were qualified for much higher levels of employment. Harvey (2010b) observes, "What could be more irrational than that?" (p. 215).

## Inequality

Income inequality is an indisputable fact. While the top 5 percent of earners have always outpaced everyone else, the margin has grown precipitously in recent years. The ratio of CEOs' earnings to those earnings of average workers now exceeds 300 to 1. Wong (2014) reports, "Chief executives of companies in the Standard & Poor's 500-stock index made an average $11.7 million last year. The average production and nonsupervisory worker: $35,239. That means CEOs are paid 331 times the average worker, according to a report released this week by the AFL-CIO, a federation of trade unions." The *amount* paid to chief executive officers may be cause for concern; the proportion paid relative to the average worker cries for an explanation. That explanation may be that the CEO is in the position of setting the vision and direction for the business and of making the major decisions. What happens when the CEOs fail at their jobs (i.e., when revenue and/or profit falls)? Well, if they have negotiated in advance, they may do quite well. Potential severance pay for 12 executives exceeds $2 billion (Green, 2013). At the present time, the income equality gap is the greatest it has been since 1928, or immediately prior to the Great Depression:

> In 1928, the top 1% of families received 23.9% of all pretax income, while the bottom 90% received 50.7%. But the Depression and World War II dramatically reshaped the nation's income distribution: By 1944 the top 1%'s share was down to 11.3%, while the bottom 90% were receiving 67.5%, levels that would remain more or less constant for the next three decades. But starting in the mid- to late 1970s, the uppermost tier's income share began rising dramatically, while that of the bottom 90% started to fall. The top

> 1% took heavy hits from the dot-com crash and the Great Recession but recovered fairly quickly: [Emmanuel] Saez's preliminary estimates for 2012 (which will be updated next month) have that group receiving nearly 22.5% of all pretax income, while the bottom 90%'s share is below 50% for the first time ever (49.6%, to be precise). (DeSilver, 2013)

There are, undoubtedly, numerous reasons for the historical trend and the current state. One small factor may be the bonuses awarded to those in the financial sector. In 2013, individuals in securities industries received $26.7 billion in bonuses, a figure that is 15 percent higher than that of 2012 (Alden, 2014). As just mentioned, this may be a minor factor, but the amount of the increase, as profits have declined, is not a trivial fact. Some of the wealthiest individuals see their wealth increase even as their work performance indicates that increases are not warranted.

Joseph Stiglitz (2012) has provided what may be the most exhaustive analysis of this problem in his book *Inequality*. His argument is that the income and wealth divides will have effects well into the future that will be threatening to some of the ideals of people of all political stripes. He (2012) writes,

> Although the United States has always been a capitalist country, our inequality—or at least at its current high level—is new. Some thirty years ago, the top 1 percent of income earners received *only* 12 percent of the nation's income. That level of inequality should itself have been unacceptable; but since then the disparity has grown dramatically, so that by 2007 the average after-tax income of the top 1 percent had reached $1.3 million, but that of the bottom 20 percent amount to only $17,800. (p. 4)

This kind of disparity is certainly cause for concern, but it is not a matter that is frequently and forcefully reported. Even if the income of the top 1 percent does not cause concern, the amount earned by the bottom 20 percent suggests that one-fifth of the US population is living below, at, or close to the poverty level. Tens of millions of Americans are working yet have little or no opportunity to live well. The incomes of most people have been stagnant for a number of years. There may be some politicians who tout the possibilities of a growing middle class, but, as we will see, that is an illusion (or a deception).

Stiglitz highlights data published by Jonathan Chait—data that are damning to the idea of upward mobility and of the chance to succeed in this country:

- Poor kids who succeed academically are less likely to graduate from college than richer kids who do worse in school.

- Even if they graduate from college, the children of the poor are still worse-off than low-achieving children of the rich. (Chait, 2011)

The deck is stacked against those from low-income families. This suggests that the old maxim that hard work and perseverance equal success is a lie: that the American dream is just that—a dream. Stiglitz (2012) adds, "A stark reflection of the inequality of educational opportunity in our society is the composition of students in America's highly selective colleges. Only around 9 percent come from the bottom half of the population, while 74 percent come from the top quarter" (p. 19). Chait maintains that there is no such thing as equal opportunity, and his data, while proving that his assertion does hold in individual cases, does indicate that the deck is stacked against those who are not born into well-to-do families. The most trenchant finding of Chait's is that achievement does little to enhance the opportunities for young people; children of wealthier parents can perform at lower levels and still come out ahead. Wealth may not be the only dynamic at play: "A white man *with* a criminal record is slightly more likely to be considered for a job than a black man with no criminal past" (Stiglitz, 2012, p. 69).

What may be most damning here, based on the available data, is that the United States is not necessarily a meritocracy. One cause may be related to an observation by Stiglitz (2012): "If we had decided to pay our teachers more, we might have attracted and retained better teachers, and that might have improved overall long-term economic performance. It was a public decision to allow public-sector wages to sink below those of comparable private sector workers" (p. 57). According to a survey, the average starting salary for education majors was $38,474 ("Average Starting," 2014). The average for accounting majors was $54,764 (for comparison's sake). Social work graduates averaged about $4,000 more than education graduates. Moreover, education majors can look forward to limited salary growth throughout their career. (More will be said about this shortly.) George Tyler (2013) indicates that the present generation of young people may be the first in the United States to have greater educational achievement than their parents yet do less well financially. That claim will deserve greater attention shortly. There are many contributing factors to the absence of meritocracy in America, not the least of which is the cost of higher education for students and their families.

Much more could be drawn from Stiglitz's book; suffice it to say that he undeniably has the bona fides (including a Nobel Prize) that necessitate he be taken seriously. One additional comment by him (2012) will be offered here: "What is different today is that the 1 percent now has *more* knowledge about how to shape preferences and beliefs in ways that enable the wealthy to better advance their cause, and more tools and more resources to do so" (p. 148). Among other things, the major media outlets are owned by a very small and concentrated group. While there are some differences among the outlets (e.g., and for good or ill, Fox News is *different* from MSNBC). Does that mean that there is no need for concern and that all data and information will be made openly public and will be featured prominently? Not at all. There is an enormous need not only to tell the stories but to examine what is occurring in the major media's ideology (used in the generic, not the pejorative, sense). Stiglitz and others help relate the stories.

Another economist, George Tyler (2013), has contributed a great deal to this discussion through his book *What Went Wrong*. As is the case with Stiglitz, Tyler offers important insights both by means of his own analysis and by means of the secondary sources to which he refers. The import of his work warrants mention here. A major component of his argument is that the US economy began to display a problematic turn in 1980 with the election of Ronald Reagan. That proved to be a watershed event that set a policy tone for more than four decades. Tyler refers to the entirety of the time from 1980 to the present as the Reagan era. He mentions work by Piketty and Saez (2003) that shows that during the Reagan era, only 5 percent of total earners realized gains that exceeded the rate of inflation and that the majority of those gains were concentrated in the earnings of the top 1 percent. Tyler (2013) reports on the impact of the recession on employment (or, rather, underemployment): "The plight of today's generation of Americans is defined by . . . wage compression. Every downturn sees fewer good jobs emerge in the subsequent recovery. Some 79 percent of the six million jobs lost in the deep recession of 2008–2009 paid more than $13.84 an hour, for example, but barely half that share (42 percent) of the four million jobs created in 2010–2012 paid as well. The rest—mostly service jobs—paid less" (p. 19). One of the problems faced by those who lost jobs and have had to take lesser ones is the state of the minimum wage. Few people can live adequately on the federal minimum (granted, some states have higher minimum wage levels) of $7.25 per hour. Analyses suggest some of the dilemmas caused by the low minimum wage:

- In 2011, the minimum wage was worth only about 37 percent of what an average worker earned per hour, not far above its lowest point, reached in 2006, in 47 years.
- A higher minimum wage would disproportionately affect women: They constitute a majority (54.5 percent) of those who would benefit, greater than their 48.3 percent share of the workforce. Historically, the minimum wage has been more important in setting a floor for women than for men.

- The vast majority (87.9 percent) of those who would be affected by the higher minimum wage are age 20 or older. A higher minimum wage would help address growing inequality, particularly as it affects lower-wage women. Between 1979 and 2009 the erosion of the minimum wage explained about two-thirds (65.5 percent) of the large 25.2 (log percentage point) expansion of the wage gap between median-wage workers and workers at the 10th percentile in wages—known as the 50/10 wage gap—among women but just over a tenth (11.3 percent) of the smaller 5.3 expansion of the 50/10 wage gap among men. For workers overall more than half (57.0 percent) of the increase in the 50/10 wage gap from 1979 to 2009 was accounted for by the erosion of the minimum wage. (Mishel, 2013)

By contrast to the United States, the minimum wage in Australia (as of this writing) is A$16.37 per hour. With the current exchange rate, the Australian minimum wage is roughly double the US rate. Tyler (2013) demonstrates that, since 1985, the growth in total employee compensation in the Netherlands, Germany, and Denmark has increased by approximately 200 percent, while in the United States, the increase has been less than 1 percent.

At the other end of the spectrum, executive compensation has grown by leaps and bounds. For example, from 1990 to 2005, CEOs' pay more than doubled the rise in the S&P 500 (Domhoff, 2013). Greenhouse (2011) quotes a source as saying, "'Pay for performance' often turns into pay without performance. Incentives are easy to game and can undermine people's intrinsic motives for doing a good job." The observation seems quite appropriate when one compares the growth in executive compensation to the growth in profits. The result is what Tyler (2013) calls "managerial capitalism."

In addition to the huge growth in executive compensation comes the realization that the wealthiest of families pay far less in federal taxes now than they did a few decades ago. One reason for this, which will be explored in a later chapter, is the reduction in the capital gains tax rate. In 1978, the rate was increased to 28 percent. At this time (as of 2009), the long-term capital gains rate is 15 percent. This change is one factor that leads Tyler (2013) to comment, "America's 400 wealthiest families paid 51.2 percent of their income in federal taxes in 1955, but only 18 percent in 2008" (p. 190). It is likely that most Americans would believe that more than 50 percent is too high a rate; it is an open question how many would consider 18 percent as too low a rate. It is also worth wondering how many citizens are aware that the richest among us pay so low a rate. Remember, Tyler's data precedes the 2009 cut of the long-term capital gains rate to

15 percent. A more recent estimate of the actual tax rate would very likely be lower than 18 percent.

Since the first term of George W. Bush, there has been a press for the lowering of taxes. Shortly after his inauguration in 2001, President Bush instituted a massive tax cut of well over $1 trillion. In a sense, a gauntlet was thrown down, and an attitude of continuous cutting began to form. The attitude has tended to be widespread across earners at almost all levels. The phenomenon, though, like the growth in real wealth, has tended to benefit the richest Americans most. The attitude has prompted David Brooks (2011), who is a conservative-leaning columnist and author, to comment,

> Moreover, many important Democrats are open to a truly large budget deal. President Obama has a strong incentive to reach a deal so he can campaign in 2012 as a moderate. The Senate majority leader, Harry Reid, has talked about supporting a debt reduction measure of $3 trillion or even $4 trillion if the Republicans meet him part way. There are Democrats in the White House and elsewhere who would be willing to accept Medicare cuts if the Republicans would be willing to increase revenues.
>
> If the Republican Party were a normal party, it would take advantage of this amazing moment. It is being offered the deal of the century: trillions of dollars in spending cuts in exchange for a few hundred billion dollars of revenue increases.
>
> A normal Republican Party would seize the opportunity to put a long-term limit on the growth of government. It would seize the opportunity to put the country on a sound fiscal footing. It would seize the opportunity to do these things without putting any real crimp in economic growth.

Brooks concludes that the Republican Party may no longer be a normal party; he has little confidence that the party will seize the opportunity. The line that appears to be drawn in the sand is that only cuts to the budget will be approved and no measures that would result in more revenue stand a chance.

One result of the attitude is that "when George W. Bush left office, 200,000, or two-thirds of all earners with taxable incomes exceeding $1 million, paid a lower tax rate than the typical taxpayer making less than $100,00" (Tyler, 2013, p. 190). Those making the lesser amount are likely to earn the money by means of salaries and wages, and they therefore pay that appropriate federal tax rate. Moreover, the totality of their earnings is subject to Social Security and Medicare taxes. Even if someone earns the $1 million in salary, only a small portion of those earnings are subject to the Social Security and Medicare taxes. For many of the wealthiest, though, the earnings are realized through capital gains and are thus subject to a lower tax rate. It must be noted that the distinction is based on a philosophical stance. If someone has the money to invest millions of dollars, the earnings from the investments are *different* in nature from salary and wage earnings—that is, if someone *labors* to earn a salary, that salary is less valuable than money received from investments. It is not that investing is not work, but it is, by definition, different from salaries and wages in such a way that the lower tax rate is warranted. Is this difference widely comprehended? If it were widely comprehended, would there be a ground swell for some sort of equity? What would federal revenues be if all earnings were treated as identical? What would be the impact of federal budget deficits?

The tax cutting dates back to Reagan's administration. However, rather than paying for tax cuts by means of budget cutting, the administration embarked on a massive program of borrowing. As Tyler (2013) points out, by 1983, Reagan borrowed $1 out of every $3 spent because the tax revenue could not support the spending (p. 194). Tyler (2013) adds, "Here are the facts: the Reagan era [1980 to the present] saw a jump to $53 trillion in overall American debt, from $5 trillion when that president took office" (p. 201). Democrats have the reputation of tax-and-spend behavior, but little has been said—in popular media or by pundits—about a borrow-and-spend strategy. Some tactics could be employed (possibly with considerable resistance). The current cap for Social Security taxation is $110,000 in earnings. Suppose that cap were raised to $150,000 but the payments were limited to the maximum rates that are presently in place. How many people would be affected? Would Social Security be solvent further into the future (provided the trust fund is not raided to pay for other federal expenditures)?

What is happening to those citizens who are part of the lower half (or more) of the earners in this country? "In 2010, 28 percent of participants reported having an outstanding loan against their retirement accounts, an all-time high, according to a survey of 110 large employers by Aon Hewitt, a human resources consultancy. And nearly 7 percent of employees took hardship withdrawals that year—roughly a 40 percent increase since the recession, while 42 percent of workers cashed out their plans rather than rolling them over when they changed jobs" (Fletcher, 2013). The obvious impact of such decisions is that these individuals will be less prepared to retire when they want to. It is a reasonable expectation that they will continue to work later in life in order to simultaneously earn salaries and wages when they are older plus contribute to retirement accounts longer in the hope that they can make up for the raid on their accounts. One aspect of this behavior that is seldom (if ever) spoken of is that, with individuals continuing to work later in life (perhaps past age seventy), there are fewer jobs becoming available for younger workers. The effects on unemployment may be palpable. The decisions by individuals (in considerable numbers) are having macroeconomic effects. Granted, the recent recession exacerbated the problem, but the slow recovery probably is not alleviating the problem.

The foregoing suggests a problem for which there is empirical evidence: "The relatively small middle class is shrinking. US Census Bureau statistics showed the share of national income in 2011 received by the three middle quintiles (60 percent) of households declined to 46.4 percent, from nearly 55 percent in 1980" (Tyler, 2013, p. 285). More Americans now describe themselves as lower to lower-middle class compared to figures as late as 2008. These data demonstrate that Paul Ryan is either ignorant or disingenuous: "Class is not a fixed designation in this country. We are in an upwardly mobile society with a lot of movement between income groups" (quoted in Zakaria, 2011). Zakaria admits that, over the most recent years, social mobility has stalled. Data presented about this illustrate that real income for most Americans has been stagnant since the 1980s. The top quintile, and especially the top 5 percent of the population, has enjoyed almost all the income growth over the past few decades. The middle-class income growth in the post–World War II decades has all but disappeared. There are no indications—based on public policy, federal taxation and spending, and corporate action—that these trends will be reversed any time soon.

Another difficulty plaguing the federal government is the impact of some budget cuts. The 2012 fiscal year budget for the Internal Revenue Service (probably the most demonized federal agency) was $300 million less than it was the previous year. The effect is that the IRS is less able to collect taxes that are owed. Rein (2012) reports the IRS estimated that people and companies underpaid in 2011 by more than $385 billion. That is an amount that would bring the federal budget deficit closer to zero. If the closing of loopholes for individuals and corporations were added to the previously stated revenue, the annual deficit might disappear altogether. As Elizabeth Warren (2014) emphasizes, these actions are guided by will and choice by the land's legislators. Of course, a similar exercise of will and choice is required to determine what the money will be spent on.

It should be stressed that the owed money is simply not being paid. Individuals and companies also hide taxable revenue in havens offshore; it is almost impossible to estimate how much *should* be paid in corporate taxes because of such activity. It could be that the annual deficit would disappear if all taxes could be collected. One thing that should be remembered is that, as Piketty (2014) says, "there is no natural, spontaneous process to prevent destabilizing, inegalitarian forces from prevailing permanently" (p. 21). In short, an end to inequality will not simply happen; it will require policy, its enforcement, taxation and redistribution, and (above all) a moral political economy grounded in justice for inequality to be eradicated. This claim will be expanded upon in the next chapter.

## Education

Nothing is more important than having a productive and effective educational system at all levels; the entirety of American society's future depends on this. Financing also affects education at all levels and in many ways. One of the most direct sources is the public funding of P–24 (preschool through graduate) education. There is no question that education is an expensive enterprise—teachers, facilities, equipment, materials, and so on all cost money, and the money to provide adequate teaching and learning is in short supply. As is true of many public (and private) financing imperatives, funding for education has been hit hard by the recent recession. Since public education is financed through tax collections (frequently property taxes for public P–12 education), the housing bubble took a toll on tax collections. If the assessed values of many homes declined, it stands to reason that the property taxes collected would decline. While property values have been rising slowly, the school funding dilemma persists. Further, the Obama stimulus package provided some short-lived relief for schools, but the infusion of money was temporary. The National Assessment of Educational Progress (NAEP) on school funding points to the difficulties experienced nationally: "Many states reduced their investment in K-12 public education in 2011. All but three states lowered their fiscal effort on education between 2010 and 2011, when they faced the fiscal cliff created by the loss of federal stimulus funds" (Baker, Sciarra, and Farrie, 2014). The national report card points to additional concerns related to base funding:

- The disparities in funding among states are vast, with average per pupil funding ranging from \$6,753 in Idaho, to \$17,397 in Wyoming. In six states (Tennessee, Mississippi, Oklahoma, Arizona, Utah, Idaho), average funding levels are below \$8,000 per pupil.
- The majority of states have flat or regressive funding distribution patterns that ignore the need for additional funding in high poverty settings. Even among "progressive" states, only eight provide more than a 10% boost to high poverty districts. In the five most regressive states (North Dakota, Vermont, New Hampshire, North Carolina, Nevada), the poorest districts receive at least 20% less funding than higher wealth districts.
- States making the strongest effort to fund public education devote more than 4.5% of their economic productivity to schools (Vermont, New

Jersey, New York), while the lowest effort states (Oregon, South Dakota, Delaware) allocate 2.5% or less.

- The extent to which school-aged children do not attend public schools raises a red flag in a number of states. In Delaware, Hawaii, Louisiana, and Washington, D.C. approximately 20% of children do not attend public schools, and the average household income of these children is often dramatically higher than that of their public school peers. Household incomes of non-public school families in Louisiana, Tennessee, Texas, and the District of Columbia are as much as two to three times higher than in the case of public school families. These data point to a potential lack of political and community support for fairly financing public education in these states. (Baker, Sciarra, and Farrie, 2014)

The National Education Association provides the most up-to-date tabular data, which shows comparisons by state according to many variables. One of the important data points concerns average teacher pay. In particular, the most recent report (National Education Association, 2014) demonstrates that from the 2002–2003 to 2012–2013 decade, 34 states experienced real average salary declines, with North Carolina seeing a 15 percent drop. The salary data are just one indicator of the state of affairs. The predicament in the state of Wisconsin in 2011 may have generated the greatest amount of press, and the news was not good for education. In the aftermath of the passage of the "Wisconsin Budget Repair Bill," tax revenues for education declined by $47 million in 2011–2012. In some districts, there were pension concessions (cuts), and in some, there were wage freezes. Given that the national average salary for a teacher is well under $60,000 a year, the burden for budget balancing falls upon the sector of the economy that can ill afford it. And it can be argued that education is one of the most important commitments a state can make to its future; poorly educated individuals result in a poorly equipped work force. In short, the highest quality education is an investment in the economic, as well as the intellectual, health of a state and of the nation.

People—informed people—should be incensed at the manner in which education has been treated in this country. And the ire should take a very different shape from its customary guise, which often includes anger at "failing" schools, "lazy" teachers, tenure, salaries, and other factors. People should become much more aware of what a political hot issue education represents. My home state of Missouri can serve as an object lesson of what can go terribly wrong in the political sphere, where education can be a literal pawn in a chess game played by a multimillionaire. Rex Sinquefield has made it a personal mission to transform the totality of Missouri politics when it comes to education. Among other things, Sinquefield is the founder of the Show-Me Institute, whose motto is "Advancing Liberty with

Responsibility by Promoting Market Solutions for Missouri Public Policy." (Much more will be said about the idea of market solutions to public issues later.) Since 2007, Sinquefield has made disclosed donations of about $28 million to Missouri candidates and issues, among which are school choice, the growth of charter schools, and the abolition of teacher tenure (see Graves and Fischer, 2014). He has also donated to politicians who want to cut, or even eliminate, the state income tax, which funds many public programs, and to gut property taxes (even as he owns a 22,000 square-foot house in the Ozarks, which sits on hundreds of acres, plus another house in St. Louis).

Sinquefield is also a staunch supporter of the American Legislative Exchange Council (ALEC). ALEC is a "free market" libertarian organization that promotes the predominance of business and business people in decision making about public affairs. The mission states that ALEC is "a nonpartisan membership association for conservative state lawmakers who shared a common belief in limited government, free markets, federalism, and individual liberty. Their vision and initiative resulted in the creation of a voluntary membership association for people who believed that government closest to the people was fundamentally more effective, more just, and a better guarantor of freedom than the distant, bloated federal government in Washington, D.C." (About ALEC, 2014). The organization's conception of justice can and should be open to question. ALEC, for example, has been behind what is called "parent trigger" legislation that would enable parents to create referenda to allow the seizure of control of schools and the firing of school administrators and teachers. There is no question that parents should be engaged in student learning, but it is at the very least an open question if parents are best suited to control schools. The Show-Me Institute provided material support for the legislative initiative.

Dissatisfaction with public schools as they exist, coupled with a lack of understanding of the challenges faced by public education have contributed to another phenomenon—privatization. There are a number of corporations that are willing to usurp the administration and operation of schools . . . for a fee. The plans usually employ voucher systems so that parents can opt out of traditional public schools in favor of privately controlled ones. Woodard (2013) observes, "*Education Week* recently reported that at the start of the decade, less than a quarter of K-12 giving from top foundations was given to groups supporting charter schools and privatization, about $90 million in all. By 2010, $540 million—fully 64 percent of major foundation giving—was directed to these private groups, including KIPP, Teach for America, the NewSchools Venture Fund, the Charter School Growth Fund, and the D.C. Public Education Fund." Teach for

America, for example, administers dozens of schools nationwide. Edison-Learning, a for-profit corporation, manages more than fifty schools.

The problematic nature of the for-profit management of schools is explored by Buchheit (2014), who suggests some specific difficulties with the structure:

1. Charter schools have not improved education.
2. The profit motive perverts the goals of education.
3. Advanced profit-making: higher education.
4. Lower-performing children [are] left behind.

As is frequently the case with consumerist capitalism, the attraction of the private sector is a siren song, attracting people who are disaffected with the public sphere and the status quo. There is no need to delve deeply into the matter of privatization here; Diane Ravitch (2013) covers the matter completely and objectively. One passage from her book sums up one of the most potentially disastrous effects of the movement: "If we truly care about the welfare of the most vulnerable children in our society, we will turn out efforts to reducing segregation and poverty. These are the root causes of poor academic performance. We must lower the child poverty rate. It is a national scandal. Other nations have figured out how to protect the well-being of children and families, and we have not. It's time to get to work on policies and programs that address root causes" (Ravitch, 2013, p. 325). The present rate of individuals living at or below the poverty level is more than 16 percent of the population. The number of children living in poverty has been increasing annually over the recent several years. Ravitch's diagnosis cannot be denied.

## Higher Education

The political economy of higher education is, if anything, more complicated than that of P–12 education. For one thing, students must pay tuition, even at public institutions. Also, states are, for the most part, directly responsible for the public funding side of budgets.

Over the last couple decades, public support (in the form of state appropriations) has decreased dramatically. For one institution—the University of Missouri—the proportion of state appropriations as a part of total financing has fallen from roughly 70 percent of the whole in 1990 to a little more than 30 percent in 2014. An obvious corollary is that tuition and fees now form a major portion of funding. (The percentage provided by indirect cost—that is, the component of external funding that the university can recover to apply to facilities and the administration of grants—has risen, indicating that the university has worked to provide some of its own funding.) The University of Missouri's plight is typical for public institutions; public support for higher education at all levels has plummeted over recent years. For example, when health services and hospitals are included, the University of Kentucky receives only about 10 percent of its budget by means of state appropriations ("Fact Booklet," 2014) An empirical study by Zhang (2009) demonstrates quite clearly that state appropriations have a positive effect on graduation rates. The matter of public funding for public education is shown to be a high-reward dynamic. As governments make demands on institutions for accountability, it is incumbent on legislators to understand the impact of their decisions on the outcomes they hope to enhance. As will be shown very shortly, colleges and universities have taken rather dramatic action to offset the decline in funding.

It is obvious that tuition rates have risen in the last several years; there has to be a way to recoup revenues lost because of the decline in state appropriations. According to data available from the National Center for Education Statistics, tuition has increased by 242 percent over three decades (in constant dollars) at four-year institutions. It should be noted that the increase at two-year colleges is just 63 percent (again, in constant dollars). An analysis published in an American Association of University Professors (AAUP) report (2013) holds,

> Much of the tuition price increase in public higher education over the last several years has been a direct consequence of reductions in state appropriations. As states have abdicated their responsibility for ensuring access to postsecondary education, students and their families have been forced to bear more of the costs in the form of higher tuition prices. Because good jobs migrate to the locations with the best-educated workforces, states such as Arizona, New Hampshire, Louisiana, Alabama, Florida, and California may be retarding their future rates of growth for decades to come.

The dire state of affairs is not likely to get better in the near future; declines in state appropriations are likely to continue for the foreseeable future. If there is a temptation to blame any increases in the costs of higher education on faculty salaries, data provide a different story. Administrative costs have largely driven the 28 percent rise from 2000 to 2012 (Carlson, 2014). What's more, the report says, "The number of full-time faculty and staff members per professional or managerial administrator has declined 40 percent, to around 2.5 to 1 . . . You can't blame faculty salaries for the rise in tuition. Faculty salaries were [essentially flat] from 2000 to 2012" (Carlson, 2014). Moreover, community colleges lost not only full-time instructors (relative to the number of students) but also part-time instructors.

Many colleges and universities have seen increases in their student populations; few have seen increases in the numbers of faculty, especially full-time tenured and tenure-track faculty.

One of the principal tactics that universities have adopted over the past several years to address the matter of institutional financing has been to alter the personnel mix. Most universities now have fewer tenured and tenure-track faculty and more of what is known as "contingent" faculty (i.e., part-time teachers and faculty who are not eligible for tenure). The concerns are not trivial; contingent faculty, particularly part-time faculty, have less contact with students and less of a decision-making role in important aspects of university and programmatic governance.

The percentage of total faculty represented by, especially, part-timers has risen dramatically. The proportion of tenured and tenure-track faculty has been falling over the years. On some campuses, the numbers of nontenure-track faculty have also climbed. Naturally, institutions do not pay benefits for the vast majority of part-time faculty, thus saving money. Also, the salaries of nontenure-track personnel are usually lower than those for tenured and tenure-track faculty. It is, of course, impossible to claim that the decline in state appropriations *causes* these phenomena, but there can be little doubt that the decline contributes to them. The warnings (stated previously) by the AAUP should be heeded, but it is an open question whether the general public—or even the parents of college-age students and the students themselves—is cognizant of the possible effects of the personnel trends. Students may wonder why they are taught by part-time instructors and not by full-time regular faculty, but they may not have a clear picture of the dynamics of staffing. There is nothing to indicate that the part-time or other contingent faculty are not qualified to teach—many, if not most, may have earned doctorates in their fields. They are not, however, full participants in the admission of students, the establishment of the curriculum, or the overall faculty governance of the academic program.

## Contradictions of Capital

Piketty (2014) explicates the principal contradiction succinctly:

> The overall conclusion of this study is that a market economy based on private property, if left to itself, contains powerful forces of convergence, associated in particular with the diffusion of knowledge and skills; but it also contains powerful forces of divergence, which are potentially threatening to democratic societies and to the values of social justice on which they are based. The principal destabilizing force has to do with the fact that the private rate of return on capital, *r*, can be significantly higher for long periods

> of time than the rate of growth of income and output, $g$. The inequality $r > g$ implies that wealth accumulated in the past grows more rapidly than output and wages. (p. 571)

Piketty's conclusion has come under fire (and has even been dismissed), but it follows from his extensive analysis, in historical and contemporary terms, of multiple variables and their relationships.

Harvey (2014) has even more to say about the contradictions of capital. In fact, he details 17 contradictions. He divides these into foundational contradictions (including use value and exchange value, and capital and labor), moving contradictions (such as divisions of labor, monopoly and competition, and freedom and domination), and dangerous contradictions (endless compound growth, capital's relation to nature, and the revolt of human nature). He explains each of the 17 and relates where contradiction resides as well as the dilemmas the contradictions create. It is neither possible nor necessary to go into the detail of his analysis, but one caveat is important: "I am not saying . . . that everything that happens under capitalism is driven by the contradictions of capital. But I do want to identify those internal contradictions of capital that have produced the recent crises and *made it seem as if there is no clear exit without destroying the lives and livelihoods of millions of people around the world*" (emphasis added; Harvey, 2014, p. 9). It is important to note that even among the most strident critics of capital, the recognition of the contradictions is rare. Better understanding of the internal consistency of capital could well contribute to a more readily adopted reform of basic economic and financial operations in the United States and across the globe.

## Neoliberalism

We will conclude this chapter with an examination of the phenomenon of neoliberalism. The first thing that must be mentioned is that neoliberalism is not a Leftist stance; it is a development of the classical liberalism of the nineteenth century tinged with twentieth-century economic theory. David Harvey (2005) dates neoliberalism back to the 1970s and says, "It holds that the social good will be maximized by maximizing the reach and frequency of market transactions, and it seeks to bring all human action into the domain of the market" (p. 3). The economic dilemma of the 1970s presented an opportunity for many economists who had a history of being fundamental anti-Keynesians. Naomi Klein (2007) refers to the 1973 Chilean coup that brought Allende to power. Allende sought the economic assistance of economists from the Chicago School to right the Chilean economic ship. Those economists already demonstrated the neoliberal tendencies that will soon be described. The 1970s presented an array of problems that did not fit the traditional economic thought and practice: "Stagflation broke the back of the Keynesian orthodoxy—as both a generative theory and as a system of government—the long-anticipated crisis for which Friedman's style of monetarist economics provided readily presentable, if ultimately flawed 'solution'" (Peck, 2010, p. 5).

These new ways of thinking, while widely held, are not considered by the entirety of one political part, but it has a decidedly ideological grounding. As Harvey (2005) makes clear, the market—especially the market that is free from regulation or limitation—is, or should be, the primal force in the political-economic life of a postmodern world. This world, this brand of postmodernism, is antithetical to a public sphere where political and economic views are articulated, debated, and accepted or rejected by means of an open discursive practice. In fact, the limits to discourse may be one of the most telling features of neoliberalism. Other theorists, such as Alain Touraine (2001), offer international perspectives that cannot be ignored: "The defining feature of capitalism is that change is managed by the market; that of socialism is the dominant role played by the state [primarily outside the United States]" (p. 9).

Giroux (2004) highlights what he calls "noncommodified public spheres" as one of the most important elements of a functioning democracy. It is in such spaces where ideas are proffered and discussed and assessed. The most important element of the public spheres is openness; these are literal and virtual places where the very nature of markets can be questioned. However, claims Giroux (and Harvey), the Left has been blind to the closed nature of neoliberalized space and has not recognized the threats to freedom and justice that have emerged. Harvey (2005) writes, "Neoliberalization required both politically and economically the construction of a neoliberal market-based populist culture of differentiated consumerism and individual libertarianism. As such it proved more than a little compatible with that cultural impulse called 'postmodernism' which had long been lurking in the wings but could now emerge full-blown as both a cultural and an intellectual dominant" (p. 42). There is more than a little irony in this postmodern push; postmodernism tends to be embraced by putative liberals who simultaneously reject the overarching political stance of liberalism (both as a positive political economy *and* as a negation of many conservative values and practices). Within that negative thrust, there rests the uncomfortable tolerance for neoliberalism as a (not particularly viable) alternative to traditional liberalism. It may be that the liberalism that supposedly gives rise to postmodernism should be called into question. As Lyotard (1984) observes, knowledge is transformed into amounts of information, and anything that cannot be so transformed has no value; knowledge, such as it is, exists to be bought and sold (p. 4). Fives (2009) offers a cogent critique of the phenomenon:

> Postmodernists are calling into question the whole project of providing universal rational moral foundations for politics . . . As some liberals have argued, postmodernists cannot avoid a "performative contradiction" whereby the attempt to state the postmodern position contradicts the content of that statement. Moreover, postmodernism descends into epistemological relativism and immoralism. And although some liberals hope to find common ground with postmodernism, so as better to identify the power relations shaping and distorting democratic debate, this article argues that liberalism and postmodernism are, in the final analysis, incompatible. However, liberals are caught in a bind. They call on participants within democratic debate to exercise certain virtues, whether 'mutual respect' or 'reasonableness.' As liberals insist on impartiality, however, they cannot offer a justification for the argument that such character traits are virtues; that is, inherently, intrinsically good qualities . . . Postmodernism must be criticized on the grounds that it stands opposed to what is intrinsically good. (p. 962)

There are implications for individuals in neoliberalism, although those implications may usually be unseen and unknown. The individual has an essential place in the political economy primarily as a consumer; the choices made by people as consumers dictate some of the microlevel successes and failures of the economy (but also fit soundly into the macroeconomy). Individuals engage in transactions that keep the political-economic engine running smoothly—at least according to neoliberals. The reach of the transaction, while not unbounded, is broad and deep. The adherents of rational choice theory and its extent—mentioned previously—may not call themselves neoliberals, but they are neoliberals, nonetheless. Education, work, marriage, and so on are transactions one engages in through the course of life. All those choices follow a very particular path—one that Harvey (2005) explicates well: "The neoliberal state [favors] strong individual private property rights, the rule of law, and the institutions of freely functioning markets and free trade . . . Individual success or failure are interpreted in terms of entrepreneurial virtues or personal failings (such as not investing significantly enough in one's own human capital through education) rather than being attributed to any systemic property (such as the class exclusions usually attributed to capitalism)" (pp. 64, 65–66).

Peck (2010), again, has a unique perspective on the history, the present, and the goals of neoliberalism: "Neoliberalism . . . has only ever existed in 'impure' form, indeed *can* only exist in messy hybrids. Its utopian vision of a free society and free economy is ultimately unrealizable . . . Ironically, neoliberalism possesses a progressive, forward-leaning dynamic by virtue of the *unsustainability* of its idealized destination. In practice, neoliberalism has never been about a once-and-for-all liberalization, an evacuation of the state" (p. 7). Peck presents the most balanced critique of neoliberalism that exists. He is able to comprehend the ironic and contradictory aims and practices of those who attempt to put the theory (if it can be called a theory) in place. He also recognizes the necessary failure of the practice, even as economists, policymakers, and market mavens insist upon it operability. What we are left with, as he points out, is a "messy hybrid" that, in many ways, is a perversion of the very idea of a free market and free consumers who can exercise choice. Those are actually fictions, and Touraine (2001) puts his finger on the cause: "*We have in reality moved from integrated national models to an international situation in which the various dimensions of economic, social and cultural life have become separated and divorced from one another*" (emphasis in original; p. 17). One might say that the dynamics have become confused to the point where a person cannot tell where the cultural ends and the economic begins.

As Giroux (2004) adds, the neoliberal ideology omits government as a positive force and nonprofit agencies as providers of assistance and insists on an authoritarian cloak that is largely invisible even as people acquiesce to the authority of the market. The ideology may extend most deeply into education, creating generations of individuals bent on optimizing transactions. The word "individual" has been employed deliberately throughout this section; neoliberalism cannot succeed within any kind of collective ethos. The ethic of success and advancement is singular. It is entirely up to each individual, acting through models of rational choice, to make it in this world. The choices extend to every aspect of life, including faith and religion: "In their individualized messages of financial blessing, televangelists tend to ignore the extent to which economic neoliberalization has produced local politics and market trends that limit possibilities for the average or 'below' minimum wage working Americans" (Frederick, 2010, p. 231).

In light of the examination of neoliberalism, some claims by economists have to be looked at rather skeptically. Sorman (2009) makes an explicit claim that economics is a science, like any other science. He goes so far as to say, "Medicine is not the only science that saves lives; economics does, too" (p. 45). But then he hedges and says that economics is a human science. If the last component of his claim is correct, then economics should have a great deal in common with disciplines that include psychology, sociology, and anthropology, among others. His (2009) claim is problematic, as is illustrated when he remarks that since 1890, the growth rate per capita has been 2 percent annually and that the annual growth rate of investments has been 4 percent annually (p. 18). As has been demonstrated here, there is no "average" citizen of the United States, at least not in any meaningful sense. Poverty has climbed, as has the wealth of the fewest among us. We can be sure that sophisticated economic analysis is powerful; we have seen evidence of that. Simplistic examinations, guided by erroneous assumptions (see Schlefer, 2012), do more harm than good by obfuscating the actual state of the political and social economy. The assertions made by ideologues who operate under a guise of science distort the real picture and misinform the populace. When complexity is the rule, it becomes more important for there to be clear and honest media and individuals to tell Americans the real story.

The present predicament is summed up accurately by Basu (2011), who critiques the entirety of today's economic systemic structure:

> A central message of [his] book is that the form of capitalism that so much of the world either relies on or aspires to is a grossly unfair system. The belief, popularized in so many books and by so much journalese, that all we need to do is work toward perfecting this system and all will be well, is a myth perpetrated, at times deliberately and at times unwittingly, in the interests of those who gain from the persistence of this unjust system . . . It is the same kind of belief that makes people feel that "redistributing the wealth" is wrong because the current distribution is somehow the right one, forgetting that the current distribution itself is, in part, an outcome of grasping, lobbying, and the bartering of favors as well as the accumulation of wealth that has occurred through inheritances passed carefully down dynastic lineages. (p. 209)

In part, the error is a matter of forgetting David Hume's maxim that one cannot infer "ought" from "is." It is here that this chapter will conclude, but some of the themes will arise again as we turn our attention to the public good.

3

# The Public Good and the Public Sphere

> The equitable, while being just, is not the just according to the law, but is rather a corrective to legal justice. The reason for this is that the law is always in a way universal, and there are cases for which it is not possible to offer a general assertion that applies to them with certitude . . . One sees clearly therefore what the equitable is, that the equitable is just and that it is superior in a certain way to the just.
>
> —Aristotle, *Nicomachean Ethics*, Book V, 11137b

Perhaps the first challenge faced in this chapter is the defining of the public good in a way that both makes sense politically and socially *and* captures (if such is possible) an indisputable description. A very brief beginning to a definition is that the public good embraces integrity, honesty, ethics, justice, and freedom. Of course, each of the components requires some explication. Integrity, which carries connotations of honor and virtue, also can be defined as being whole and complete. Being honorable is something most people can recognize, but virtue may mean different things to different individuals. That will warrant exploration. Honesty is a characteristic that almost all can recognize; a question that may arise, though, is whether complete honesty is called for in every situation. Ethical behavior is also usually recognizable by most of us, but it has come under some question in recent years. Justice and freedom, as is evident from the discussion in Chapter 1, are common rhetorical tropes but are used in malleable ways, especially politically. Some extended treatment of these characteristics is necessary before specific examples can be discussed.

## Integrity

What may come to mind first when one hears about integrity is personal integrity in a professional setting. There are frequently norms of action and behavior associated with various fields of work, including medicine, law, education, and so on. People are expected to act with integrity in the contexts of the various professions and their norms. There may be penalties when individuals fail to uphold the norms. Santoro (2013), in addressing the profession of teaching, emphasizes that integrity is not merely a concern while an individual is at school; it is an essential component of identity, of self. Santoro (2013) suggests a model that illustrates how personal integrity, integrity in teaching, and professional integrity interrelate. The intersection of the three components marks the goal for teachers. Santoro (2013) maintains that when an individual leaves teaching, professional integrity may disappear, which can lead to a diminishing of the other elements of integrity (p. 565). The model, plus the possibility of the diminution of self-integrity, can occur in the context of most professions.

Personal and professional integrity may, according to some, be considered something of a prerequisite for certain fields. Tyreman (2011) claims that such is the case when workers are in the business of caring for vulnerable individuals and populations. Tyreman speaks principally about nursing, but the same applies to all health care (and, one could argue, social service) professions. Tyreman (2011) is especially concerned with recent changes in the work of health care, where multiple disciplines and fields of work are involved in the key matters of things like patient care:

> A . . . reason for revisiting integrity concerns the changing nature of Western healthcare. Modern healthcare has become heavily reliant on multiprofessional and cross-disciplinary work. The roles of individuals acting professionally is very different today from how it was three or four decades ago. Even in primary care, it is rarely one individual who has sole responsibility for a patient; practice nurses, pharmacists, physiotherapists, and so on, work with doctors in a team to provide effective care. So is there still a place for the individual to demonstrate integrity or is it inevitable that healthcare behaviour should be codified and good practice only defined in terms of bureaucratic standards? (p. 108)

One concern that can arise is whether the norms for integrity are shared across the disciplines. Another concern is whether the matter of integrity is equally embedded in identity and self across the fields of work. Even if the latter is the case, do the definitions of identity share enough in common that patient care is optimally provided?

The foregoing addresses ideals and proposed norms for integrity in action and as part of identity, but there remain questions and concerns about integrity in practice. Some measures can be provided for consideration. A search of the Medline database reveals that there have been more than 3,000 journal articles that have been retracted for a number of reasons. Moreover, only 327 articles were retracted from 1966 through 1999. From 2000 to the present, a total of 2,673 have been retracted. One reason for the increase in recent years may be a heightened sensitivity to problematic research and publication. Another potential reason could be increased numbers of errors and misconduct in scientific work. Chatterjee (2014) writes, "Incidences of scientific misconduct, acceptance of such misconducts among scientific community and academia are increasing. Reproducibility and trustworthiness of even 'landmark' research and publications have reached worryingly low levels. The biotech company, Amgen, found it could reproduce only 6 of 53 such 'landmark' studies in cancer research. Previously, a group at pharmaceutical company Bayer managed to repeat just one-fourth of 67 similarly important papers" (p. 693).

Many commentators have speculated on reasons for the increases in problematic work; the suggestions include the enormous amount of money that is at stake for corporations in the development of new pharmaceuticals and treatments, as well as the intense pressures on faculty members to publish and attract external funding in order to be promoted and earn tenure. These kinds of observations have implications for personal and professional integrity among scientists here in the United States and around the world.

## Honesty

Honesty is certainly related to integrity, but it carries some specific elements as a virtue, in both personal and professional milieux:

> such considerations would seem to engender difficulties for understanding the virtue-ethical status of *honesty*—about, precisely, whether honesty is best regarded as an epistemic or as a moral virtue. On the one hand, the logical object or "target" of honesty would seem to be *truth*, in which case honesty has the belief-to-world direction of fit—and some concern with truth might be expected of the honest agent. Further, while agents might be considered epistemically defective by dint of failure to seek truth on this or that matter, it is not always obvious that we should regard them as *morally* dishonest on this account. On the other hand, if honesty is taken to imply commitment to *truthfulness*, it seems clear that we do morally blame agents for lying or concealing the truth. (Carr, 2014, p. 4)

For the public good to function, we must link honesty with truthfulness, which includes the avoidance of deception or concealment. The definition is connected with politics, for example, since people have a right to expect that officials—elected or appointed—be truthful in their statements and actions. If they are not truthful, democracy itself becomes endangered; it is difficult for the populace to have confidence in what is being told to them. Of course, truthfulness in itself has limitations related to the public good. As Lynch (2004) points out, it is opposed to the good if someone pursues the truth about the most effective ways to torture another human being (p. 50; praise for the enhanced interrogation that occurred during the war in Iraq is precisely the kind of negative example Lynch has in mind).

It should be noted here that, in the context of the public good, lying for altruistic reasons is not a major concern. Of course, one should dissimulate if complete honesty might lead to harm to another person. That action might be said to be public in some way, but it is something quite different from normal political, economic, or (in general) public speech. A politician who has no intention of, say, upholding the regulations of the Environmental Protection Agency (EPA) does not act in the public good by lying and saying that he or she will uphold those regulations. Similarly, an activist does not advance his or her cause when he or she misrepresents the actions of, for example, a coal mining company. The deceptions are self-serving; they are antithetical to the discourse that is needed in public debate. Let us presume that, as a citizen, I want to hear the most trustworthy information about the topics I find important. A speaker who lies loses my trust, not simply on the matter at hand but in that person's discursive practice generally. Lynch (2004), says, "If there is no such thing as being right, wrong, or even in-between, then we can't really disagree in opinion" (p. 161). As a citizen, I must be willing to take the responsibility to sort out meaning in legitimate disagreements, since honest persons can interpret events or actions differently without engaging in deceit. All that signals is that I must seek out more speech so that I can make determinations of trustworthiness.

## Ethics

There are, of course, numerous ethical schools of thought. At the outset, and in keeping with what has been said previously, we can consider virtue ethics. Such a manner of considering the right ways to act dates back to antiquity; in Greek philosophy, a set of virtues—including courage, prudence, and so on—defined the worth of a person. The ultimate goal in the ancient world was eudaimonia: "*Eudaimonia* means, literally, to be possessed of a good demon, and this conveys the idea of extreme good fortune on the part of its possessor. One possessed of *eudaimonia* was thought by the ancients as blessed beyond measure, as having won something of supreme worth and, at the same time, something very elusive and hence rare" (Taylor, 2002, p. 108).

We can date the more modern concept of virtues at least as far back as the beatitudes of the Gospels. The principal difference between the ancient and modern virtues is that the modern sort is defined mainly by moral action. Where courage would have been valued in Greece and Rome, generosity, mercy, purity of heart, and so on tend to be prized in modern ethics. In both cases, virtues are normative; they designate qualities that one should possess to be considered an ethical or "good" person. A distinction between ancient and modern virtues, though, is that in ancient times, the virtues included skills that distinguished one person from another. In modern, particularly Christian, virtue ethics, it is the qualities that people not only possess but act on (relative to others) that constitute distinguishing features. The Christian tradition is a change from the older Judeo-Christian standard represented by, for example, the Ten Commandments. Those commandments demand abstention or restraint, while the beatitudes emphasize positive qualities. As is the case with most ethical theories, there are opponents who negate the validity of the school of thought; virtue ethics is no different. Perhaps the most notable critic of virtue ethics is MacIntyre (2007), who finds it questionable that a set of normative qualities can adequately define a person and the ethical standards according to which that person can live.

Among modern philosophers, virtue ethics has fallen somewhat out of favor. There are other ways of thinking that have greater currency; only a couple varieties will be mentioned here as examples. One, which is associated primarily with Emmanuel Kant, is deontology, or ethics based on rules and their adherence. Kant's principal idea is that people must act out of duty—to oneself and toward others. Perhaps the best known and most often mentioned of Kant's conceptions is the "categorical imperative." According to this imperative, one must always act in such a way that the action should be exemplary of a universal law; one must always treat oneself and another as an end, never as a means; every person must act as though he or she is legislating the universal concept of ends. Some, following Kant, have taken deontology to be absolutist, but there is an error to that way of thinking. One example of Kantian ethics is that one should never lie. An example that arises is a murderer coming to one's door seeking the person he wishes to kill. Some absolutists maintain that if one knows where the intended victim is, one must tell the murderer. Such a belief is fallacious, as Eagleton (2004) has shown. An overriding duty is to treat others as ends, and that entails keeping the intended victim safe. Therefore, one must err on the side of lying in this conflict of duties, since keeping the other safe outweighs telling a lie. The absolutist stance is negated by this example.

Another contender for primacy in modern ethics is consequentialism. The gist of this way of thinking is evident in the name; the consequences of one's actions (or *in*actions) are most important. If an individual acts deliberately to harm another person and does so, then there are fairly clear outcomes that result from the first person's actions. The case of Bernie Madoff might be mentioned here. He willfully defrauded many people to the tune of about $50 billion. As a result, many of his victims lost all that they had; some committed suicide. There is no question that Madoff acted unethically. Many more examples could be given. As a school of ethical thought, however, the matter is not merely deciding on a case-by-case basis whether particular acts are ethical or not; it is whether this method of judgment is sufficient for a theory. Some, notably Samuel Scheffler (1994), maintain that it is not.

Utilitarianism, articulated in the nineteenth century, has not disappeared in the twenty-first century. As stated by the likes of Jeremy Bentham and John Stuart Mill, utilitarianism provides the structure by which the greatest happiness for the greatest number is provided. In part, happiness has been defined as pleasure, but it has also included "good" for the greatest number of people. As many utilitarians hold, "good" is agent neutral; it is a matter of providing not for the poorest or the most needy but for the greatest proportion of the population. A criticism has been that since the poor constitute a minority, their needs are not adequately provided for in classical utilitarianism. A worry that has been expressed by some philosophers, including Bernard Williams (1995), is that utilitarianism carries an elitism that renders it too selective to be a general theory of ethics. The principal tenets of formal utilitarianism are not adhered to by many within the realm of practical ethics today, but vestiges of the program do remain, as we will see, within concepts of justice.

For the purposes of establishing and maintaining the public good, it probably becomes evident that there can be some frustration with every theory of ethics (and be sure that this brief outline does not describe every theory). Where there may be some aspects of a program that appears reasonable and doable, there may be perceived difficulties with each program. For a genuine public good to become manifest in our society, we may have to select the most advantageous elements of a variety of theories while abandoning the most problematic components of each theory. For example, we may well determine that there are virtues that we hope to instill in citizens; we may want generosity, kindness, prudence, and other virtues to be integrated into people's lives. We may also desire that people be truthful: that honesty is the rule in our discourse and our actions. This can include demands that politicians not lie or dissimulate when they communicate with the populace: that they be straightforward with regard to their intentions if elected and in office. (Realistic expectations may allow for some opaqueness when it comes to national security but only within those limits.) There should also be demands of truthfulness in business dealings and on the parts of those speaking and acting on behalf of corporations. Certain duties can also be identified as well, and we should expect that others (and ourselves) adhere to some version of the Kantian categorical imperative. The first imperative could well be treating people only as ends, not as means.

It is a combination—but not just any combination—of the features of theories and the traits demanded that can best serve the public good. In short, the goal is to locate the most efficacious behaviors and beliefs that will heighten the ethical treatment not just of other individuals but also of other groups and segments of the population. One lesson from Chapter 2 is that the current behavior of people and corporations is falling short of achieving the best lives for *all* citizens of the United States. The failings frequently entail information and informational behavior. The failings can be in the area of dissimulation—deceit, hypocrisy, duplicity, or subterfuge—in order to gain advantage over people, or it can be in the area of hiding what is occurring (especially when what is happening has a deleterious impact on people). The public good is a concept that is opposed to those failings, whether deliberate (which may be more often the case) or inadvertent.

## Justice

Justice was discussed in Chapter 1; only a bit more will be said here. Regarding the public good, we should pay close attention to what Michael Sandel (2009) has to say: the important questions about justice "are not only about how individuals should treat one another. They are also about what the law should be, and about how society should be organized" (p. 6). Sandel (2009) also argues against utilitarianism as a means of achieving justice:

> The utilitarian approach has two defects: First, it makes justice and rights a matter of calculation, not principle. Second, by trying to translate all human goods into a single, uniform measure of value, it flattens them, and takes no account of the qualitative differences among them . . . A just society can't be achieved simply by maximizing utility or by securing freedom by choice. To

> achieve a just society we have to reason together about the meaning of the good life, and to create a public culture hospitable to the disagreements that will inevitably arise. (pp. 260, 261)

Sandel is speaking of "classical" utilitarianism, but the solution is a latter-day version of the theory that incorporates discourse about what really achieves a more universal (or as widespread as possible) level of happiness or the good life. Nothing less actually helps to realize the goals of the public good as envisioned here.

In his articulation of justice, Philip Pettit (2014) paraphrases Keats by saying, "Justice is freedom, freedom justice" (p. xxiii). In elaborating on his maxim, he adds, "Justice in the narrower sense—that is, social justice—is the virtue of a national or domestic framework in which people's relationships with one another are subject to a just social order: one, intuitively, that gives people the resources and protections of equally free citizens" (pp. xxiv–xxv). The addition of freedom to the concept of justice adds, at least according to Pettit, an egalitarian component. Pettit (2014) actually emphasizes freedom above all and maintains that, among all competing versions of justice, a republican (not to be confused with party politics) model serves best: "The republican theory of justice, like any plausible alternative, will argue for the nurture and care of the society's infrastructure, both institutional and material, since this will affect the extent to which people can exercise and enjoy basic liberties" (p. 84). To this we can add that freedom of access to information of all sorts is likewise necessary for the justice spoken of by Pettit.

The previous addresses concepts of justice as it applies to individuals and society. There is also the matter of what individuals contribute to a just society—that is, justice is not abstract; it is a value that comes about by means of personal action (people do not merely sit and wait for just action to surround them). Let me suggest, in keeping with the ethical imperative written of, an Aristotelian foundation for just action. Each of us should ask what is required to achieve the good life—what virtues, what actions, what thoughts and beliefs lead us to live the good life, defined as righteous, generous person concerned for others, respectful of rights, and guided by acting on the basis of the characteristics that define that good life. According to Ricoeur (2000), just action considers the other along with the institutions in which each of us encounters the other. He (1992) has said that one of our obligations is to live the good life, with and for others, in just institutions (p. 172). Ricoeur's stance is a phenomenological one. While phenomenology is a complex philosophical theory, suffice it to say that a vital aspect is the relation between self and other and the understanding of both that comes from the introspection of experience, consciousness, and perception. We live our lives consciously and intentionally in a world where others also experience life as conscious and intentional beings. The realization of the responsibility to others adds dimensions to justice.

## Freedom

Freedom and justice are almost inextricably related; they are separated here as a way to emphasize the importance of each to the public good and to the public sphere (and the open communication that is essential to the latter). Freedoms are, of course, enumerated in the US Constitution, but the Constitution does not contain every freedom that people might hold dear. In the context of the public good, concentration here will be placed on freedom of information. For a member of the polity to be able to participate fully in democracy and governance, there must be a high level of freedom. The absence of freedom to information affects civic discourse and, among other things, the outcomes of elections. The discursive practice engaged in by all people must be marked by the possibility of critique (not merely criticism, which can block out the speech of others). Openness of discourse is, perhaps, the principal hallmark of freedom of information; anyone should be able to say anything, as long as there is equal potential for refutation, rebuttal, denial, and correction. As it stands, people say and write things that are false; there has to be the opportunity to counter falsehoods with truth.

When it comes to information, access is a vital component of freedom. One must be able to read, see, and hear the speech, especially political speech, in order to become genuinely informed and to be able to *act* within that state of being informed. Does this claim include false or erroneous statements? Pettit (2014) would say that it does and would disagree with the caveat, "But does all bad or failed research really need to be accessible to all? Non-health professionals may not fully understand the research, which could cause anxiety. Anyone in a profession that requires access to research should have it, but it may be good to introduce a registration system so that only those who need to see the results can do so" ("Publish and Be Damned," 2012, pp. 24–25). Granted, a difficult predicament is raised here; should those who might misuse information still have access to it? The dilemma that really underlies the predicament is whether people should have the power of self-determination when it comes to what is done with the information. People could misuse valid information almost as easily as invalid information. Without the access, there is far less of a chance for just action by the populace, especially when the decision is based on an idea that some may not fully understand. That excuse could provide a slippery slope down which democratic and, in the words of Pettit (2014), republican action might slide.

The terminology that has been used so far may itself be problematic. "Information" is poorly defined and, to be useful, should probably be replaced by words that carry richer conceptual denotations and connotations. Speaking of communication, rather than information, is more meaningful since communication embraces all media and forms of human action. Communication is intentional as well; there are purposes that are both personal and social. A narrower term, but one that is also intentional, is knowledge. We live in a communicative society, but there is a subset that is concerned with knowledge growth, knowledge sharing, and knowledge organization. In all instances, and for all conceptual frameworks, freedom remains essential. Lor and Britz (2007) examine what is required for the development of a knowledge society and conclude, "In our view it is very doubtful whether a country can progress towards a knowledge society under conditions of severe restrictions of freedom of information. The development of content and human capacity is critical to the development of a knowledge society. Both require freedom of information" (p. 396).

## Public Sphere

Does the public good require a locus, a space where it can flourish? There are many who answer yes to that question, even if the locus is to be both physical and virtual. Beginning with Jürgen Habermas (1989), the concept of a public sphere regained attention. The idea certainly did not begin with him; the eighteenth-century coffee shops in England and (especially) the salons in France presented places where discussions could occur. In Paris, the discussants read newspapers, pamphlets, and other (sometimes surreptitiously published) works. Public opinion was formed through debate among these discussants and the matter they read. The conversation was thus characterized by publicity, in the sense of debate taking place in the open. In fact, Habermas (1989) emphasizes, "An opinion that is public in the strict sense however can only be generated in the degree that the . . . domains of communication are mediated by a third, that of *critical publicity*" (p. 248). He recognizes the difference that time and social change make, though. The communicative structures of the eighteenth century cannot, and should not, be replicated today. He (1989) realizes that "mediation is possible on a sociologically relevant scale only through the participation of private people in a process of formal communication conducted through intraorganizational public spheres" (p. 248).

In short, the discursive public sphere is a modern development for a couple key reasons. One reason is the more technological nature of French debate. Print allowed for the mass production of newspapers as well the pamphlets and the quasi-anonymous works that circulated in the late eighteenth century. The other factor is recognized by Warner (1992): "The transformation [of the public sphere] . . . was a cultural rather than a technological one; it came about not just with more use of print but rather as the language of republicanism was extended to print contexts as a structuring metalanguage" (p. 380). The culture of print as a communicative medium reached ascendancy in conjunction with the kind of republican ethos that Pettit (2014) describes. In today's world, communicative action is rendered complex by the many media that exist and are employed. Quite literally, the interactions that symbolize the lives of people now are mediated, and the mediations are not continuous but disjointed. The complications, noted by Garnham (1992), are exacerbated by the market of the media and the economic power that underlies the media and their ownership and operation. Also, and Garnham (1992) is almost prescient in recognizing change, "Current technical developments in communication . . . are legitimated in terms of a desirable move away from mass communication and back towards forms of interpersonal communication that are seen as inherently more desirable and liberating" (p. 367). Social media are, even them, foreseen.

Not everyone agrees with Habermas's idea of the public sphere (or, rather, not everyone agrees that the public sphere originated, was transformed, and exists as Habermas claims). Kellner (2000) takes Habermas to task for his idealism and the difficulties that presents for democratic participation. Habermas's emphasis on the actions by, and impact on, private citizens is one of the challenges Kellner identifies; the spheres that developed in the eighteenth century were populated by the white middle class of the dominant religious affiliation. They were not, by construction, diverse and, so, were not populist. Roberge (2011) criticizes Habermas for not being sufficiently "cultural" in his examination of the public sphere. Roberge (2011) maintains, "Society is neither rational nor irrational; that is, degenerating in a sea of mere amusement. On the contrary, it is ambiguous and complex in its meaningful orientations, and this explains why such a concept as the aesthetic public sphere is certainly appropriate in today's discussions of social scientific nature" (p. 448). In fairness to Habermas, it is nearly impossible for one thinker to anticipate all possibilities; he did, though, call attention to the public sphere(s) legitimacy.

As is indicated previously, discursive practice is integral to the operation of the public sphere. People must be able to speak freely, but there is also an obligation placed upon everyone to listen and to weigh what is said. Habermas has also created an ideal for the creation and maintenance of discourse ethics. His (1990) aim is to establish norms that include phenomenological praxis, which entails recognizing moral phenomena as moral phenomena (p. 47). This is a very demanding obligation that places a burden not just on philosophers but on everyone who wishes to contribute to moral organizational and interorganizational action. Habermas (1990) expresses precisely what he intends by discourse ethics: Discourse ethics, then, stands or fall with two assumptions: "(a) that normative claims to validity have cognitive meaning and can be treated like claims to truth and (b) that the justification of norms and commands requires that a real discourse be carried out and this cannot occur in a strictly monological form, i.e., in the form of a hypothetical process of argumentation occurring in the individual mind" (p. 68).

To be effective in practice (and not merely in principle), the participants in discursive practice must agree to the tenets of discourse ethics and the previously stated assumptions. For example, if we envision a city council meeting, we assume that all speakers are making normative claims that have a close relation to truth claims (which does not automatically mean that claims can be taken *to be* true but that the speaker is acting in good faith to the extent that the claim can be evaluated on the same basis as truth claims). The group can then assess the claim openly and honestly and judge its merits and demerits through open discussion. As part of the next step, "Only those norms can claim to be valid that meet (or could meet) with the approval of all affected in their capacity as participants in practical discourse" (Habermas, 1990, p. 93). While Habermas (1994) is creating an ideal for discursive practice, he readily recognizes that claims can be more or less fallible and that the actual practice engaged in is almost always going to be context sensitive (p. 25). In emphasizing the practical side of his ideal, Habermas (1994) adds some conditions: "Anyone who seriously engages in argumentation must presuppose that the context of discussion guarantees in principle freedom of access, equal rights to participate, truthfulness on the parts of participants, absence of coercion in adopting positions, and so on" (p. 31). These are very stringent conditions.

Some commentators point out limitations with Habermas's ideal and do so cogently, even as they may agree with that ideal:

> Whose opinion "counts," whose opinion is valid, is not merely a question concerning the quality of an opponent's argument, but also a question of whether that person meets the "standards" for inclusion within a discourse. The discourse concerning abortion is exemplary in this respect; activists from both sides of the debate discount not only the arguments and opinions of their opponents, but also the opponents themselves—they are often seen

> as crazy, immoral, or fanatical, as people not worth the effort of a conversation. (Murphy, 1994, p. 132)

A political example that exists today is the battle between mainstream Republican politicians and affiliates with the Tea Party. Tea Party officials and candidates simply believe that the mainstream is not sufficiently conservative, and most are loath to compromise on any issues. There is no acceptance of the legitimacy of other participants in discourse. What occurs in the previous instance is the active or tacit rejection of Habermas's (1990) principle of universalization: "(U) *All* affected can accept the consequences and the side effects its *general* observance can be anticipated to have for the satisfaction of *everyone's* interests (and these consequences are preferred to those of known alternative possibilities for regulation)" (p. 65). There is support for Habermas's principle:

> There are, in other words, *two dimensions* to a reasonable moral compromise: What I will call (1) the conflicting interests dimension and (2) the conflicting evaluative views dimension. First, taking for granted some account of interests that people have, I must be motivated to accept that others' *interests* make normative claims upon me. This means that, faced with an intractable conflict of interest, I ought to be willing to compromise on my own particular interests according to some principles of fair accommodation. This is what (U)'s *welfarist constraint* does. (Though (U) goes even further: It makes reference to interests *necessary* to the justification of norms.) Second, in the face of intractable evaluative disagreements about what counts as an interest, I must be motivated to grant that others' *views* make normative claims upon me. According to how I propose to read (U), this is what (U)'s *requirement of agreement* does. (Abizadeh, 2005, p. 209)

Abizadeh's commentary is equally idealist; stating an ideal, by Habermas or anyone else, does not render the conception of discourse ethics invalid. Rather than idealist, we should view the program as potentially normative (as Habermas intended). In fact, it may be the people who are best situated to legitimate and demand the normative practice.

In some of his later work, Habermas has elaborated on discourse ethics and its operation in authentic settings. As Goode (2005) has pointed out, the later work is more explicitly accepting of the role of the "other" in situations of speech intended to lead to action. The alteration, as Goode (2005) notes, is both a more open acknowledgment of political-cultural discursive settings *and* a maturation of Habermas's critical theory (p. 72). Discourse ethics becomes an orientation to a moral point of view, rather than an overt and narrow articulation of a universal ethics. He quotes Habermas (1998): "The four most important features are: (i) that nobody who could make a relevant contribution may be excluded; (ii) that all participants are granted an equal opportunity to make contributions; (iii) that the participants must mean what they say; and (iv) that communication must be freed from external and internal coercion" (pp. 43–44). Idealistic or not, this kind of discourse ethics is foundational to the public good.

Following these tenets of the public good, specific settings and situations can be examined.

## Religion in America

Given that millions (possibly most) Americans identify themselves directly or indirectly with some religious sect, it is impossible to ignore the role religion plays in any investigation of the public good. This is not to say that any particular religion—or even religion in general—is an absolute necessity for the public good, but religion is undeniably important to culture, society, politics, and most other facets of life. It is also not to say that secular life is not important, even vital, to much of the human action in the United States. The place that religion has in society is, in itself, neither positive nor negative. People do act, though, in the name of religions, and some people do speak on behalf of religions. Those factors mean that analysis of religion and the public good warrants critique. A rise in some kinds of religious fervor is a worldwide phenomenon, of course, but attention here will be on the place of religion in the United States. George W. Bush benefited greatly from the votes of religiously minded—specifically Christian—people, for example. His success may call into question any claims of the secularization of public action and public being.

To be sure, this section does not represent an antireligious rant. Religion, though, is a major force in the lives of Americans and can contribute to the public good in many ways. For one thing, when there are disasters or serious mishaps, many congregations pool resources to help those afflicted by storms, floods, and other natural events or to aid individuals and families who suffer from accidents, diseases, or other life-altering predicaments. Those beneficent acts must be noted in any discussion of the public good, whether one is affiliated with some religion or one rejects organized religion (or, indeed, rejects religion entirely). The assistance may take the form of clothing and blankets, funds to provide food and water, and even taking people into one's home as a means of providing shelter. Almost all religions and sects engage in these charitable acts when situations call for the provision of assistance.

Congregations frequently behave as communities, perhaps aiming first to the provision of the needs of congregation. This kind of behavior should not be surprising; communities frequently look to their own first when needs arise. In fact, if people act in the name of God to do good works, it would be bordering on the venal to criticize the works. Without question, commentators and observers do criticize the actions of those who would act uncharitably, or even with hostility, in the name of religion. There has been a considerable amount of discussion about the thoughts of Christopher Hitchens, Richard Dawkins, Sam Wallis, and others. There is no need to delve into a critique of them here. Suffice it to say that whenever there is, say, violence committed in the name of God or a religion, the public good is diminished. All humanity is diminished whenever violence is committed for any excuse. Whether religious or secular, there are moral imperatives that provide guidance for the treatment of fellow human beings; those imperatives are genuinely aimed at fostering public good.

### *Prosperity Theology*

There is a movement within Christianity—associated more often than not with Pentecostalism—that emphasizes material life on earth. The movement is usually referred to as "prosperity gospel" or "prosperity theology." The message is rather simple and causes concern to secular and religious observers alike. For example, Pastor Fernando Garay, of the Casa del Padre church, "talks about jobs and houses and making good money . . . money is 'really important,' and besides, 'we love the money in Jesus Christ's name! Jesus loved money too!'" (Rosin, 2009, p. 39). Garay's church operates on a relatively small scale, but the message is not fundamentally different from that of larger operations. Garay had, prior to his ministry, worked for the mortgage lender Countrywide, which has been the focus of numerous lawsuits. Rosin (2009) adds, "One theme emerging in these suits is how banks teamed up with pastors to win over new customers for subprime loans." (p. 42). Rosin reports on some members of Garay's congregation who got in over their heads with mortgages and had to default. According to Garay, it is the real Christians who succeed with their home purchases. Others, by implication, must bear the brunt of being poor Christians and being poor materially.

Rosin (2009) reports on the members of the congregation who desperately wanted to own their own homes and would plead with Garay to help them. Garay himself noted that mortgage payments could be as much as $1,500, which was the total income of the buyer. The congregation members figured they could rent out part of the home to make ends meet. One buyer rented to two additional families, who all lived in the house, but the buyer still couldn't make the payments. Rosin (2009) says that Garay sometimes told people "the loans were going to kill them, but they would plead, 'Please help me, *please*. I want a house.' Because he was an increasingly prominent pastor at the time, many people who came to see him assumed he was the president of the bank and could protect them, he recalls" (p. 45). Of course, he could do nothing to protect the people. These experiences call into question the opinions of those such as Rick Santelli (see Chapter 1); it is by no means always the greed of the buyer that causes the problem; some entity is making the loan, and that entity has a great amount of information at hand.

There are critiques of the prosperity gospel, apart from those in secular literature. One critic is Gregory Hollifield (2011) who asserts, "Whatever it is that one does for the Master, he or she does because the Master graciously sought him out and gave him the opportunity to serve" (p. 53). Hollifield (2011) adds, "Whatever one receives for any labor in Christ's vineyard, it is graciously given as far more than one deserves. From beginning to end, it is a story of grace. From beginning to end, preaching should retell the story of God's grace" (p. 53). Additionally, Daisy Machado (2010), professor of church history at Union Theological Seminary, states,

> It is this very inability to perceive our faults and honestly to define what is the good, as well as our inability to define as a nation and a people to live this "good life" within and outside our borders, that continues to serve the kind of neoliberal ideology that undergirds our current economic system [see Chapter 2]. In reality, capitalism in the United States is a deeply entrenched ideology (belief system) that has survived and benefited from slavery, immigrant labor, and other forms of exploitation. (p. 723)

These kinds of criticisms stand in stark relief compared with the rhetoric of the prosperity gospel. One more critique by researchers into the background of followers of this brand of theology is telling: "Our observations reinforce the long-standing claim that SES [socioeconomic status] plays a pivotal—and complex—role in the social patterning of religious beliefs. More generally, these findings add to the growing literature about SES and beliefs in a personal God that influences outcomes in daily life" (Schieman and Jung, 2012, p. 751).

Some descriptions may help depict some of the outcomes of this particular take on ministry. The home of Jan and the late Paul Crouch (who died in 2013), heads of the Trinity Broadcasting Network (TBN), was more of a monument to the TBN founders than anything else. TBN describes itself as thus: "TBN is now the world's largest Christian television network. Across America and around the world TBN is carried by TV stations and cable systems to millions of homes. As a matter of fact, TBN is featured on over 5,000 television stations, over 70 satellites, the Internet and thousands of cable systems around the world. And the number continues to grow!" ("The TBN Story," 2014). The home page of their website has a button to "Donate now," and it is noted that they will take PayPal, MasterCard, and Visa. In the spring of 2014, TBN was sponsoring a "Praise-A-Thon," a telethon aimed at raising additional money. Since TBN is categorized as a church for tax purposes, it is an easy matter to get financial data on donations and assets.

National Public Radio (NPR) has been able to gain some information on another large-scale network that is also classified as a church—Daystar Television. NPR reports that they were able to analyze "six years of Daystar balance sheets. They show the network took in $208 million in tax-deductible contributions and gave away $9.7 million in direct grants, not $30 million [as minister Marcus Lamb claimed]. It works out to charitable giving of about five percent of donor revenue" (Burnett, 2014). As NPR reports, there is little, if any, indication that Daystar actually offers religious services, although the television network claims to provide gospel-based programing all day, every day. As is the case with TBN, there is a "Giving" button on the home page, which offers ways to donate online, by telephone, and by mail.

Another of the largest of the prosperity gospel ministries is that of Joel Osteen, whose Houston-based Lakewood Church has a capacity of approximately 16,000. Osteen also has a television presence and has written a number of bestselling books. Osteen's church underwent a move to a renovated space in 2005 and now is a 16,000-seat megachurch complete with jumbotron so that Osteen's face can be seen by the congregation.

### *Concerns*

There is no political problem, necessarily, with citizens who are adherents to a religious doctrine. There is not even a grave issue with people living postsecular lives. Where difficulties arise is when there is no tolerance—no freedom—regarding which doctrine individuals choose to follow and/or when there is any effort to suffuse the American polity with a single doctrine.

There are, however, numerous statements linking Christianity to the tenets of Tea Party political positions and support for candidates for offices. The statements come from grassroots and national sources. Skocpol and Williamson (2012) report on interviews that reveal many Tea Party supporters identify themselves as affiliated with evangelical Christian churches. Many also look to the Bible for guidance in political life and as inspiration for, among other things, the US Constitution. This does raise a political conundrum in terms of both Tea Party "dogma" and the dilemma of having power for the first time: "Thinkers from the time of the American Revolution—behind them, Locke and Montesquieu—have realized that there can be no elite to govern us for our benefit. Though a few individuals are a little more objective than the rest of us, no one knows, on the basis of past behavior, how anyone—not even oneself—will behave under temptations that, having newly come to power, one has never known before" (Weidhorn, 2013, p. 227).

In the quest for a solution to the problem, which touches upon all the aforementioned characteristics of the public good, we can turn to Charles Taylor (2011):

> There must be equality between people of different faiths or basic belief; no religious outlook or (religious or areligious) Weltanschauung can enjoy a privileged status, let alone be adopted as the official view of the state. Then . . . all spiritual families must be heard, including in the ongoing process of determining what the society is about (its political identity), and how it is going to realize these goals (the exact regime of rights and privileges). This . . . is what corresponds to "fraternity." (p. 35)

### *On the Other Hand*

Religion and religious activity can also be sources of good in communities and beyond. There are spokespeople who exert formidable efforts to ensure that the public good is recognized and realized. People from many sects preach goodness, both for self and for others. The following is a rather lengthy quotation from a recent book by Pope Francis (2014); it concisely summarizes the place and role of religion within the public good:

> I would like to reflect on two fundamental values: freedom and service. First of all: be free people! What do I mean? Perhaps it is thought that freedom means doing everything one likes, or seeing how far one can go by trying drunkenness and overcoming boredom. This is not freedom, Freedom means being able to think about what we do, being able to assess what is good and what is bad; these are the types of conduct that lead to development; it means always opting for the good. Let us be free for goodness. And in this do not be afraid to go against the tide, even if it is not easy! Being free always to choose goodness is demanding, but it will make you into people with backbone who can face life, people with courage and patience . . .
>
> The second word is *service*. In your [Jesuit] schools you should take part in various activities that accustom you to not retreating into yourselves or into your own small world, but rather to being open to others, especially the

> poorest and the neediest. They accustom you to working hard to improve the world in which we live. Be men and women with others and for others, true champions at the service of others. (pp. 122–23)

The difference between Pope Francis's admonition and that of the gospel of prosperity is that his vision is outward directed, while prosperity gospel is inward looking.

Marcus Borg (1989), an Episcopal theologian, adds to the message of Pope Francis:

> In times when we have a strong sense of having sinned, the common meaning of the word *mercy* can have deep meaning. But think of the larger meaning the Kyrie would have if it used the word *compassion* instead: "Lord have compassion on us, Christ have compassion on us, Lord have compassion on us." Each time we say it or sing it, we would be reminding ourselves of our need for God's life-giving and nourishing quality, reminding ourselves that this is the character of God. God is not primarily a threatening judge to whom we appeal for mercy, but a life-giving and nourishing reality who wills our well-being and the well-being of the whole of creation, just as a mother wills the well-being of the children in her womb. And we are reminding ourselves that this is how it should be. (p. 131)

Borg preaches of a love of God for everyone.

Others offer messages of hope grounded in faith. This is a message that those who believe take to heart, and it is a message that is widely shared. Joel Osteen (2013), for example, writes, "The Scripture says, 'Rain falls on the just and the unjust.' I'd love to tell you that if you have faith and you love God, then you'd never have any difficulties. But that's not reality. I can tell you when the storms come, if you've got your house built upon the rock, if you've got an unshakable confidence in God, if you know the Lord as your shepherd, then storms will come, but you will not be defeated" (p. 221). The foregoing is not intended to advocate a particular vision of religious faith or belief. These words are presented so as to demonstrate that religion plays many roles in people's lives. There is no one kind or brand of faith held by the American people or propounded by ministers. The messages are not all equal, and the purpose of this section is to demonstrate that the public good may or may not be represented by those who espouse religion as something essential to people's lives. As is the case with everything that becomes part and parcel of people's lives, there are variations that must be evaluated and must be assessed according to their own merits and by use of critical acumen.

## Constitution: Cruel and Unusual

### *Execution*

On April 21, 2014, the Oklahoma Supreme Court issued stays of execution for two death row inmates: Clayton Lockett and Charles Warner. At issue was the source—which was not revealed—of the drugs to be used for the executions. As Andrew Cohen (2014) reported,

> Things got complicated because there are two high courts in Oklahoma—one that focuses on "criminal" matters and one that focuses on "civil" matters. The criminal court, the Oklahoma Court of Criminal Appeals, said it had no jurisdiction to look at the injection secrecy matter. The civil court, the Oklahoma Supreme Court, said that the Court of Criminal Appeals did have jurisdiction. There was open conflict between the courts. The state Supreme Court criticized the Court of Criminal Appeals for not accepting the appeal and for not halting the executions. The criminal appeals court criticized the state Supreme Court for intruding upon what its judges considered the purely "criminal" matter of execution protocols. (Cohen, 2014)

Mary Fallin, Oklahoma's governor, said that she would only abide by the original decision of the Court of Criminal Appeals and that the executions would proceed as scheduled.

The attempted execution of Clayton Lockett proceeded on April 28, 2014. The first drug, a sedative, was administered. A doctor pronounced him unconscious, but within a couple minutes, Lockett began to writhe against his constraints. He lifted his head and attempted to speak. The procedure was halted, but Lockett died of a massive heart attack several minutes later. After the convulsions were under way, the curtain was drawn, and the members of the press were unable to witness anything further. The execution of Warner, scheduled for later that evening, was stayed for a time. The next day, Governor Fallin announced that an independent inquiry would be launched. The Eighth Amendment to the US Constitution explicitly prohibits cruel and unusual punishment, but it is obvious the Lockett suffered terribly before he expired. Since Governor Fallin insisted that the execution take place—even in the face of questions regarding the drug cocktail that would be used—it seems reasonable to expect that she be at the center of any independent investigation. The Oklahoma legislature must be subject to examination as well, primarily because members threatened the justices of the civil court with dismissal if they did not cease their challenge of the criminal court decision.

In short, everything that could go wrong in a public action did go wrong. Moreover, there is moral and ethical, if not legal, culpability resting at the feet of elected officials in Oklahoma. Their planned execution was not the first to be questioned on the basis of the efficacy of drugs that would be used in lethal injections. The questioning relating to the shortage of drugs that were used for years is not new. Mottor (2007) raised concerns: "Clarence Ray Allen was executed through lethal injection in California [several years ago]. The execution log showed that he was given anesthesia at 12:18 a.m. However, the anesthesia did not have its intended effect, and respirations did not cease until the pancuronium bromide was injected at 12:27a.m. Thus, Allen likely felt the excruciating pain associated with the administration of pancuronium bromide" (p. 287). Other examples could be offered, but the ones described here suffice and should demonstrate clearly that the public good is not being served by official governmental action that affects the lives of human beings.

In 2000, Illinois governor George Ryan declared a moratorium on the death penalty, out of concern that some individuals on death row might actually be innocent. It should be noted that Ryan had previously been a staunch supporter of the death penalty but became convinced that it may lead to intolerable injustices. In 2011, Ryan's successor, Governor Pat Quinn, signed a bill that abolished the death penalty in the state of Illinois (making Illinois the sixteenth state at the time to do so). It is obvious that some public officials in the United States are sufficiently concerned that the public good is not being served and that drastic action has had to be taken. The decisions by those officials call into serious question the heavy-handed actions of individuals such as Governor Fallin. Not only is the ethical matter brought into stark relief, but also the oaths of such individuals to support the US Constitution must be considered.

### *Solitary Confinement*

In many instances, solitary confinement is used in prisons as a discipline and control mechanism. The inmate is removed from the general prison population and placed in a small cell where there is little or no contact with other humans. Usually, the inmate has no reading materials or writing implements either. The period of time someone may be placed in solitary confinement can be quite lengthy. Brian Denson (2014) reports on a prisoner who was confined to solitary for 23 hours and 20 minutes a day for 27 months. The prisoner, Joshua Robert Brown, was confined for possession of a weapon, and he sued the Oregon Department of Corrections. While the Ninth Circuit Court of Appeals acknowledged that Brown was subjected to "atypical and significant hardship," it denied his appeal (Denson, 2014). A typical solitary confinement cell is bare, to say the least (usually consisting of a small bed, a bare toilet, and a washbasin).

Cockrell (2013) recognizes that there is insufficient data on the physical, emotional, and mental effects of solitary confinement on individuals but observes, "A very high number of inmates in solitary confinement get severe headaches. Other physical symptoms are chest pains, weight loss, diarrhea, dizziness, and fainting. There are many psychological symptoms: decreased ability to concentrate, confusion, memory loss, visual as well as auditory hallucinations, paranoia, overt psychosis, violent fantasies, anxiety, depression in huge numbers, lethargy, and trouble sleeping. Attempts to commit suicide are not uncommon" (p. 213). Cockrell notes that the impact can be exacerbated for the mentally ill. Arrigo and Bullock (2008) conclude, "Prisoners with preexisting mental illnesses are especially vulnerable to the destructive psychological effect of segregated housing. The lack of adequate medical and psychiatric care—in prisons in general and in supermaximum security units in particular—compounds these problems. In addition, convicts in the SHU are uniquely susceptible to physical and verbal abuse by staff. These hostile conditions of confinement increase the risk that prisoners will suffer emotionally crippling effects from punitive and administrative isolation" (pp. 636–37).

It appears clear from what research that has been conducted (although much more inquiry is needed) that there are serious deleterious consequences for inmates who are subjected even to short-term stays in solitary confinement. The psychological and medical research that should be conducted ought to inform legal determinations about prisoners' Eighth Amendment rights. (Note that as of May 3, 2014, there were no items in the Medline database that included the term "solitary confinement.")

## Regulations and Courts

Federal agencies and US courts have a decided impact on the public good. The scope and depth of the impact is immense and covers far too large a territory that can be covered exhaustively here. Some examples can serve to enforce some of the points made here and can be topics for reflection. One issue that has captured attention very recently is that of network neutrality (hereafter referred to as "net neutrality"). The Federal Communications Commission (FCC) defines this principle as thus: "The 'Open Internet' is the Internet as we know it, a level playing field where consumers can make their own choices about what applications and services to use, and where consumers are free to decide what content they want to access, create, or share with others" ("The Open Internet," 2014). It may be surprising to discover that this principle has come under fire and has been challenged. At this time, the enactment of net neutrality is open to dispute and eventual interpretation:

> In January 2014, the D.C. Circuit struck down the antiblocking and antidiscrimination rules in *Verizon v. FCC*. The court held that the FCC had the statutory authority to enact the rules, but that the agency had unreasonably interpreted sections of the Communications Act and had regulated broadband providers as "common carriers" despite declining to classify them as such, in violation of that statute. While the immediate result was a loss for the FCC, the court's holding on the agency's statutory authority charts a path for the FCC to follow in drafting new Open Internet rules that could withstand judicial review ("Telecommunications Law," 2014, p. 2565).

Of course, the court ruling, unless and until it is challenged in a higher court, constitutes the law for the time being. That said, there is no doubt that the ruling is in opposition to the public good. In some ways, the ruling follows Supreme Court decisions, such as *Citizens United*, that effectively equate corporations with persons. The argument put forth by Verizon is that net neutrality limits First Amendment protections that would allow the corporation to conduct its business. The public good issue aside, as Crawford (2014) says, "To apply a heightened First Amendment standard when a court is reviewing an ordinary economic regulatory program, merely because there may be some indirect effect on private speech caused by the challenged regulations, would return us to the *Lochner* era and sharply undermine congressional authority" (p. 2344).

It must be mentioned that the personhood of corporations is an aberration of conservative opinion among Supreme Court justices. In a 1978 Supreme Court decision in the case of *First National Bank of Boston v. Bellotti*, Justice William Rehnquist wrote a dissenting opinion that established one possible position on the issue: "A State grants to a business corporation the blessings of potentially perpetual life and limited liability to enhance its efficiency as an economic entity. It might reasonably be concluded that those properties, so beneficial in the economic sphere, pose special dangers in the political sphere. Furthermore, it might be argued that liberties of political expression are not at all necessary to effectuate the purposes for which States permit commercial corporations to exist" ("Justice Rehnquist's Dissent," 2014). In recent decisions, the majority of the Supreme Court has chosen to ignore Rehnquist and effectively rule not only that a corporation is, to many purposes, a person but also that the corporation is a potentially immortal person—that is, the "rights" according to corporations exist as long as the corporation exists (which could be centuries), *and* the corporation's rights exist regardless of the views of all its members and even, at times, the rights of all its members. So the rights extend to the top management of the corporation and are *added* to their rights *as individuals*. The rights accorded to the top management of corporations effectively exist as double rights, thus debilitating the rights of dissenting members of the corporation plus the rights of all individual citizens. Three months after the *Citizens United* decision in 2010, a circuit court issued a ruling in the case of *Speechnow.org v. Federal Elections Committee* that would further open the floodgates of donations by means of a variety of mechanisms (see Vogel, 2014, p. 34).

The Supreme Court today comprises a majority of conservative justices—some more conservative than others. The most unapologetic is probably Antonin Scalia, who has exerted a tremendous influence over court decisions over the last couple decades. One element of Scalia's conservatism is what he claims is a strict interpretation of the text of the Constitution. He is an opponent of the interpretive style of viewing the Constitution as a living document, primarily because of the interpretations of the adherents of that way of thinking. As he (1997) writes, "This might be a persuasive argument if most of the 'growing' that the proponents of this approach have brought upon us in the past, and are determined to bring upon us in the future, were the *elimination* of restrictions upon democratic government. But just the opposite is true" (p. 41). Lawrence Tribe (1997), however, says that "Justice Scalia is by no means faithful to this approach" (p. 66). A similar conclusion is drawn by Murphy (2014; whose book should be read with careful attention to the technical side of Scalia's record). The most damning critique of Scalia is offered by Ronald Dworkin (1997): "Justice Scalia has managed to give two lectures about meaning with no reference to Derrida or Gadamer or even the hermeneutic circle, and he has set out with laudable clarity a sensible account of statutory interpretation. These are considerable achievements. But I believe he has seriously misunderstood the implications of his general account of constitutional law, and that his lectures therefore have a schizophrenic character" (p. 115). It is in the circumstances that decisions are being made at this time.

Many decisions rendered by the court are marked by 5–4 votes, with conservative and liberal justices voting together, but there are occasional surprises offered by the Roberts court. For example, in 2012, the court—primarily behind Justice Roberts's vote and majority opinion—refused to strike down the Affordable Care Act as unconstitutional. The decision was a surprise given that the oral arguments and the questioning by some justices, especially Scalia, appeared to be opposed to the act. The decision was certainly not simple; it was ultimately multifaceted (although this is not the place to review the entirety of the opinions). The upshot is that the act has been able to proceed. In another case, however, the court was, perhaps, more closely beholden to its conservative majority. As Tolson (2014) concludes, "Sixteen years ago, the Supreme Court pointed to the Voting Rights Act as the paradigmatic example of a remedial scheme appropriately tailored to address harmful discrimination in voting. In *Shelby County v. Holder*, the Court backtracked on this position, finding that the preclearance regime lacks the same constitutional foundation that existed when the Act was first passed in 1965" (p. 438). Localities were no longer under the obligation to ensure the rights of minorities; sufficient progress had been made in making equality the rule.

Much more could be written about regulation and the courts. For example, the matter of financial and banking regulation could fill a book (and, indeed, has filled several; see Sorkin, 2009, for example). In many instances, the argument made is opposed to regulation in the name of free enterprise. It has been shown clearly, however, that the financial industry, left to its own devices, will not act in the interests of the public good. The basest inclinations of humans—individually and/or collectively—have to be controlled so that there will not be domination by the few over the many.

## Politics: Influence

Let us assume (and the assumption is, believe it or not, a valid one) that lobbyists inform a legislator about issues of the day and interests of which one should be aware. To this extent, and in this way, lobbying can serve a positive purpose. The nature of lobbying at this time extends well beyond an informative factor and can easily slide into the corruption of the deliberative process for which legislatures are responsible. Lobbying is actually big business in itself, with about $3.27 billion spent on direct lobbying in 2012 (about twice as much as was spent in 2001; Choma, 2013). It should be pointed out that the figures reflect only the lobbying expenditures at the federal level. Many industries spend a great deal of money trying to influence state legislatures. Also, let it be known that some industries' efforts pay off better than others. Lobbying does also have its negative side, which Rowbottom (2013) explains succinctly (from a British perspective):

> While lobbying can provide benefits, there are several different reasons why we might be concerned about the effects of lobbying. The first is that meetings behind closed doors provide a setting where officials might make a deal with interested parties in return for some benefit. Here the concern is with the potential for corrupt exchanges to be made. This can arise with any industry, for example where a company agrees to make a large political donation or employ a minister's relative in return for some policy benefit. (pp. 254–55)

With the amount of money expended each year for access to legislatures, it might be naïve to expect that no favors are exchanged for that access.

Lawrence Lessig may be one of the most articulate and aggressive critics of the systemic kind of corruption that exists right now. Explaining what he refers to as "dependence corruption," he (2011) writes that when congressmen are not dependent on the people for decision making, "that independence gets corrupted when a conflicting dependency develops within Congress" (p. 231).

Peter Schweizer (2013) has a somewhat different take on the place of money in politics. The customary view is that money corrupts politics; he turns the table—politics corrupts money. His thesis is that businesses and interest groups do not *bribe* politicians; politicians *extort* money from the interest groups. Green (2013) interviews former senator Russ Feingold:

> It's not like businesses and business leaders call up politicians and beg them, could I please give you some money? It goes the other way, which is that people are called constantly by politicians when you have a system like this, or their representatives, or their allegedly independent agents. And it's more like extortion than it's like bribery. So my theme today, I hope, on this podcast is that the corporations and the business community that are trying to make jobs and make money in this country for people are victims of the Citizens United decision. And it's put the extortion possibility at an all time new level of danger.

The money expended does not begin and end with lobbying. Fields (2013) points out, "Congressional campaigns are incredibly expensive. Just over $1 billion was spent on House races in 2012, estimates a report by opensecrets.org, a website maintained by the Center for Responsive Politics. There was more than $700 million spent on Senate races" (p. 558). Schweizer observes, "During the 112th Congress, a senator needed to raise an average of $10,476.451 and a representative $1,689,580 to clinch the coming election" (p. 33). Add to these figures the amounts spent on the presidential campaign and state and local races, and we arrive at a figure in excess of $3 billion. Campaigning and lobbying account for more than $6 billion spent in some years. An ethical system of influence expenditures would cost a fraction of that amount, and corruption could be minimized (there will always be some degree of corruption when human beings and substantial sums of money come together). Self-policing by the House and the Senate could further limit the corruption and bring back a culture of integrity to the business of legislating. The impact of the money, the lobbying, and the failures of integrity leads to a problem identified by Light and colleagues (Light, Lexehin, and Darrow, 2013):

> It is our thesis that institutional corruption has occurred at three levels. First, through large-scale lobbying and political contributions, the pharmaceutical

> industry has influenced Congress to pass legislation that has compromised the mission of the Food and Drug Administration (FDA). Second, largely as a result of industry pressure, Congress has underfunded FDA enforcement capacities since 1906, and turning to industry-paid "user fees" since 1992 has biased funding to limit the FDA's ability to protect the public from serious adverse reactions to drugs that have few offsetting advantages. Finally, industry has commercialized the role of physicians and undermined their position as independent, trusted advisers to patients. (p. 590)

The far-reaching implications of the failure of will and integrity become clear; the American people (and the citizens of the world) are those who end up with the short end of the stick.

Are people aware of the amount of money that is required for candidates to win elections? Are people aware of where the money comes from? Recently, the dynamic of campaign funding was upset, shocking most political reporters. Eric Cantor, the current Republican House majority leader, lost the Republican primary race in Virginia to David Brat (supported by the Tea Party) even though Cantor outspent Brat by several orders of magnitude. Brat did gain support from well-known, very conservative figures, such as Mark Levin and Laura Ingraham. It is, of course, impossible to attribute Brat's victory to any one single factor, but voter turnout was horrendously low. Only about 65,000 people, out of an electorate of about 750,000, voted in the primary. (The low turnout has only been mentioned in general terms in most of the mainstream media reports; rather, many reports speak of a resurgent Tea Party movement even though incumbent Republican candidates have tended to win their races in this primary season.) Brat, in what some would call a venal claim, attributed his victory to a miracle from God, an especially egregious statement given that Cantor is Jewish (for more, see Cassidy, 2014). The upset victory by Brat renders the general election later in 2014 an even more interesting race.

In addition to lobbying, there may be efforts by individuals or groups to exert influence over political races. In the 2004 Kerry-Bush presidential race, the Swift Boat Veterans for Truth (SBVT) managed to twist John Kerry's Vietnam War record to convince at least some people that Kerry falsely earned honors for his actions. In a close election, rhetoric such as that propounded by the Swift Boat group can make a substantive difference. Reyes (2006) analyzes the message of the group and concludes, "What one sees in the SBVT ad, then, is a rhetoric of realism that adroitly takes advantage of Vietnam remembrance in order to dismantle the ethos of a man who chose to serve" (p. 593). After the election, the Federal Election Commission attempted to investigate the SBVT ads, but the damage had already been done. The lack of integrity and truthfulness may have played a role in changing history.

Nichols and McChesney (2012) report that in 2012, television stations would stand to benefit to the tune of about $5 billion thanks in large part to the spending by political action committees (p. 11). Gulati (2012) takes the critique of political action committees (PACs) a step further:

> Democratic government is threatened, however, when a select few individuals or interests have a greater voice in the process and on public policy outcomes. Yet interest groups and wealthy individuals have been more than eager to help candidates finance their campaigns, and candidates desperate to win office or stay in office are eager to accept their assistance. This longstanding practice creates numerous opportunities for corruption of the electoral process and American democracy and, in turn, calls to control the influence that vested interests have over candidate agendas and public policy and to create a more competitive electoral environment. But with each new attempt at reform and subsequent reform of the reforms, candidates, organized interests and wealthy individuals identify new ways to circumvent the spirit of recent campaign finance reform laws and channel substantial amounts of money into the electoral process (p. 409).

The *Citizens United* and *McCutcheon* cases have already been discussed. Such Supreme Court decisions render election reform not only more difficult but also almost impossible. It is likely the mechanisms like Super PACs and leadership PACs will be the rule for the foreseeable future.

## Politics: Corruption

Ferguson (2012) maintains that "over the last thirty years, under Democrats as well as Republicans, the United States' political-economic system has lost its way" (p. 276). Ferguson (2012) expands on his criticism, noting in particular the Obama administration:

> The first troubling sign was his personnel appointments. Not a single critic or voice of reform got a job—not Simon Johnson, Nouriel Roubini, Paul Krugman, Sheila Bair, Joseph Stiglitz, Jeffrey Sachs, Robert Gnaizda, Brooksley Born, Senator Carl Levin, none of them. Instead we got Larry Summers, the man behind nearly every disastrous policy that created the crisis, fresh from making $20 million from hedge funds and investment banks, as director of the National Economic Council. (pp. 300–301)

In short, people who might be trusted to oversee the financial system of our nation have largely been ignored, even as voices of dissent outside the political internal structure. One can surmise that Obama has failed when it comes to providing a culture of integrity and ethics for the administration. Commitment to the public good has to be questioned when the same people who have ignored that public good are still, or once again, within the administration. The opportunity for genuine change was lost before there could be new blood.

Another issue that is included here in the section on corruption is the matter of voter identification laws. A number of states have passed laws that require potential voters to possess and show state-approved identification cards. The first possible matter of concern is whether voter fraud is ubiquitous (or at least is sufficiently prevalent that restrictions on citizens' franchise should be materially limited). Kahn and Carson (2012) have an answer to that concern: "A new nationwide analysis of 2,068 alleged election-fraud cases since 2000 shows that while fraud has occurred, the rate is infinitesimal, and in-person voter impersonation on Election Day, which prompted 37 state legislatures to enact or consider tough voter ID laws, is virtually non-existent." Another site includes more specificity: "Between 2000 and 2010 there were 649 million votes cast in general elections and 13 cases of in-person voter impersonation" ("Get the Facts," 2014). The factual evidence reveals that the impetus behind the state laws is a particular ideology, and there is also the possibility of pandering to a particular segment of the public. There is an absence of integrity, truthfulness, ethics, and freedom evident in this antidemocratic, and antirepublican, political action. The body politic suffers mightily when the same individuals who scream for evidence in other instances ignore the preponderance of evidence that militates against voter ID laws.

One may ask what lies behind the abominable legislation that undeniably will result in the disenfranchisement of not simply some Americans but Americans of certain racial and socioeconomic groups. Wilson and Brewer (2013) have conducted some inquiry into the public opinion that may have influenced the horrendous legislation (their findings may shock some readers):

> We find significant effects for the usual suspects of ideology and party identification, but we also find important patterns related to racial attitudes and political information. Support for voter ID laws is strongest among Republicans, conservatives, and those with higher levels of racial resentment, as well as with regular Fox News viewers and those who perceive voting fraud as common. It is especially strong among those conservatives who are most familiar with voter ID laws. Opposition is strongest among Democrats, liberals—especially those with higher levels of familiarity with the laws—and those with lower levels of racial resentment, as well as those who see fraud as rare. We also find that exposure to the argument that voter ID laws

> might prevent eligible voters from participating in elections reduces support for such laws. (p. 980)

The passage of the laws indicates a failing of the public good; the rights of people are being trampled upon in ways that are reminiscent of the days of poll taxes. Without active dissent, the restrictions on voting could someday target other groups.

## Education

Rhetorically, few things are associated with the public good with the frequency and the emphasis of education. It tends to be a political maxim that education of today's youth is the most important investment in the nation's future. In actuality, commitment falls short of the rhetoric. Financing of education was addressed in the last chapter; this chapter focuses on the policy and practice of education as they can contribute to the public good. (Of course, funding is integral to success according to any measure or definition, but other factors will be covered here.) The No Child Left Behind Act (NCLB) of 2002 is one feature of education of the past several years that deserves some attention.

Fritzberg (2004) examines the early financial aspects of the NCLB legislation in light of the assessment of schools according to the provisions of Title 1 of the act. He finds that, in a number of states, more than half of the schools fall short of the standards, yet the funding to assist schools is inadequate to make a difference. Edmondson and D'Urso (2009) offered some constructive advice as the act was facing reauthorization: "Our analysis critiques the underlying assumptions of this policy and proposes different possibilities for education policy, particularly the potential for policy to: (1) provide possibilities for all citizens to engage in democratic life, (2) provide access to information, and (3) to embrace the complexities of learning and literacy" (p. 79). Unfortunately, their advice has not been followed, and NCLB has, more or less, fallen by the wayside with the Obama administration. In its fundamental concept, NCLB had something to recommend for the enhancement of elementary and secondary education; in practice, it never lived up to the stated promise of improvement based on meaningful assessment.

The Common Core State Standards are now the hot discussion item in elementary and secondary education. Not surprisingly, there is some controversy attached to it (it may be axiomatic to say that controversy will follow any and all large-scale recommendations for standards). The goals for the Common Core are expressed graphically and include such elements as building knowledge in the disciplines, writing from sources, text-based answers, and building an academic vocabulary. Tienken (2011) expresses skepticism regarding the Common Core:

> Where is the evidence to support the rhetoric surrounding the CCSS? This is not data-driven decision making. This is a decision hoping for data. I am not aware of many contemporary professions that operate this way. The main evidence offered by the NGA and CCSSO to make the case for a cause-and-effect relationship, or any significant relationship for that matter, between test scores, economics, and the need for national curriculum standards amounts to nothing more than a statistical house of cards. (p. 60)

Not everyone (not surprisingly) agrees with Tienken, even though many educators and policymakers share his concern. Some, though, have hope that the Common Core will be able to resolve some challenges and offer some benefits related to students' learning. That hope does tend to be tempered by some skepticism regarding standards-based approaches to education. The conclusions of Kornhaber and Griffith (2014) are typical:

> Views of equity inform educational policy and therefore inform the actions and resources that shape children's possibilities. To understand whether a reform aimed at equity is succeeding on its own terms or, beyond that, meeting larger social aims, it's necessary to understand what is within its conceptual purview. The Common Core rests on an equal conception. Its purview is thus to distribute equal resources across schools. It is therefore reasonable to evaluate the Common Core against this goal. If it were achieved, the Common Core would reinforce arguments for meritocratic distribution of opportunities in a way that is not now possible. However, attaining this goal is unlikely to reduce the disparities in student outcomes associated with sociodemographic variables or to enable all students to graduate high school ready for college and career. Given its equal conception, the Common Core cannot close achievement gaps, any more than the same icing will transform different cakes. Policies and resources aligned to an expansive view of equity are needed to foster more equal chances of school and life success for children from disparate circumstances. (p. 20)

Will the Common Core be the public good panacea that many policymakers are seeking? Probably not, but it may hold some promise to be a set of reasonable standards that can enhance the possibilities for learning.

Beyond standards, an issue that educators, parents, and policymakers are dealing with now is the privatization of schooling. There are several companies that have taken over the management of elementary and secondary schools in recent years. The form of privatization is frequently the establishment of charter schools. In one sense, the growth of charter schools has been an outgrowth of some demand for school choice (although the dynamic of school choice is much broader and more complicated than privatization). One factor that must be considered with respect to charter schools is whether the managing entity is a not-for-profit organization (which could be a university) or a for-profit corporation. In the latter instance, there, of course, must be a potential for profit, other educational considerations aside. As Witte (2004) points out, the growth of for-profit education management organizations (EMOs) accelerated after the passage of NCLB. He (2004) also explores some of the experiences of teachers in different environments: "On a Wisconsin teacher survey of more than 2,300 charter and noncharter teachers, the one overwhelming difference is on any and all measures of autonomy. Charter teachers have and desire considerably more autonomy in all aspects of their jobs. It is by far the most often cited reason for joining charters, and charters reward the teachers with considerable classroom and school control" (p. 1053).

EMOs definitely have their critics, and Diane Ravitch may be among the most vocal. Among other concerns she (2013) has is that the original supporters of NCLB have become supporters of for-profit education in the United States. The concern, as she explains it, has to do with the potential for education falling prey to the neoliberal disasters described in Chapter 2. If profit is the primary motivation for the enterprise, where do diversity, concern for students with special needs, and those who are challenged in other ways fit into the business model? If profit, for example, is based on particular measures of performance, then the elimination of pupils who, for example, have learning disabilities would make business sense. The overall, or average, student performance rises when only high performers are admitted. Ravitch (2013) also suggests the Obama administration's Race to the Top program has continued the ineffectiveness of NCLB. As she (2013) concludes, "The corporate reform movement has capitalized on the American public's infatuation with consumerism. Consumerism is as American as apple pie. People shop for their shoes and their jeans and their homes, say reformers, why not shop for their children's schools? Competition may produce better shoes and jeans, but there is little evidence that is produces better schools" (p. 319). So we must ask if the public good is served by privatization, and the answer may not be as elusive as some seem to think.

## Higher Education

Education at all levels can and should contribute to the public good, but higher education has a particular role to play. Unfortunately, colleges and universities have been subjected to the negative effects of neoliberalism. The following assessment by Radice (2013) applies to the United Kingdom but could easily be said about US higher education: "Those outside the managerial élite have been increasingly subjected to the process of deprofessionalisation or proletarianisation, which has affected not only the rest of the UK public sector, but also fields such as legal practice, accountancy and architecture . . . The traditional model of autonomous professional partnerships in these fields is giving way to a corporate private enterprise model in which only a small minority (predominantly white and male) retain control, while the rest become salaried workers managed from above" (p. 415). In the United States, there has been an increase of nonacademics selected to lead colleges and universities. Influential individuals, like Derek Bok (2003), decry the commercialization of higher education and the effects of diminishing learning for the sake of learning.

Commercialization is a bit of an understatement when it comes to a major challenge facing higher education. It was demonstrated in the last chapter how public support for public higher education has been diminishing over the last few decades; funding has to come from somewhere. If more of the financing will come from corporate sources, some compromises (at the least) will occur. Some of the compromises may be reflected in the curriculum; those areas that are not market-driven may see support dwindle in the future as STEM (science, technology, engineering, and mathematics) fields thrive. The study of literature, history, sociology, anthropology, and so on could be seen as somewhat expendable—at least to the point where they have no opportunity to grow and develop. What matters is the locus of decision making. Those who are in management positions could well employ a set of criteria for expenditures that is based on neoliberal principles of markets and transactions. On the other hand, a recent survey demonstrates that students' majors constitute a hiring criterion only 44 percent of the time. Moreover, where the student graduated from is used only 10 percent of the time ("Survey Results Detail," 2014). It is apparent that employers are using a broad spectrum of criteria when they hire entry-level personnel. The behavior calls into question some of the decisions being made on college and university campuses.

Looking at the bigger picture, Gregorian (2005) suggests that higher education is facing six major challenges:

1. The information-glut . . . and the fragmentation of knowledge;
2. the curriculum crisis, including the liberal arts;
3. the commercialization of research;
4. the evolution of a two-tier system of faculty, with full-time and part-time members;
5. concerns about quality, especially in schools of education; and
6. the changes that distance learning and e-learning [will] bring (pp. 77–78)

Each of the challenges is severe, and each has far-reaching implications. We can address the last challenge at this time. First, for-profit learning is not new, but until recently, the institutions were rather small in number and in enrollment. Technology has enabled colleges and universities to grow in both ways. It should be noted that in the 2009–10 year, for-profit institutions received about $32 billion from the federal government (primarily in the form of student financial aid). However, "They also charge far higher tuition fees than comparable state universities. Yet they spend much less per student on instruction. Indeed, they typically spend a lot more on marketing their courses than they do on teaching them. This may explain why the majority of students on their degree programmes drop out long before they graduate" ("Why Do Americans," 2013). At the time of this writing, the University of Phoenix, the largest for-profit university, has about 300,000 students. This compares to about 36,000 students (still a substantial number) for a competitor, Capella University. With hundreds of thousands of students in for-profit colleges and universities, there is reason for traditional higher education to be concerned.

Of course, distance and online education is by no means limited to for-profit institutions. There are numerous not-for-profit colleges and universities that are primarily online, for example. Southern New Hampshire University has an enrollment of more than 17,000 students. Additionally, many colleges and universities with traditional campuses have online operations. Columbia College (Missouri) is a liberal arts college with roughly 1,000 students on the main campus but an additional 24,000 students in nationwide and online programs. This recollects another of Gregorian's concerns; much of Columbia College's instruction is provided by part-time adjunct teachers. The operation may be well managed, but most students do not have the opportunity to learn from full-time faculty members. Columbia's mode of operation is by no means unique; many colleges and universities enhance their enrollments by having online offerings. The students provide needed financial support for institutions, and the costs of instruction are controlled by employing part-time and adjunct teachers. The quality of instruction and of students' experiences is an open question. One factor that is particularly questionable is the degree to which out-of-class contact with faculty members and other students enhances learning. If research would find that these interactions were valuable, important questions related to the public good would be raised. One major question to be asked is whether large-scale online education is inherently neoliberal of construction and operation. That question cannot be asked here, but it needs to be a concern to all who care about education.

Given what is said previously, it is no wonder that Gardner (2005) wonders if educational goals are being marginalized. To clarify his point, he (2005) articulates the goals:

> First of all, human knowledge is among our most precious possessions; we owe it to our predecessors and successors to privilege this human creation. Second, education is the sphere designated by society as the guardian, transmitter, and accumulator of that knowledge; if colleges do not carry out this mission, no other body can step into the breach. Third and often forgotten, the greatest gifts that we provide to our students are the appreciation of such knowledge, the capacity to think with and about it, and the potential to add to that knowledge in whichever sphere they eventually enter. All the rest is incidental. (p. 101)

Gardner appreciates that the neoliberalism that threatens higher education can do irreparable damage to the futures of students. That realization also lies behind Budd's (2009) statement of the purpose of higher education: "*the pursuit (in the form of teaching, learning, inquiry, and service beyond the institution) of knowledge and truth within an ethical and democratic institution*" (emphasis in original; p. 5). The public good deserves no less.

## Discussion

The essential and needed characteristics of the public good—integrity, honesty, ethics, justice, and freedom—have been mentioned previously. It is apparent that their absence is a cause for considerable concern. For example, as Ferguson (2012) notes, "At the peak of the [housing] bubble, the *average* annual income of a Goldman Sachs employee was $600,000; and even within investment banking, incomes are heavily skewed toward the very top" (p. 215). These observations may draw some criticism from conservative commentators, but a few things must be emphasized with respect to the public good characteristics. They are neither Left nor Right leaning. The characteristic of integrity, for example, include personal responsibility, which is a feature that those of all political stripes can support. It would also be difficult to imagine people on any point on the political spectrum who would disagree with the fundamental purpose of higher education. I mention these examples (and refer to the entirety of the chapter) to stress that what is actually of consequence is adherence to the characteristics, to efforts at doing what is right.

There are some conservative scholars who have taken stands on the matters that concern us in these pages. Richard Posner (2010), a federal judge, claims, "At the root of the financial collapse, then, was a failure of regulation, compounded by unsound monetary policy and deregulation, nonregulation, and lax—excessively permissive—regulation of financial intermediation" (p. 79). It may be that extreme libertarian sentiments would run counter to Posner's analysis, but the absence of regulation is not necessarily a classical liberal stance. It is quite clear that the lack of responsible regulation has resulted in a heavy cost for all citizens. When positive action is required to ensure that the polity is not harmed, that action is the responsible mode of behavior. There are times when the government must do something in order to make certain that the property and possessions of Americans can be preserved in the face of such attacks as the greed of corporations. Posner (2010) adds what may be one of the most important statements that should be shared here: "But capitalism is not a synonym for free markets. It is the name given to a complex economic system with many moving parts" (p. 1).

The phenomenon of greed complicates the usual social-economic dynamics that are spoken of. In short, greed is by no means necessarily good. In fact, while it may enrich some individuals, it can damage, even impoverish, others in society. Bernie Madoff was greedy, and he wrought severe misfortune upon investors. Unscrupulous lenders managed to persuade potential borrowers to sign on for mortgages that eventually forced the signers out of their homes. Rick Santelli was seriously mistaken to think that all blame rested with the signers. There is no doubt that some borrowers were irresponsible and thought that they could play the system. But it should be remembered that the financial structure is indeed systemic; the creation, and then the bursting, of the bubble was not because of a very few rogue individuals. The policies of several companies developed mechanisms whereby people were taken advantage of. Maybe Santelli would not have been fooled by mortgage instruments that were designed for the sole purpose of making an initial sale (with no care at all for the futures of the borrowers), but few people are professional financial analysts. Robert Frank (2011) presents an explanation that must be heeded by any analyst: "Darwin's view of the competitive process was fundamentally different. His observations persuaded him that the interests of individual animals were often profoundly in conflict with the broader interests of their species" (p. 17).

Frank concentrates on what he calls the "rational libertarian," who considers, among other things, what kind of world and society that rational person will ideally choose to live in. In other words, this libertarian considers personal preference but extends that preference to society and adds not only the personal goals he or she may have but also the world he or she will live in. That may include noninterference with personal goals but could also add the nondomination of any citizen. Each individual, then, would have access to personal goals and not be subject to the interference not only by government but also by corporations and individuals who might also be able to exercise interference and domination. Frank (2011) says, "A rational libertarian who reflects carefully about the traditional libertarian position will find it difficult to defend" (p. 211). In the Darwinian analysis, admitting that the behavior of individuals may harm the whole, rational limits must be a component of a free society (one in which people are free from the domination of entities or individuals). Doing harm to others is, then, unacceptable.

The position that Frank adopts is a fundamentally ethical one. In one sense, he is echoing Adam Smith, with regard not to *Wealth of Nations*, but to his *Theory of Moral Sentiments*. Smith (2000 [1759]) articulates his predilection for benevolence toward others in that work. He also maintains that self-interest, while prudent within our economic lives, is nothing more than a stepping stone to a moral and virtuous life. In other words, Smith also believes in living a just life with and for others. Self-interest is not blind to the social milieu and the lives of other individuals. At this time, it should be mentioned that, while the moral stance advocated here is something short of absolutism, the idea of relativism is by no means advanced. Drawing from Steven Lukes (2008), the belief that truths are relative when taken from moral and ethical thought is weak for three reasons:

> The first, and the weakest, is that if people accept relativism, then they will lack the motivation to accept basic moral principles, even those forbidding such things as murder . . . The second reason is that relativism threatens to deprive us of moral confidence: of the sense that we are *right* to condemn the actions of wrongdoers and to think that their victims are entitled not to be wronged. And the third reason is that relativism removes the sense of *conflict* between apparently conflicting moral judgments by suggesting that since they are relative to different standards, they do not really conflict. (pp. 17–18)

It is unstated by Lukes, but the importance of his message arises from its being communicated in a general medium and not so much as part of an institutionalized mechanism of "approved" scholarship. That means that his work is, to an extent, outside the bounds of high education's limitations, outside the customary tenure and promotion review. Misztal (2007) praises such work and goes so far as to warn that "there are those who believe that the role of the intellectual has been undermined by the processes of institutionalisation, professionalisarion, and the commercialisation of intellectual life . . . There are [though] other voices claiming that the death of the intellectual are greatly exaggerated . . . or even false" (pp. 14–15). The debate itself signals a problem though. That there are those who believe there is no public intellectual is a sign to the world of intellectuals. Without doubt, there is work—there are even fields—where the principal work is communicated in technical language so that progress is possible. In other areas, there is a need for communication aimed at intelligent readers; moreover, the communication should offer suggestions of actions that people can take to change our predicament for the better. That communication, to be worthwhile and successful, must adhere to the tenets of the public good outlined here; those works have the potential to make a difference in the body politic.

# 4

# Informational Failures

No medium, no single source, can cover every item that someone might claim to be newsworthy or vital to making decisions. Now the excuse has been stated; every television network, every newspaper, and every blogger can throw up collective hands and plead overload. They can add another caveat as well; readers cannot possibly pay attention to everything. If they want to lend some credence to the claim, they can cite cognitive load theory (although this is usually something to which academics resort). Fundamental psychological states of humans are such that when automatic schemas are developed for application, memory can be rendered more efficient; when the schemas are not developed (or are underdeveloped), individuals must employ a greater amount of working memory: "In sum, schema development reduces the constraints of a limited capacity working memory in two ways. First, a highly complex schema can be manipulated as one element rather than as multiple interacting elements when brought into working memory. Second, well-developed schemata are processed automatically, minimizing the demands of cognitive resources to tackle the task at hand" (Plass, Moreno, and Brünken, 2010,p. 14).

The academic apology is seldom employed in the popular media or those locations where the media are collected (including such places as public libraries). A different rationale may be used at times. For those remaining print resources (such as some newspapers and books) and broadcast media, including television and radio, space and time are real constraints. In part, the limitation is an economic one; a newspaper cannot afford to print unlimited pages. Also, a television network cannot devote endless hours to news coverage (save in genuinely exceptional instances). Even in the blogosphere, the creators of messages are aware of the attention spans of potential readers. At all times and in all media, there will be selections made; the decisions represent an extremely complex dynamic that must be investigated to be understood. This chapter is devoted to the selectivity (which is not always transparent) so that the lacunae can be explored.

In particular, there are stories and events that receive little press but could be integral to assisting people in making voting decisions or in developing opinions about policy issues. To an extent, polling data can be explored to figure out public awareness of any number of matters. Those data are a beginning; they indicate what could be delved into more deeply.

## The US Military

At times, there are informing successes that alert people to events related to democratic operations in the United States. Some successes are related to the US military. When military forces invaded Iraq in 2003, there were many events and statements that placed considerable pressures on people's attention. In fact, the pressures began with the rationale for the invasion itself. There is an extensive essay in Wikipedia on the invasion with facts that have been vetted by a number of individuals. The movement of troops and materiel into Iraq began on March 19, 2003, but forces were gathering in Kuwait on February 18 (2003 invasion of Iraq). A CBS News/*New York Times* poll taken in January of 2003 found that 63 percent of respondents wanted the president to seek a diplomatic solution to the dilemma. At the time of the poll, the UN inspectors had not reported their findings. When people were asked what the United States should do if no weapons of mass destruction were found by the inspectors' January 27 reporting date, 77 percent stated that the international community should continue the search for the weapons. The Americans polled, though, did believe that Iraq *had* the weapons (85 percent answering in the affirmative). The new agencies polled citizens repeatedly about approval of taking military action against Saddam Hussein; the lowest mark of approval and the highest mark of disapproval for such action occurred just prior to the invasion. Poll figures reported by the ages of respondents demonstrated that the generations who could have been in combat were most opposed to invasion and most favorable to diplomacy (Cosgrove-Mather, 2003).

Artillery attacks on Baghdad began on March 30. A CNN.com report stated, "More than 40 satellite-guided Tomahawk cruise missiles were fired from U.S. warships in the Red Sea and Persian Gulf, military officials said. F117 stealth fighters, which carry two 2,000-pound bombs apiece, also were involved in the strikes, though apparently on a target other than Saddam" (Chilcote, King, and Starr, 2003). The day before the State of the Union address, Hans Blix, chief UN weapons inspector, spoke to the United Nations, updating ambassadors on the state of inspections at that time. Blix reported that there remained numerous concerns about weapons in Iraq but that the inspections team was progressing in its task and was identifying some (but few) weapons and munitions enrichment facilities. His recommendation was that the inspection process be allowed to conclude its work (see "Transcript of Blix's Remarks," 2003). "'If they have any—and still, that's a big if—I would doubt that they would use it because a lot of countries and people in the world are negative to the idea of waging war,' Blix said. 'If the Iraqis were to use any chemical weapons, then I think the public opinion around the world would immediately turn against Iraq, and they would say, as well, that the invasion was justified'" ("Blix: Iraq Unlikely," 2003). Taking the opinion of Blix into consideration, the reality is that US and international forces did not encounter any serious resistance nor weapons of mass destruction. The distance from the Kuwait-Iraq border to Baghdad is approximately 346 miles. News outlets reported that forces entered the center of Baghdad on April 7, more than two weeks after setting out from Kuwait. There are few, if any, reports on the absence of any Iraqi weapons strikes on invading forces.

A majority of Americans appeared to believe that Iraq had weapons of mass destruction, and President Bush uttered the famous statement, "The British government has learned that Saddam Hussein recently sought significant quantities of uranium from Africa" in his January 28, 2003, State of the Union address (Bush, 2003). People of various political stripes have argued whether or not the president was lying when he uttered those words. The answer to the question is, of course, important, but the effects of the statement may be even more important. To an extent, it strengthened the resolve of many who were disposed to believe that there was a cause for the invasion. In other words, belief in the utterance was one more piece of perceived evidence for the correctness of a certain position. A genuine examination of the matter has a foundation in Steven Pinker's linguistic analysis of the phrasing of the statement. Bush said that the British government "learned" of something Saddam may have done. According to Pinker (2007), "*Learn* is what linguists call a factive verb; it entails that the belief attributed to the subject is true" and that in "the usual sense, especially in the perfect tense with *have*, is factive; it means 'acquired true information'" (italics in original; p. 7). Citizens, hearing the statement within the context of the State of the Union address, which is supposed to be vetted by several government agencies, could be expected to believe what was said. The president's address was followed closely by a speech by Secretary of State Colin Powell to the United Nations on February 6, 2003, in which he enumerated weapons violations on the part of Iraq. Powell (Weisman, 2005) said, "There were some people in the intelligence community who knew at the time that some of these sources were not, and shouldn't be relied on, and they didn't speak up. That devastated me." All the speeches and addresses at the time (2003) were reported uncritically just as they were delivered. The popular media failed the US public utterly.

The address, however, was not the sole informing instance, especially for officials and reporters who were privy to other data at the time. In fact, members of the intelligence community were very skeptical of the claim. At the time of the address, there was no consensus on the issue of acquiring uranium, so it cannot be said that President Bush was lying at the time (and no claim can or should be made with any degree of certainty). When later questions were raised about the president—and, by extension, the US government—having *learned* something ostensibly true, the language shifted. In a July 17, 2003, report in *The Economist*, it was written, "'The British have said that,' says Condoleezza Rice, the national security adviser" ("In the Grips," 2003). The difference is not trivial and is not merely a language game. In 2003, Joe Wilson was working for the National Security Council in Niger. Wilson had experience with Saddam's reign in Iraq in the 1990s and stated that he was aware that the dictator presented a genuine concern. In a July 6, 2003, op-ed piece in *The New York Times*, Wilson (2003) recounted that, after his 2002 mission to Niger, "It did not take long to conclude that it was highly doubtful that any such transaction had ever taken place." The invasion had already occurred, though, and international troops were entrenched in Iraq by July 2003.

Meanwhile, in a March 25, 2003, report by "Democracy Now," Kurdish officials said that the US bombing resulted in the deaths of 150 of their people ("Kurdish Officials Say 150 Killed," 2003). Timelines of the invasion are presented by CNN ("Gulf War to Iraq War," n.d.) and *The New York Times* (Crichton, Lamb, and Jacquette, 2011), but neither mentions the Kurdish report. It is indeed an open question to what extent American citizens were aware of the event. The popular media failed to inform people about something that went against the grain of the almost universal positive news about the occurrences in Iraq. A Google search (on July 25, 2014) using the terms "bush iraq war mission accomplished" results in 1,740,000 hits. Most of the retrievable items are retrospective pieces. One of the items, reported by MSNBC, stated, "While the speech was well-received at the time, the war lasted another eight years. Congress decided to send in 20,000 more troops into the country in 2007. The war claimed the lives of at least 190,000 people—the bulk of whom were civilians, in addition to 4,488 U.S. soldiers and 3,400 U.S. contractors" (Frumin, 2013). Did people believe on that day (May 1, 2003) that the war in Iraq was over? By 2006, according to an Opinion Research Corporation poll, conducted for CNN, only 9 percent of respondents believed that the mission was indeed accomplished. By contrast, 44 percent said the United States would never accomplish its goals in Iraq ("Poll: Vast Majority Believes," 2006).

The lack of confidence in the war effort was not something that was widely announced.

Not long after the US invasions of Iraq and Afghanistan, a program of the capture and removal of suspects who were believed to have terrorist links was instituted. This program, called "extraordinary rendition," was designed to relocate the detainees to other countries where the suspects could be interrogated. The interrogators were residents of the country of relocation. Open Society Foundation (OSF) details the process:

1. At least 136 individuals were reportedly extraordinarily rendered or secretly detained by the CIA and at least 54 governments reportedly participated in the CIA's secret detention and extraordinary rendition program; classified government documents may reveal many more.
2. A series of Department of Justice memoranda authorized torture methods that the CIA applied on detainees. The Bush Administration referred to these methods as "enhanced interrogation techniques."
3. The CIA's Office of Inspector General has reportedly investigated a number of "erroneous renditions" in which the CIA had abducted and detained the wrong people. A CIA officer told the Washington Post: "They picked up the wrong people, who had no information. In many, many cases there was only some vague association" with terrorism.
4. German national Khaled El-Masri was seized in Macedonia because he had been mistaken for an Al Qaeda suspect with a similar name. He was held incommunicado and abused in Macedonia and in secret CIA detention in Afghanistan. (Horowitz and Cammarano, 2013)

There have been reports of extraordinary rendition over the years, but it is likely that a small minority of American citizens are fully aware of the extent and nature of this questionable action by the CIA. Fewer still may understand precisely what happened to the people who were seized and relocated.

As horrific (and secretive) as was extraordinary rendition, official US policy should concern citizens even more. In 2002, Deputy Assistant Attorney General John Yoo wrote a memo in which he said, "We conclude that these [international] treaties do not protect members of the Al Qaeda organization, which as a non-State actor cannot be party to international agreements governing war" (Yoo, 2002). The interpretation is very selective and is highly questionable; treaties generally are intended to protect individuals in times of war. Attorney General Alberto Gonzalez (2002) shortly thereafter confirmed the interpretation in a memo to President Bush: "I also advised you that DOJ's opinion concludes that there are reasonable grounds for you to conclude that GPQ [the Geneva Convention on

Prisoners of War] *does not apply* with respect to the conflict with the Taliban. I understand that you decided that GPW does not apply and, accordingly, that all al Qaeda and Taliban detainees are not prisoners of war under the GPW" (emphasis added). The way was opened up for waterboarding, electrodes attached to genitals, the subjection to extreme heat and cold, and other measures that could only be described as torture. As is the case with many such actions, a few major news outlets covered these stories, but full descriptions appeared in only a few sources. Once again, many citizens may have been unaware of the actions taken by the US government. A rhetorical ploy is evident in these memos: it has been stated numerous times, including by the president, that the United States is at war, yet combatants are not deemed to be prisoners of war. Linguistic and cognitive elasticity must be used in order to have anyone accept the points made in the memos.

In a short time from now (as I write this), the United States will begin a major withdrawal of troops and materiel from Afghanistan. The prevailing fear is that the country will devolve into ethnic and tribal battles. The fear is legitimate, given the centuries-old history of conflict in Afghanistan (a country that has geographic divisional challenges such as mountains, passes, valleys, and other features that render continuity, and even travel, challenging). What will the impact of the Taliban be at that time? No one can predict this:

> "It is a characteristic of this kind of warfare," Gen. John R. Allen, the commander of NATO forces in Afghanistan, told reporters at a Pentagon news conference. He said that in a counterinsurgency conflict like the one in Afghanistan, where American forces are fighting insurgents while training Afghan security forces, "the enemy's going to do all that they can to disrupt both the counterinsurgency operation, but also disrupt the integrity of the indigenous forces." American commanders say that the Taliban have in some cases infiltrated Afghan security forces to attack Americans, but that most cases are a result of personal disputes between Afghans and their American trainers. (Bumiller and Kopicki, 2012)

General Allen appears to be prone to the error of almost all his predecessors (and ignorant of the viewpoints of many Americans); US military personnel stay in order to maintain order and peace. Even *with* the presence of the military personnel, there is an absence of peace and order that he himself confesses to. Party affiliation aside, one can question the strategic and tactical wisdom of the people in charge of military operations in Iraq and Afghanistan.

In fact, that question could have been—should have been—asked at the time of the initial invasion of Iraq. There are, though, accounts of problematic dilemmas that have plagued the military efforts in the Middle East. In June 2010, Michael Hastings (who, sadly, died in an car accident three years later) wrote an article on General Stanley McChrystal for *Rolling Stone* magazine. The article pulled no punches on McChrystal, his subordinates, or their overall attitude to counterinsurgency (McChrystal's own strategy in Afghanistan). In particular, Hastings chronicled the structural difficulties plaguing fighting a war and attempting to apply diplomacy:

> Part of the problem is structural: The Defense Department budget exceeds $600 billion a year, while the State Department receives only $50 billion. But part of the problem is personal: In private, Team McChrystal likes to talk shit about many of Obama's top people on the diplomatic side. One aide calls Jim Jones, a retired four-star general and veteran of the Cold War, a "clown" who remains "stuck in 1985." Politicians like McCain and Kerry, says another aide, "turn up, have a meeting with Karzai, criticize him at the airport press conference, then get back for the Sunday talk shows. Frankly, it's not very helpful." (Hastings, 2010)

Hastings also recounts McChrystal's disdain for Richard Holbrooke, a state department official in Afghanistan, referring to him as a wounded animal, and also criticized Karl Eikenberry, former US ambassador to Afghanistan. McChrystal offered his resignation from his post in Afghanistan to President Obama on June 23, 2010 (one day after the online appearance of Hastings's article), and he retired one month later. Almost all news outlets carried the story of the resignation, and many quoted Hastings in doing so. This is an example of informational success inasmuch as the news was universally covered and reported.

Various sources also covered the ignominy of General David Petraeus, successor to General McChrystal and eventual head of the CIA. Petraeus became entangled in an extramarital affair. A number of individuals became involved in the fallout from the controversy. There is no need to recount the matter of harassing emails, their sources, nor the involvement of civilians, government employees, and military personnel. Suffice it to say that the details quickly became sordid and led to Petraeus's resignation as director of the CIA and a serious diminution of his reputation. Coverage of the story extended from blogs (Read, 2012) to CNN (Pearson, 2012). Again, the story was deemed newsworthy, so all sources covered it in some way.

An open question has to do with what happens to military personnel after their deployments. The case of one man provides an object lesson. Sergeant Jerrald Jensen was on duty in Iraq when an improvised explosive device (IED) exploded, shattering the lower half of his face. He underwent reconstructive surgery and was deployed once again, this time to Afghanistan, where he was severely injured again. Nermeen Shaikh, in an interview with Amy Goodman on the radio program "Democracy Now," stated, "When he [Jensen] got home, he faced a less than honorable discharge after he tested positive for the drug amphetamine. He asked to be retested, saying his many Army prescriptions might be to blame. But his commander refused and instead gave Jensen the maximum punishment, cutting his rank to private, docking his pay and canceling surgery to fix his face so he could spend weeks mopping floors, picking weeds and scrubbing toilets" ("Other Than Honorable," 2013). Jensen was obviously abandoned by a military in which he served and for which he gave a substantial part of his life. Apart from "Democracy Now" and David Phillips's (2013) items, almost no media attention has been given to Jensen's plight, which demonstrates not only the brutality of the war but also the treatment of fallen soldiers by the US military. The ploy of which the military is culpable is certainly egregious; American citizens should be made aware of it.

Another fact of which many Americans may not be aware is that "955,609 (about 36 percent) of our total Active Duty/Reserve/National Guard forces of 2,656,300 have deployed to Iraq or Afghanistan during this period. 651,622 (24.5 percent) have one deployment during this period, and 303,987 (11.4 percent) have deployed more than once" (Powers, 2005). That report covers only the first five years of the conflict; recent estimates suggest that about five hundred thousand military personnel have been subjected to multiple deployments. Simple statistical analysis holds that the chances of physical injury are much greater the longer one is in a combat zone. Further, the chances of suffering emotional and psychological trauma likewise accelerate. A question the citizens should be asking is how many veterans are suffering from psychological problems. Barnes (2008) has reported, "An estimated 300,000 veterans among the nearly 1.7 million who have served in Iraq and Afghanistan are battling depression or post-traumatic stress disorder. More than half of those people, according to the study conducted by the Rand Corp., are slipping through the cracks in the bureaucratic system, going without necessary treatment." Again, with the passage of time it is probable that more personnel are suffering trauma, and that more are going untreated.

The wars have taken a serious toll that tends to fly under the radar of the media and the awareness of the American people. Haiken (2013) provides data on this matter:

> Many of these suicides involve older veterans; 69 percent of the suicides recorded were by veterans age 50 and older. But another way to look at this is that 31 percent of these suicides were by veterans 49 and younger. In

other words, by men in the prime of life. And then there are the shockingly common active duty suicides. Just two weeks ago, the military released data showing that suicides among those on active duty hit a record high in 2012. There were 349 suicides among active duty personnel—almost one a day. That means there are now more suicides among active duty soldiers than there are combat deaths.

Haiken (2013) quotes Williams (2012), who adds to what we can and should know:

> The military said Friday that there had been 154 suicides among active-duty troops through Thursday, a rate of nearly one each day this year. The figures were first reported this week by The Associated Press. That number represents an 18 percent increase over the 130 active-duty military suicides for the same period in 2011. There were 123 suicides from January to early June in 2010, and 133 during that period in 2009, the Pentagon said. By contrast, there were 124 American military fatalities in Afghanistan as of June 1 this year, according to the Pentagon.

One voice that has been critical of US foreign policy over the last several years, especially the decisions that brought on the conflicts in Iraq and Afghanistan, is that of Andrew Bacevich. In his book *The Limits of Power* (2009), he details many of the actions that have had negative, or deleterious, effects for the United States and the Middle East. His book received considerable attention in magazines and journals, and the reception was mixed. Some praised him for bringing many facts to the fore, but others criticized him for what he *did not* include (the position of Israel, in particular). The meat of his critique is summed up late in the book: "That a career intelligence official like [Robert] Gates or a retired Marine four-star like [General James] Jones will question the core assumptions informing standard national security practices is by no means an impossibility. It's just not especially likely. One might as well look to the CEOs and Detroit's Big Three to promote mass transit as a preferred alternative to the automobile" (p. 186). One of his most important observations is that the depression that began in 2007 was unlike the Great Depression in that there was the simultaneously occurring massive expenditures of wars on two fronts. There was a loss of wealth and jobs, along with the cost of the conflicts (variously estimated at something between $ 1 trillion and $3 trillion). Domestic recovery and growth has naturally been stymied by the massive federal spending. As Bacevich (2009) says, the economic trouble, along with the national security problems, creates a dual challenge of massive proportions (pp. 184–85). The degree of coverage of the previously stated is questionable.

At the time of this writing, the US government is contemplating firing on Syria because of purported evidence of the Assad regime's use of chemical weapons. There is no doubt in the mind of any moral human being that the use of chemical weapons is a heinous breach of international law, but the nature and appropriateness of a national response by the United States is not a simple matter. A very recent report (Clement, 2013) states that a *Washington Post*–ABC News poll illustrates public opposition to military strikes (by about a 3-to-2 margin). About 66 percent of political independents express opposition (there is little difference between Democrats and Republicans). Apparently, the reluctance of Britain and France to engage Syria affects the opinions of US citizens. Another factor that is far less frequently reported is that Iran is a close ally of Syria; no one can predict how Iran might respond to bombings or other military action. Very few commentators have written about parallels between the Middle East and the Balkans of today. There is an enormous amount of uncertainty and instability in the Middle East at this time; there could and should be informed voices recounting historical lessons.

## The US Government

The rich are different from you and me. For example, in 2013, my personal federal income tax rate was 18.9 percent (I am not a millionaire). In 2011, Mitt Romney paid a rate of 14.1 percent. According to Carter (2012), writing for the left-leaning *Huffington Post*,

> Mitt Romney paid an effective tax rate of 14.1 percent in 2011, according to a tax return filed on Friday, a relatively low tax rate resulting from exotic deductions, the special tax treatment for his Bain Capital retirement package and the low tax rate on capital gains. Romney also opted not to deduct millions in charitable contributions from his tax bill in order to maintain a pledge from August that he has paid at least 13 percent in federal income taxes for each of the past 10 years. Romney's income was $13,696,951 in 2011, and he paid $1,935,708 in taxes. Romney's income for the year was more than 263 times larger than the U.S. median household income of $51,914.

Most middle-class taxpayers are unable to take advantage of many deductions, and most middle-class citizens are wage earners and so pay specified tax rates. One may wonder how many Americans are aware that in 1997 (as a result of the Taxpayer Relief Act of 1997), the long-term capital gains tax rate fell from 28 percent to 20 percent. The rate fell to 15 percent in 2003 with the passage of the Jobs and Growth Tax Relief Reconciliation Act of

2003. With the capital gains rate cut of nearly 50 percent over the past several years, those individuals whose income source is investments are likely to pay lower tax rates than millions of wage earners. Warren Buffett, one of the wealthiest individuals in the world, recognizes the inequity of this kind of taxation: "No household making more than $1 million each year should pay a smaller share of their income in taxes than a middle class family pays. This is the Buffett Rule—a simple principle of tax fairness that asks everyone to pay their fair share" ("The Buffett Rule," 2012). How would people respond if asked about this "rule"? The White House website (see "The Buffett Rule," 2012) has a calculator function; an individual or family can calculate the effective tax rate on earnings *and* find out how many millionaires paid a lower tax rate.

The revenue collected by the US government is a reflection of many factors. The marginal capital gains tax rate is one of the factors. Suppose the rate had remained constant at 28 percent; Romney may have paid nearly twice as much in taxes in 2011. The total difference in tax collections in 2011 could have been approximately $25 to $40 billion (based on simple extrapolation). The IRS estimates that approximately $300 billion in personal income taxes owed go unpaid each year, and the amount is rising (Cauchon, 2008). Something similar occurs with corporate income taxes, as Klinger (2013) reports: "Consider Pfizer's track record. The drugmaker increased its offshore profits by $10 billion in 2012, boosting its offshore stash to $73 billion—all of it untaxed by Uncle Sam. Like most pharmaceutical companies, Pfizer registers its patents in a low-tax offshore haven, and then charges a high price for the use of this 'intellectual property.' Doing so, it shifts all of its U.S. profits offshore, avoiding U.S. taxes and bloating its overseas bank account." If all taxes that were owed happened to be paid and if the capital gains tax rate had not been reduced, the federal government would be collecting considerably more than an extra $400 billion a year right now. Furthermore, Medicare and Medicaid fraud costs the government large sums each year: "The Centers for Medicare and Medicaid Services, or C.M.S., estimated that in 2010, the two programs together made more than $65 billion in improper federal payments. An April 2012 study by a RAND Corporation analyst and former C.M.S. administrator estimated that fraud and abuse cost Medicare and Medicaid as much as $98 billion in 2011" (Konrad, 2012). All of a sudden, without budget cuts, the federal government budget could become more than half a trillion dollars more efficient. Numbers tend to be reported, and there may be some hand-wringing in published items, but little is said about responsibility—personal, corporate, or legislative.

There is more to the money trail. According to Morgenson (2013), the top one hundred CEOs made (as a median) $14 million each in total compensation. This figure is mentioned so that poverty data can be placed in perspective. About seventy thousand individuals could have received $20,000 from what those top CEOs made. The US Census Bureau calculated that in 2011, the poverty rate in America was more than 16 percent (almost 20 percent for children). The percentage translated into 49.7 million people living in poverty (see "Census: U.S. Poverty Rate Spikes," 2012). The rate has been reported in some venues, but poverty is still an almost invisible problem in most of the United States. Millions of people tend not to see—or tend not to notice—the poorest among us, except for the homeless people who sleep on city streets or panhandle as people walk to and from their workplaces. Many more poor Americans live in suburbs or small rural towns, though. Sources as diverse as FoxNews.com, National Public Radio, and *The Huffington Post* all report that four out five Americans live near poverty at some time in their lives. It appears that the new American dream may be to escape poverty for the entirety of one's life. While the data are reported in diverse outlets, this is a story that one may not see on the above-the-fold headlines of many newspapers or see as the lead story on broadcast news channels. The amount of time devoted to Jodi Arias or George Zimmerman dwarfs stories on poverty in the United States.

Awareness of global poverty may be even lower among US citizens. Facts that ought to frighten everyone in the developed world are, perhaps, unnoticed: "The United Nations Food and Agriculture Organization estimates that nearly 870 million people, or one in eight people in the world, were suffering from chronic undernourishment in 2010–2012. Almost all the hungry people, 852 million, live in developing countries, representing 15 percent of the population of developing counties. There are 16 million people undernourished in developed countries" ("2013 World Hunger," 2014). "Chronic undernourishment" translates into life-threatening malnutrition. One cannot even speak of "quality of life" when considering the lives of people who wonder if they will have something to eat from one day to the next. Meanwhile, pundits that include Tom Brokaw opine that earning $250,000 a year in the United States doesn't make one "rich." The percentage of tax filers (federally adjusted gross income) in 2009 making $200,000–500,000 is a mere 2.3 percent of US filers (see Reeve, 2012). It may be that someone earning $250,000 would like to have a larger or nicer house or apartment, or to have a luxury car, or to dine out at expensive restaurants more frequently, but the amount still sets one far apart from a family earning the median income. No amount of spin can alter reality.

Regarding a matter that is somewhat related to poverty, the Affordable Care Act (bastardized as "Obamacare"), there is serious confusion among Americans. According to a Kaiser Family Foundation poll conducted in August 2013, only 57 percent of respondents indicated that they are certain it is, in fact, law and that it is being implemented. A total of 13 percent answered that it has been either repealed by Congress or overturned by the US Supreme Court. Moreover, "Public opinion on the ACA as a whole continues to tilt negative this month, with 37 percent saying they have a favorable view of the law and 42 percent expressing an unfavorable view" ("Kaiser Health Care Tracking Poll," 2013).

At the present time, there is a serious concern regarding surveillance conducted by the National Security Agency (NSA). The concern is well founded, at least according to documents leaked by Edward Snowden (who, at the time of this writing, is looking for a nation that will grant him political asylum). The leaks aside (or *because* of the leaks), the US Senate has been holding hearings about the massive NSE collection of phone conversations and email messages. Many documents have very recently been declassified, but questions linger. The rationale for the collection of data has been the effort to uncover illegal, even terrorist-related, activities. The effectiveness of the data collection program is unclear, though (see Dilanian, 2013).

The current surveillance is not new; in 2005, there was massive eavesdropping on phone calls made by American citizens without the courts' approval, established by the Foreign Intelligence Surveillance Act (FISA) of 1978. The decisions of the courts are not reported, so there are no security concerns attached to the decisions. Moreover, the vast number of requests made of the FISA court is approved, so there is little need to bypass this official channel. The bypassing of the court is not included in the USA PATRIOT Act, which was passed very soon after the 9/11 bombings, so there is no lawful excuse or rationale for not using the court to secure the approval of surveillance of domestic-to-domestic communication. According to a *New York Times* report, "Justice Department lawyers disclosed their thinking on the issue of warrantless wiretaps in national security cases in a little-noticed brief in an unrelated court case. In that 2002 brief, the government said that 'the Constitution vests in the President inherent authority to conduct warrantless intelligence surveillance (electronic or otherwise) of foreign powers or their agents, and Congress cannot by statute extinguish that constitutional authority'" (see Risen and Lichtblau, 2005). The illegal actions led Greenwald (2011) to write, "The lawbreaking could not be clearer, yet virtually nobody in the political and media class was willing to call those acts 'criminal,' much less to demand legal investigations or prosecutions" (p. 2). Greenwald refers to the "media class" alongside politicians as a way to link the two together when it comes to informing the public of the serious consequences of government action. Again, the informing mechanisms fail the US citizenry.

It needs to be said that the amount of coverage a story gets does not necessarily equate to the public being completely informed about the matter. The case concerning Bradley (Chelsea) Manning has been in the news for a few years now, but there are some key elements of his circumstances and deeds that have not been made clear. Just prior to this writing, Manning has been found guilty in a military court on several of the charges against him. He was found not guilty of the most serious charge of aiding the enemy. There is a possible reason for that judgment; Manning did not leak any documents classified as "Top Secret." In the words of Daniel Ellsberg, the documents Manning did provide to WikiLeaks were categorized, in Pentagon parlance, as "merely secret." Both the Manning and Snowden leaks were, according to the two men, released so that the American public would be fully aware of some of the actions the US government has been responsible for, including the procedure and outcome of extraordinary rendition, among other actions. It has been noted by more than one commentator that the oath taken by service personnel and officials is to the US Constitution, not to any particular administration.

## Commentary

General commentary on any number of topics also displays some of the problems with popular press and so-called pundits. As is known by most people, there are left-leaning and right-leaning publications, and their perspectives are usually quite different from one another. The Occupy and Tea Party movements have been discussed previously, but these are two topics that demonstrate the differences in coverage and comment. An article in *The Progressive* by Rothschild (2013) quotes Lisa Graves, executive director of the Center for Media and Democracy and former legislative strategist on national security for the ACLU, as saying, "The government has built a giant domestic surveillance apparatus in the name of homeland security that has been unleashed on ordinary Americans expressing concern about the undue influence of corporations on our democracy" (p. 21). This is a generic critique, but the article further points out that there have been official mechanisms (such as the Homeland Defense Bureau of the Phoenix Police Department to shield Jamie Dimon, CEO of JPMorgan Chase [the nation's largest bank], from protests). Rothschild (2013) also reports that Phoenix detective Jennifer O'Neill "made it her job to monitor possible 'terrorist' activity by Occupy Phoenix connect with Dimon's visit" (p. 21). Another left-leaning article in PR Watch states,

> In October of 2011, Jamie Dimon, president and CEO of J.P. Morgan Chase, had plans to travel to Phoenix for a "town hall" event with 2,000 of his

> employees at Chase Field (home of the Arizona Diamondbacks, located in downtown Phoenix). As Dimon is one of the most powerful men on Wall Street and the head of the largest bank in the country—a bank that played a key role in the collapse of the U.S. economy in 2008—JP Morgan Chase Regional Security Manager Dan Grady contacted Arizona Counter Terrorism Information Center personnel on October 17 (the day before Dimon's scheduled visit), to ensure a smooth landing for Dimon in Phoenix (Hodai, 2013).

Rothschild (2013) also reports on an email sent from a private citizen to the Phoenix Police Department: "'Dear Sir or Madam,' the e-mail began. 'Please consider leaving the Occupy movement alone. They speak for me and I suspect a large portion of America who are upset with corporate greed and the ability to purchase politicians and their votes. We are going to take America back for its citizens, and would probably be better for your careers not to get in the way. Thanks, David Mullin" (p. 23). Rothschild (2013) continues, "Within minutes of sending his e-mail, Mullin caught the attention of the Phoenix Police Department's assistant chief of the Homeland Security Division, Tracy Montgomery, who wrote in an e-mail: 'Interesting e-mail threatening our careers. Anyone know the name?'" (p. 23). Many outlets, including the *Arizona Republic* (see Wiles, 2011) and CNN (see Barr, 2011), make no mention at all of the Phoenix Police Department and its squelching of protest. It is not that the content of Dimon's speech was not newsworthy but so were the collateral events that accompanied his visit to Phoenix, particularly in light of the Phoenix Police Department's clearly documented activities.

Both *The Progressive* and right-leaning *American Spectator* included articles about the Boston Marathon bombing in their June issues. Conniff (2013), in the pages of *The Progressive*, turned her attention to what she saw as a negative side of the events: "After the Boston Marathon bombing, our national atmosphere turned toxic. The lurid cable news coverage, the 'we are at war' grandstanding by Republicans, the shutting down of a major metropolitan area, and the collapse of bipartisan efforts on gun safety all bode ill for society. Weirdly, the biggest beneficiary of the bombing seemed to be the National Rifle Association" (p. 14). On the other hand, *The American Spectator*'s Flynn (2013) writes, "Noncitizens such as Tamerlan Tsarnaev possess civil rights far beyond what actual citizens enjoy. Chief among these is to hide one's illegal activity from law enforcement . . . Coincidentally, in 2004, more than four out of every five Cambridge voters supported the 'Curb USA Patriot ACT' ballot measure" (pp. 32, 33). Tsarnaev actually had permanent resident status, which does ensure considerable rights of the holder of the status. His brother, Dzhokhar, is a naturalized citizen, a fact not mentioned in *The American*

*Spectator*. Also, Tamerlan Tsarnaev was shot dead by police. The rhetoric in both articles discredits the reporting of *news*; each is filled with invective, albeit aimed at different targets. The writers might claim that they are not reporting facts but offering editorial opinions. Does that excuse the discourse? No, and the body politic is the worse for the employment of the rhetorical extremes.

If the rhetorical excesses constitute a contest between the two publications, *The American Spectator* is the hands-down winner. The magazine's editor, R. Emmett Tyrrell Jr. (2013), writes,

> April is no more and on comes May with good news for Our President. Just as sequestration began to bite, Holy Islam's barbigerous inmates, incarcerated in tropical Guantanamo with all expenses paid, have gone on a hunger strike! At least half of the boys have given up solid foods, *even desserts!* Many are not brushing their teeth, and some are refusing to flush the toilet. What does it all mean? Considerable savings for the federal government, and a big help with sequestration for our Muslim-educated President. (emphasis added; p. 10)

Tyrrell also refers to the Tsarnaevs (who are/were undeniable criminals) as the "Brothers #%!@*" and John Kerry as "Jean-François Kerry" and calls for public hangings. This discourse is not even remotely civilized and is an insult to every intelligent reader, regardless of one's political preference. If his rhetoric is to reign, one could as easily refer to "Herr McConnell" or "Baron Romney." These epithets would be every bit as offensive as the puerile discourse of Tyrrell. *The American Spectator* fails Americans and America by diminishing all that the nation is supposed to stand for.

## Tea Party and Occupy Movements

The issues on which FreedomWorks concentrates are numerous, but a theme runs throughout: the demand that government be removed from as many financial matters as possible, including health care, retirement, taxation, and so on. The word "freedom" in this rhetoric is used as a thematic counterpart to "government." An interpretation could follow that government means (or is the semantic equivalent to) oppression. Therefore, there must be a diminution, if not elimination, of government involvement in many programs for freedom to thrive. Environmental matters also capture the attention of FreedomWorks. (In actuality, it is not the environment that is the focus of attention; it is energy.) There is criticism, for example, of the Environmental Protection Agency (EPA) for its "war on coal," "war on affordable energy," and support for green sources of energy.

The language used directs the audience to the opposition between freedom and prosperity, on the one hand, and government and waste, on the other. The intention of using information to persuade should not, by its nature, allow for overt internal inconsistency, but practices may present selectively "correct" and "incorrect" stances regarding important issues.

An extensional outcome of the inquiry here is an examination of the effects of informational expressions on the beliefs and opinions held by those who identify themselves with the movements. One issue, global climate change, reflects the informational/discursive practices that the Tea Party and its members employ. In a *New York Times*–CBS poll, 53 percent of those self-identifying as Tea Party supporters said that global warming will have no serious impact on the environment, and 8 percent said it does not exist. Respondents to the poll overall included 22 percent who stated global warming would have no serious impact and 3 percent who said it does not exist (number of respondents = 1,253, October 1–5, 2010). At a 2010 candidates forum in Indiana, one attendee said, "'[Global warming] a flat-out lie,' Mr. [Norman] Dennison said in an interview after the debate, adding that he had based his view on the preaching of Rush Limbaugh and the teaching of Scripture. 'I read my Bible,' Mr. Dennison said. 'He made this earth for us to utilize.'" (Broder, 2010). Both the author of the *New York Times* article and the Tea Party member infuse language with images of religion and scripture.

The populist bent of the Tea Party is articulated by Angelo Codevilla in his denouncements of an American ruling class. Codevilla's (2010) questions are those that should be asked in any political system, including, "What is the right way for human beings to live? By what standard is anything true or good?" (p. 29). The ruling class, according to him, presumes to know better than do the people, which gives the members of the class a right to rule. Codevilla, however, does not identify the "rulers," save to mention some of the past (such as Woodrow Wilson and his effort to build the League of Nations). By implication, there is no conservative ruling class, but people such as former Massey CEO Don Blankenship, the Koch brothers, casino owner Sheldon Adelson, Fox News executive Roger Ailes, and others do wield considerable power over people, their informational sources, and their attitudes. Influential individuals have opportunities to make statements that can reach large audiences and may affect opinion and action in everyday life. For example, Sean Hannity used his radio program to interview and endorse Ted Cruz, a Tea Party sympathizer from Texas, for a Senate seat. His show is heard by millions and has influenced some listeners.

Two of the most distinctive rhetorical practices associated with the Occupy movement are the mic check and hand gestures. The former refers to a low-tech means of disseminating information using the collective vocal power of a group. It begins with one person yelling, "Mic check." Surrounding people respond by yelling "mic check" in unison. This is repeated until the crowd of participants is sufficiently loud to reach the desired audience, at which point the original speaker begins his or her statement, broken into short segments that are repeated in a call-and-response manner until the message is broadcast in full. The mic check was used across the Occupy movements, at general assemblies as well as during protest actions. Like the mic check, hand signals were used across Occupy movements. These include wiggling fingers upward in the air to signal approval or downward to signal disapproval. Other gestures signified the point of information or requested the dialogue be sped up, and a block gesture indicated the willingness to leave the movement if the suggested issue or statement was approved by consensus (90 percent of those present). The Occupy movement has arguably been less successful than the Tea Party in transmitting clear messages of political change outside their enclaves, yet there's an important caveat that while the Tea Party seeks to alter and disseminate messages, the Occupy movements are determined to alter practices. This is borne out in their processes of democracy—general assemblies, hand signals, and mic checks.

There are some similarities between the Tea Party and Occupy, most notably the populist character of both. While there is a substantial amount of money behind the Tea Party, much of the activity is spread across the nation and concentrated in small but numerous groups of dozens of people who tend to have localized concerns. Skocpol and Williamson (2012) demonstrated the populist nature most clearly. Their observations of grassroots meetings of local Tea Party chapters (and they found that there are several hundreds of them, usually with memberships of less than one hundred each) show some particularities: (1) demographics show homogeneity (older, white citizens, many of whom are retired and many of whom have had US military connections), (2) a consistent concern for the fiscal future of the United States (stated primarily in terms of budget deficits), and (3) a commitment to look for candidates for public office who share their concerns. This said, they (2012) also found that there are some disagreements among the citizens identifying themselves with the movement. The most frequent point of disagreement is over social issues, with a majority of those with whom they spoke expressing a far more serious concern over the fiscal issues.

The principal difference between the two movements has been that the Tea Party groups—along with the financing from wealthy activists like the Koch Brothers, Sheldon Adelson, Don Blankenship, and others—have translated stated complaints of grassroots organizations into the election of specific candidates for state and national offices. The Occupy movement was quite successful at raising attention among people to the inequities of wealth distribution, but, in a sense, the movement was also something of a failure. There was no clear legislative activist agenda and no cogent plan to work toward the election of candidates. One reason for the distinction between the two movements—a distinction that is seldom discussed—is that the Tea Party manages to articulate a number of complaints, along with potential solutions to the complaints, that could move into the electoral venues. Occupy was, and is, fundamentally an individualistic plaint that has been almost impossible to translate into what could be called an electoral platform. Comprehension of the differences between the two movements would require a thoroughgoing analysis of not only the reasons behind the movements but also the outcomes of the plans that the participants (and their well-financed supporters) had for future action.

## Higher Education

Higher education is a topic that many people—within and without the academy—have opinions about and want to share. In general, the opinions offered are negative and express criticism of faculty, students, curricula, and other particulars of the educational environment. While the criticism extends well back in time, the more contemporary comments can begin with Allan Bloom's bestselling book, *The Closing of the American Mind.* From its publication in 1987, it has been seen as a prophetic message by many (usually on the political right) or as a bête noir (customarily by those on the political left). According to Bloom's critique, students are unaware of the master works of the past (literary and philosophical) and so have little guidance as to how the good life should be defined and lived. Even more damning, students at all educational levels have been mistreated by being told that literary, philosophical, and especially, moral relativism are the most legitimate means by which to live. Such relativism destroys enduring truths, which should be the hallmark of higher education. For example, with respect to the political and human issue of feminism, Bloom (1987) writes, "The souls of men—their ambitions, warlike, protective, possessive character—must be dismantled in order to liberate women from their domination" (p. 129). Besides being insulting to men *and* women, Bloom is engaged in dissimulation that could only be considered deliberate on the part of one so learned.

Reception of Bloom continues, long after the book's publication and the passing of the author. Errors continue to abound as to the meaning of the work and what Bloom intended in his book. For instance, Ellwanger (2009) says, "Many critics suggest that Bloom is invested in constructing a culture of values. This is a grave error. Rather, he is interested in reestablishing the value of culture. Note that *culture* is not plural here. For Bloom, the privileging of a distinct culture is essential for the healthy functioning of the modern liberal democracy" (p. 477). Ellwanger is correct is assessing Bloom's purpose, but he does not admit to the limitations of Bloom's vision, the reactionary nature of Bloom's argument, and the stubbornness with which Bloom defends his own correctness. Lazere (2009) takes the opportunity of the revisiting of Bloom's work to acknowledge the many academic critics who have dismissed *The Closing of the American Mind*, and he is also correct in noting that a number of the critics show little sign of having read Bloom. Lazere (2009) cogently observes, "Bloom simply co-opted the Frankfurt [School of critical theory] critique for the political Right by detaching mass culture from its conservative role as an arm of corporate capitalism (with the essential role of ceaseless stimulation of selfish desires and unbridled consumption to hype up profits) and presenting it as an autonomous entity serving only 'liberal' moral relativism—a trick that has been picked up by countless other conservative culture warriors to let corporations off the hook for fostering moral and social lassitude" (p. 505). Bloom was indeed more concerned with the political than the cultural, although far too many readers accepted his putative cultural attack (perhaps because of a shared political ideology).

Critical works about higher education are legion, and there is by no means space and time here to discuss them all. Only a few more will be mentioned here because they fit the mode of informational failure that characterizes this chapter. The books to be mentioned are quite different in intent and content, but they are representative of error and, in one instance, dissimulation. Mark Bauerlein is concerned, as is Bloom, about the future of a democratic nation and expresses his views of technology in *The Dumbest Generation* (2008). He states, "Democracy requires an informed electorate, and knowledge deficits equal civic decay . . . [Knowledge] supplies a motivation that ordinary ambitions don't. Voting in every election, reading the op-ed pages, sending letters to politicians, joining a local association . . . they don't advance a career, boost a paycheck, kindle the dating scene, or build muscle and tan skin" (pp. 212, 214). What raises Bauerlein's hackles? Digital media and the Internet. The ready access to the "trivial" and the entertaining stunt critical acumen by shoving aside the meaningful and filling consciousness with mindless popularized content about fashion, sports, reality shows, pseudocelebrities, and so on. These numbing yet absorbing and meaningless kinds of distractions lead young Americans away from the topics that are at the heart of civil society.

An exposition of Bauerlein's argument is not simple; it can even give rise to unease. Is the attention of young people occupied with the Kardashians, Snooki, *The Bachelorette*, and other less-than-serious things? Yes. Is the attention of middle-age people also so occupied? Yes. Is a minority of the population well informed about politics, culture, international events, and the serious business of the day? Yes. Does Bauerlein make sport of the attention-grabbing media that do not contribute to "an informed electorate?" Yes. Does the blame for the attention deficit rest with technology? No (or, at least, certainly not entirely). The present generation is actually more educated than preceding ones. In 2012, 33.5 percent of Americans age 25–29 had earned bachelor's degrees; in 1995, the figure was only 24.7 percent (see Lewin, 2012). Given these data, it may not be the digital age that is to blame for the reading/cultural/political ignorance among America's young people. One should examine what percentage of the population at various points in time composed what may be called literati (or cognoscenti for that matter). It is estimated that one in seven Americans *cannot* read; they are illiterate (Britt, 2009). A 2002 study by Kirsch and colleagues (Kirsch, Jungeblut, Jenkins, and Kolstad, 2002) demonstrated that at that time, 40–44 million US adults had literacy skills at the lowest level defined by the test (p. 16). It is painfully obvious that if there is a challenge relating to the creation and maintenance of an informed citizenry, it is *much* more complex than Bauerlein suggests.

A recent polemic on higher education is William Bennett and David Wilezol's *Is College Worth It?* (2013). In part, their work addresses "return on investment" (ROI); do graduates get what they pay for by attending a college or university? They mention that the ROI factor is due to a combination of factors:

> The problems have metastasized at many levels, including
>
> - the federal government's role in student aid,
> - the accountability and transparency of the universities and colleges,
> - poorly performing high schools, and
> - uninformed consumers (both students and their parents). (p. xii)

Their fundamental point is that graduates, for the most part, end their college careers undereducated, underprepared, and deep in debt. There is no doubt at all that many graduates complete degree programs and face underemployment (perhaps unemployment in their chosen fields) and crushing student loan debts. What is not mentioned is whether higher education at the bachelor's degree level is *supposed* to prepare graduates for immediate employment is select fields. What would be the result if colleges and universities taught students such things as logical thinking, the understanding of the fundamentals of mathematics, scientific literacy, arts, literature, and history? Would students be less prepared for life after graduation? Bennett and Wilezol (2013) answer these questions (without providing evidence or reason), "In today's colleges, much of what is taught in the humanities and social sciences is nonsense (or nonsense on stilts), politically tendentious, and worth little in the marketplace and for the enrichment of your mind and soul" (p. viii). The matter of political tendentiousness is tossed out, as it is in many of these antieducation diatribes. The avowedly right-leaning *Washington Times* supports the opinions of the book, stating,

> "Is College Worth It?" is a book that should be read by everyone. No parent should write a check and no student should declare a major without first reading this book. For the graduating class of 2013, I fear this book has come too late. You can read it in your parents' basement while you are looking to find a job with that degree in anthropology. But for those who have graduated high school and are heading off to college this September, there is still time. If you are more of a hands-on type, think about deferring for a year and working as an apprentice in a skilled trade. (DesRosiers, 2013)

Reviewers of the book should, at the very least, evaluate the claims on their merits rather than echo a failed political harangue.

There may be some presumptions Americans have about education in the United States. One could be that the purpose is to optimize the learning of all students at all levels and across all fields of study. That may be accomplished, at least in part, by having a public system of education, including higher education, the purpose of which is to open the opportunities for learning and advancement to as large a population as possible. How would the majority of people react to discover the following (Bond-Graham, 2013): University of California "regents recently approved a new corporate entity that will likely give a group of well-connected businesspeople control over how academic research is used." They have created a corporation—Newco—that is designed to revamp how the products of research conducted at the university reach the public. Some wonder if the oversight of this entity will be less than transparent and if the mission of the university will be harmed by the selective dissemination of research results. No other news outlets have reported on this vote by the regents. California is the nation's most populace state, and the University of California system is enormous; would the citizens of the state (would anyone concerned with the present condition and the future of higher education) be interested in the news?

Perhaps the best-known polemicist against higher education in recent years has been David Horowitz. He appears to have made it his mission to select some institutions and individuals as not living up to his own standards for conservatism (sometimes in the guise of "fairness"). He has written several books over the past years that demonstrate his prejudice and his vituperative anger. These include *One-Party Classroom*, *The Professors*, *Indoctrination U.*, and *Reforming Our Universities: The Campaign for an Academic Bill of Rights*. While much can be said about his ad hominem attacks on universities, the purpose behind the last mentioned book deserves attention. Horowitz has been behind the founding and continuance of the organization Students for Academic Freedom. The name of the group is apparently intended to be irony free. The statement of the Academic Bill of Rights is stated as follows:

## Academic Bill of Rights

### I. The Mission of the University

The central purposes of a University are the pursuit of truth, the discovery of new knowledge through scholarship and research, the study and reasoned criticism of intellectual and cultural traditions, the teaching and general development of students to help them become creative individuals and productive citizens of a pluralistic democracy, and the transmission of knowledge and learning to a society at large . . .

### II. Academic Freedom

2. *The Practice* . . . This means that no political, ideological or religious orthodoxy will be imposed on professors and researchers through the hiring or tenure or termination process, or through any other administrative means by the academic institution. Nor shall legislatures impose any such orthodoxy through their control of the university budget.

This protection includes students . . .

1. . . . No faculty shall be hired or fired or denied promotion or tenure on the basis of his or her political or religious beliefs.
2. No faculty member will be excluded from tenure, search and hiring committees on the basis of their political or religious beliefs.
3. Students will be graded solely on the basis of their reasoned answers and appropriate knowledge of the subjects and disciplines they study, not on the basis of their political or religious beliefs . . .
5. Exposing students to the spectrum of significant scholarly viewpoints on the subjects examined in their courses is a major responsibility of faculty. Faculty will not use their courses for the purpose of

> political, ideological, religious or anti-religious indoctrination. (see Academic Bill of Rights, n.d.)

We can take one excerpt from the Academic Bill of Rights for review: "This means that no political, ideological or religious orthodoxy will be imposed on professors and researchers through the hiring or tenure or termination process, or through any other administrative means by the academic institution." Recently (in 2011), a foundation financed by conservative billionaire Charles Koch pledged $1.5 million to hire faculty in Florida State University's economics department. In exchange for the funding, representatives of the foundation would be able to screen and approve candidates for positions to ensure that they would promote "political economy and free enterprise" (Hundley, 2011). Faculty review would be subservient to the approval of those representatives. Hundley (2011) reports, "Bruce Benson, chairman of FSU's economics department, said that of his staff of 30, six, including himself, would fall into Koch's free-market camp." It appears that the Academic Bill of Rights does not apply when faculty pass tests relating to conservative orthodoxy. This incident is emblematic of Horowitz's dissimulation; he utters complaints when people do not agree with him or are not sufficiently pure in their ideology. Students' rights should, without a doubt, be respected. That said, the atmosphere in a class might be considered uncomfortable for a student when that student states a factual error and is corrected by the teacher. If the Academic Bill of Rights necessitates accepting such statements as valid, then it is anti-intellectual and in opposition to all that is reasonable. Likewise, Horowitz's condemnation of faculty should be examined closely to ensure that the similar exclusion of truth and genuine inquiry do not occur. Gutmann (1999) offers what may be the most cogent rebuttal possible to Horowitz's stance: "Treating every moral opinion as equally worthy encourages children [and university students] in . . . false subjectivism . . . This moral understanding does not take the demands of democratic justice seriously" (p. 56).

There are some other recent publications as well. One is Charles Murray's *Real Education* (2009), which takes a look at schooling more generally. His book begins with an assumption that has little, if any, validity or evidence behind it: "The educational system is living a lie. The lie is that every child can be anything he or she wants to be" (p. 11). *If* that is a common message in schools, then they are indeed doing students a disservice. Even the brightest students may be blocked from success by circumstance (political, economic, or cultural). That said, if the schools' message is that hard work in school and efforts to learn can make a positive difference in students' lives, that message *should* be true or it is society, not schools, that is failing. Murray's (2009) thesis is that there are four realities that must be recognized if schools are to realize genuine reform:

1. Ability varies.
2. Half of the children are below average.
3. Too many children are going to college.
4. America's future depends on how we educate the academically gifted. (pp. 12–13)

The axioms are either tautological or silly. Of course, half the children are below average, but what level of achievement constitutes "average," and can that level rise? The last statement is elitist in the extreme, given that many students have little opportunity to demonstrate their ability. Schools in depressed urban and rural areas do not offer even the brightest students chances to accomplish academic excellence. The amount of money expended per pupil varies so greatly that blanket statements such as Murray's appear absurd. For example, in the 2008–2009 year, the state of Arizona spent $8,006, while Connecticut spent $15,502 (*Digest of Education Statistics*, 2012, Table 194). Spending more may not ensure opportunities for students, but there is probably a critical amount of money needed to provide such opportunities.

Murray has his apologists; Schrag (2009) writes,

> Many on the left fear that by admitting the role of academic ability they pave the way, either for letting schools off the hook, or for blaming the victims for their lack of academic prowess. Surely, the important point here is that regardless of whether one attributes the plight of the disadvantaged to social forces or to bad luck in the genetic lottery, they have done nothing to deserve their ill fortune. (Likewise for the privileged, of course.) There is no philosophical basis for behavioral geneticists to use their findings to oppose universal health care or a more progressive income tax. Neither the cause of education nor that of social justice is served by denying Murray's initial claim, that every kind of ability varies from person to person, including academic ability. (p. 374)

Others have also reviewed Murray's book favorably. It seems that the readers ignore many of Murray's dicta, such as, "Children still lower in the distribution of linguistic and logical-mathematical ability—the bottom third of the distribution is a rough demarcation of the group I am talking about—are just not smart enough to become literate or numerate in more than a rudimentary sense" (p. 44). Murray, in a fashion that is typical in his book, is quite selective in his argument. There probably are students who, through no fault of their own, cannot achieve at high levels academically.

Should they be forgotten by society? Also, are the teachers in schools the best and the brightest in society? The average salary for teachers in 2010 in my home state of Missouri was $45,317. Bramwell (2013) reports that the average *starting* salary for accountants is $53,300—a salary $8,000 higher annually than the *average* salary for elementary and secondary teachers in Missouri. What society values is what society gets (and deserves?). What is the value of elementary and secondary education to American society, and should "the best and the brightest" be attracted to teaching?

A fitting conclusion to this section is to leave the reader with some words by a classical liberal, F. A. Hayek (2011 [1960]): "Knowledge is perhaps the chief good that can be had at a price, but those who do not already possess it often cannot recognize its usefulness" (p. 498).

## Science

In some ways, informing failures in the realm of the sciences are akin to those in education; the shortcoming resides in failing to provide thoroughgoing inquiry into serious matters and allowing what might be called a "folk psychology" to reign. The area that may have received the most attention in recent years is that of climate change. According to a Gallup poll conducted in 2013, 15 percent of respondents believe that climate change will never happen. On the other hand, 54 percent believe that it has already begun (Saad, 2013). The poll records beliefs and opinions, but belief does not equal truth. Climate expert Michael Mann published data analysis some time ago that does indeed demonstrate changes in the global climate over the most recent centuries. When some statisticians disagreed with his method, he reanalyzed the data, adopting the assistance of an expert statistician. The import of his results did not change. Nonetheless, Mann's work has come under fire, in large part by politicians who disagree with the policy implications of addressing the reality of climate change:

> This, of course, has made Mann a big target of climate-change deniers. While most of them attack the graph—failing in their attempts, I'll note—some have taken a more personal tack. Two groups, the far-right *National Review Online* and the Competitive Enterprise Institute, have made this personal indeed. In a frankly disgusting article be Mark Steyn, the NRO accused Mann of academic fraud. It even compares him to the ex-Penn State University coach Jerry Sandusky, *a convicted serial child molester*. Steyn got this comparison from an article by Rand Simberg in the CEI's blog, who called Mann "the Jerry Sandusky of climate science . . . [who] molested and tortured data." (Plait, 2013)

The vast numbers of climate researchers of repute agree with Mann and refer to his work positively (see Budd, 2007, for a complete discussion of Mann's plight).

Another almost constant point of contention is evolution. For the most part, the dispute arises on account of a less-than-complete understanding of what scientists mean by evolution. In a nutshell, Darwin's hypothesis of evolution by natural selection is accepted as a sound working hypothesis among the biological community. Evidence—some of which has been provided by Darwin himself—does indeed suggest that animals and insects adapt to altered surroundings by developing or changing their physiology or other aspects within a very few generations. The alterations may be as simple as a bird developing a larger and stronger beak so as to be able to eat different foods. Some microbiologists have demonstrated that bacteria can alter their characteristics very quickly, in part because the time between generations is so short. The evolution of humans, as just about all scientists agree, is much more complicated, in part because of the nature of the factors that have evolved—including brain size and complexity, the nature of social change, and other aspects. A 2012 Gallup poll reports that 46 percent of respondents say that God created humans in their present form, though ("Evolution, Creationism," 2012). The report includes some data from a 2005 poll, in which 54 percent of respondents state that creationism should be taught in schools. A fundamental difficulty with the opinion is that creationism is not science; while it could be taught as a social phenomenon, scientists will overwhelmingly agree that it should not be taught within a scientific context. Was Darwin absolutely correct more than one-and-a-half centuries ago? Few scientists would answer in the affirmative to that question, but Darwin was not the only person arguing for some hypothesis regarding evolution. Today's scientists are examining more recent and completely developed theories about evolution, including Mendelian evolution, which explains the actuality of evolution more fully than Darwin could.

Apart from science programing in broadcast media and some journalistic reports, evolution is seldom mentioned in popular discourse. There are, of course, dissenting voices, but that dissent seldom receives sympathetic scientific approval. The same absence of approval tends to be the case when nonscientists broach the topic. Recently, the noted philosopher of mind Jerry Fodor and his colleague Massimo Piattelli-Palmarini published a book titled, *What Darwin Got Wrong*. Without delving too deeply here, it suffices that a reviewer, Massimo Pigliucci (2013), sums up the gist of the book's shortcoming succinctly: "I'm afraid that the only results of *What Darwin Got Wrong* will be to provide even further ammunition to creationists (despite the self-conscious disclaimer of the authors in that respect) and to once again set back the relationship between philosophy and science. It will take much work by philosophers of science to repair the damage." The difficulty that arises when those outside science (Thomas Nagel [2013] included) offer observations on evolutions is that they are seen by scientists as complete outsiders who have nothing cogent to say. The dispute, however, tends not to be so simple, and some scientists break with their colleagues and pay close attention to the dissenters. The dispute is almost never mentioned in popular media, though, when sides must be black or white, wrong or right (instead of wrong *and* right). Can learning, can civil discourse, take place when the democratic ideal of open conversation is thrown aside?

## Elections and Money—Oligarchy?

On January 21, 2010, the US Supreme Court decided the case *Citizens United v. Federal Election Commission*. The justices ruled, in a 5–4 vote, that political action committees (PACs), even those established by corporations, cannot have their speech restricted:

> Although the First Amendment provides that "Congress shall make no law . . . abridging the freedom of speech," §441b's prohibition on corporate independent expenditures is an outright ban on speech, backed by criminal sanctions. It is a ban notwithstanding the fact that a PAC created by a corporation can still speak, for a PAC is a separate association from the corporation. Because speech is an essential mechanism of democracy—it is the means to hold officials accountable to the people—political speech must prevail against laws that would suppress it by design or inadvertence. (*Citizens United*, 2010, p. 3)

As many have said, a major result of the ruling is the equation of corporations (that establish PACs) with people—that is, exactly the same allowances are provided for both entities. The primary result of the ruling is that floodgates of funding have been opened, so election spending after the ruling has exploded. Justice Stevens, in a dissenting opinion, wrote,

> The basic premise underlying the Court's ruling is its iteration, and constant reiteration, of the proposition that the First Amendment bars regulatory distinctions based on a speaker's identity, including its "identity" as a corporation. While that glittering generality has rhetorical appeal, it is not a correct statement of the law. Nor does it tell us when a corporation may engage in electioneering that some of its shareholders oppose. It does not even resolve the specific question whether Citizens United maybe required to finance

> some of its messages with the money in its PAC. The conceit that corporations must be treated identically to natural persons in the political sphere is not only inaccurate but also inadequate to justify the Court's disposition of this case. (*Citizens United*, 2010, pp. 1–2)

The results of the ruling have already been felt in the 2012 elections.

For a complete and nonpartisan account of the spending of the elections, refer to *Dollarocracy* by John Nichols and Robert McChesney. They estimate that as much as $10 billion was spent on national, state, and local elections. Both the Democratic and Republican parties are laid bare in the book, and neither comes off as morally or ethically superior. They (Nichols and McChesney, 2013) acknowledge that in the popular press, "the corporate control of the economy and corporate domination of government itself get barely a nod" (p. 5). They (2013) also write, "In 2012, Democrats received 500,000 *more* votes in House races than Republicans did, but thanks to aggressive redistricting following the 2010 election and effective targeting of spending by Karl Rove and other, the Republicans maintained a landslide-caliber 34-seat advantage" (emphasis in original; p. 15). Nichols and McChesney were not the only observers to notice the discrepancy. Shortly after the election, Stone (2012) stated, "Although the Republicans won 55 percent of the House seats, they received less than half of the votes for members of the House of Representatives. Indeed, more than *half-a-million* more Americans voted for Democratic House candidates than for Republicans House candidates. *There was no split-decision.* The Democrats won *both* the presidential election and the House election. But the Republicans won 55 percent of the seats in the House." There is no need to refer further to *Dollarocracy*; suffice is to say that Nichols and McChesney's analysis is complete and effective in demonstrating the absence of informing.

Another recently published book (*Collusion: How the Media Stole the 2012 Election and How to Stop Them from Doing It in 2016*) by Bozell and Graham addresses a similar topic but by no means from a nonpartisan perspective. Early on, they (Bozell and Graham, 2013) quote an unnamed source who stated that in order to win, not on his accomplishments, Obama "will have to kill Romney" (Burns, 2011). Bozell and Graham claim that this quotation was not mentioned in the "liberal" media, but the piece was picked up by *USA Today*, PBS, *The Washington Post*, and other outlets. They (Bozell and Graham, 2013) then criticize the media for the extensive coverage of Herman Cain's extramarital affair, which (they say) ended his presidential campaign. What they fail to include is that Cain was indeed culpable and that news outlets of all political stripes ran the story. Bozell and Graham (2013) then state that Bill Clinton's affairs did not receive such attention, but even *People* magazine covered the Paula Jones incident. Also (they [2013] do not mention this), Clinton was impeached (but not convicted) during his presidency. That incident was covered extensively by all broadcast and print sources. Instead, they (2013) write that the Cain affair "is not the way allegations against a Democrat are handled" (p. 12). One has to go back in time, but all outlets covered Gary Hart's indiscretion. Bozell and Graham are extremely selective in what they report and in how they report it. They do a disservice to truth in the process of informing.

More recently, another US Supreme Court decision (a 5–4 vote) also affects elections, campaigning, and financing. On April 2, 2014, the court, in *McCutcheon v. the Federal Election Commission*, determined, "The District Court denied their [McCutcheon and the Republican National Committee] motion for a preliminary injunction and granted the Government's motion to dismiss. Assuming that the base limits appropriately served the Government's anticorruption interest, the District Court concluded that the aggregate limits survived First Amendment scrutiny because they prevented evasion of the base limits" (*McCutcheon v. FEC*, 2013). The result of this ruling is nearly as sweeping as that of *Citizens United*. The aggregate donations that can be made by a single individual to candidates and party committees were struck down. Under previous regulations, a donor was limited to contributions to no more than 18 candidates and a total of $48,600 in direct contributions. Individual donors are now able to give a maximum amount of money to as many candidates as the individual chooses, allowing wealthy donors a great amount of flexibility in affecting election outcomes. On the one hand, the donor cannot give unlimited money to a single candidate or party committee. On the other hand, the donor can give the maximum legal amount to preferred candidates in every federal election every year. That donor can still give huge amounts to political action committees (PACs).

While billed as a First Amendment issue, the reality is that only the wealthiest Americans can "speak" to such an extent in elections. Sheldon Adelson boasted that he gave about $100 million in the 2012 election and warned that he would spend more to get candidates elected and legislation passed. This ruling is essentially party neutral; a wealthy individual could donate to Republicans or Democrats. In fact, "As *The Washington Post*'s Robert Barnes and Matea Gold explain, defenders of the limits worry that such a ruling could dramatically increase the power and size of joint fundraising committees, which harness the fundraising power of different political committees. For example, the Obama Victory Fund joined together the DNC and Obama campaign last election cycle" (Sullivan, 2014). Regarding "free speech," Justice John Roberts came down on the side of erring in favor of eliminating some limits: "The overall limits 'intrude without justification on a citizen's ability to exercise "the most fundamental First Amendment activities,'" Roberts said, quoting from the court's seminal 1976 campaign finance ruling in Buckley v. Valeo" (*McCutcheon v. FEC*, 2014).

While most newspapers covered the decision (as would be expected with any Supreme Court action), this matter is complex and esoteric. It is not an easy matter to explain clearly that the wealthiest individuals can exercise control of elections in multiple ways. It is not beyond imagination that one person (or family) could spend hundreds of millions of dollars ensuring that particular candidates get elected. The number of people who could exercise such influence is small. As a matter of free speech, the opposite intention of rhetorical support for both *Citizens United* and *McCutcheon* could be seen as disingenuous. The United States is on the verge of transformation from a democracy (putative or genuine) to an oligarchy—a form of government where a few people control or dominate. This is a matter that tends not to be reported in mainstream media, although the possibility becomes more and more possible each time contribution limits are eroded and the wealthiest among us inch closer to becoming oligarchs.

## Summary

It may be that a full accounting of the failures of informing could fill a book, but the contents of this chapter suffice to provide a clear demonstration of the shortcomings (usually deliberate). Truth telling is an intentional act; intentionality requires not merely *doing* something but developing beliefs and testing those beliefs for what Alvin Goldman (2004) calls "veritism." Veritism, for Goldman, is an essential component of social epistemology—a means by which we reach knowledge of things through the actions not just of ourselves but also of all those who inquire into a particular matter. One way we reach a true understanding of an issue is by weighing those things that many people talk and write about. The measure includes both empiricism (testing the actuality of occurrences) and reason (applying thought and logic to the arguments and statements that are made). If a speaker provides evidence for what he or she says, then that evidence can be evaluated (is it accurate, is it complete, does it relate fully to the point in question, etc.). Once spoken, the speaker's words and argument can be tested by logic and reason. If the speaker's words pass both tests and do so to a degree that surpasses what others have said, then those words have a veritistic, or truth-bearing, quality. The foregoing presents a primary evaluative measure of informing. These qualities are much more stringent than simply agreeing that what was said is something of which the hearer or reader had no prior awareness. Novelty is by no means an effective assessment tool.

The method of evaluation is only one task for the citizen who wants to be able to deliberate fully and critically on important topics. The *content* of what is said is the matter of evaluation. Yes, there must be a reliable way to assess statements and claims, but that reliable way is *applied* to what is said. The principle purpose of this chapter is to demonstrate that, when that critical evaluative method is applied, some things are found to be decidedly wanting. A secondary outcome of the analysis in this chapter is that the noninformative discourse presented to Americans almost constantly is all too frequently accepted uncritically. As Nichols and McChesney (2013) observe, "news" programing can well consist of the opinions of pundits who are pressing their own interests accepted by a news host (who offers no critical evaluation of what is said). The dilemma described here is dire, and the body politic is in need of some potentially corrective process. The status quo has become intensely entrenched, and the corporate control of news does not bode well for change. These challenges provide the fodder for the next chapter. There is the possibility for recapturing deliberative democracy, but it will require attention and effort on the part of the citizenry. It is now time to explore the potential.

## Discussion

Identifying a locus for the challenges is difficult, if not impossible. To mention only one factor, it may be that the preferences of the media and journalists are different from those of the public in general. That, in itself, is not an explanation for failures; media may report on the important issues that will affect the body politic, but people may prefer to spend their limited attention on other things, including celebrity news and reality TV programing. There is much greater complexity in the larger scheme of things. For example, Boczkowski and Mitchelstein (2013) state, "The new gap also poses challenges to two other roles that news organizations play in the public sphere: providing information and providing spaces for public deliberation" (p. 5). The latter point may be the more important point (and Habermas might agree). While newspapers, blogs, and other social media are indeed attempting to create deliberative space, success is decidedly limited at this time. There may be opportunities for technology to enhance the deliberative actions of people, but it is likely that the spaces will have to be deliberately constructed and managed so as to create civic discourse where it does not presently exist.

There is not space here to address the concentration of ownership of information-related companies. (For astute commentary and analysis on this important issue, refer to McChesney (2013) and Noam [2009].) As for the first point, it may actually indicate a problem in itself. That issue will be addressed in the next chapter.

# 5

# Informational Potential

We have encountered numerous problems, and at the center of the problems enumerated here has been some kind of informational failure. As the previous chapter details, there are absences of detail or reportage as well as misinformation and disinformation. All the examples belie a dishonesty or a failure of truthfulness; in short, the instances show that the public good is ignored or violated by the inadvertent or (worse) the deliberate falseness that intentionally misleads people. All the foregoing points to shortcomings dealing with informing of the public. The thesis that has guided the present analysis is that truth, accuracy, integrity, and the other hallmarks of the public good are necessary for the body politic to function democratically. Falling short of the goals fails the nation and the political functioning of the state—functioning that is essential to the achievement of the promise of America's history. Many sources are cited here that demonstrate clearly that there have been many failures in informing the people of the nation. That said, there is the potential to rectify many of the problems that have been described. In this chapter, the potential will be examined carefully; the solutions are not simple, though. Moving toward achievement of the objective of an informed populace will require, to some extent, a sea change in behavior on the part of all who would report and comment on the challenges we face.

## What Is Informing?

The potential for a remedy for some of the challenges and problems discussed so far relies, in part, on defining precisely what "informing" is. Budd (2011) offers some definition of information that fits well here:

> Definition: Information is meaningful communicative action that aims at truth claims and conditions.

> Statement of Theory: Information is comprised of those communicative actions (and only those communicative actions) that can be evaluated by a population—defined as the intended or potential hearers of the communication—as meaningful. Meaning is not limited to pure semantics, but includes context and history within evaluation. Further, information is true in that there is warrant for the communicative action, that this action includes no deliberate deception or omission, has inherent evaluative components, provides evidentiary justification, and is fundamental to ethics. (p. 70)

The key elements of this definition include the requirement of being meaningful, of constituting a truth claim, and of being able to be evaluated. According to this definition, such communicative actions such as *dis*information or *mis*information do not count as information. Those other actions do not carry the intention of communicating meaningful and truthful claims. As such, they aim to deceive, not to inform.

Any informational potential that is worthy of being considered must follow the previous definition, at least in spirit. That is to say, someone can make an honest error, can believe in the efficacy of what is said, but can still be unintentionally mistaken. The mistakes can be corrected, even by the original speaker; Disinformation and misinformation, since they are not intended to be truth claims, are not easily corrected except by investigation, usually by a third party. In part, informational failure is a personal failure; we fall short as individual agents and as actors according to what Aristotle called *phronesis*, or practical wisdom. As Schwartz and Sharpe (2010) tell us, "Ethics, said Aristotle, was not mainly about establishing moral rules and following them. It was about performing a particular social practice well—being a good friend or parent or doctor or soldier or citizen or statesman—and that meant figuring out the right way to do the right thing in a particular circumstance, with a particular person, at a particular time. This is what took practical wisdom" (pp. 5–6).

Certain specific features of the previous advice must be emphasized. First, the potential humans have to inform is a component of ethical responsibility. It is, as Schwartz and Sharpe say, doing the right thing in the right way. It is also part of the agency of each of us, the action that each of us undertakes. As part of agency, the ethical responsibility is rooted in choice. Christine Korsgaard (2009) clarifies precisely what this means: "The necessity of choosing and acting is not causal, logical, or rational necessity. It is our *plight*: the simple and inexorable fact of the human condition" (p. 2). The potential for realizing participatory democracy, for an ethical economic and financial state, and for actualization of the public good rests with the choices and actions of each individual. This means that a great deal of the responsibility for the future and its situation rests with each of us; we must make the right choices for the right reasons. Moreover, each of us exercises checks and balances over each other. Suppose I speak publicly with the intention of deceiving all who hear me. I have thus abdicated the responsibility just detailed. If I make a claim, you should not merely take it at face value. You must affirm or disaffirm my claim and speak out about what you discover. At this time, we are not in a position to presume that everyone who speaks, writes, or utters a claim is following Aristotle and acting upon *phronesis*.

What does it mean to act, to choose to do the right thing for the right reason? Many of the examples found in the previous chapters fall into this category of deceit; what we need to address is the possibility for correction and the revision of claims and statements that fall short of the goal of truthfulness (which, as we have seen, is a hallmark of the public good). Organizations such as the Center for Investigative Reporting and FactCheck.org are very helpful in providing some balance to claims that are made. These organizations can be consulted to provide correctives to what is said in the press or by organizations whose actions warrant scrutiny.

Here is an example of the usefulness of such organizations: The Center for Investigative Reporting states, "Over the last five years, more than $600 million in college assistance for Iraq and Afghanistan veterans has been spent on California schools so substandard that they have failed to qualify for state financial aid" (Glantz, 2014). The institutions include such universities as the University of Phoenix, which charges high tuition and has low graduation rates, as well as unaccredited programs in a vast array of fields that do not have success in placing people in jobs. A spokesperson for the University of Phoenix said only that veterans choose to attend the institution but would not relate completion rates for veterans. The center also finds that the cost of an associate's degree in California from the University of Phoenix is ten times as high as a similar degree from a California community college. There are very few checks by the federal government on the accountability of many of the institutions receiving GI Bill money; there does not even appear to be a requirement that the institutions be accredited. However, as the center reports, the state of California has barred many institutions from receiving state student aid funds. Since the GI Bill is support by federal taxes, there is definite cause for concern about the efficacy of the institutions recruiting veterans and the accountability for the success of the students. Federal oversight appears to be lacking in this area. This is merely one example of the potential that is realized by some organizations attempting to operate for the public good.

In the political realm, FactCheck.org helps point out where there may be disingenuousness (or worse) in venues such as political advertisements.

In reporting on the Republican run-off election between Paul DeMarco and Gary Palmer in the summer of 2014, DeMarco ran an ad that stated, "***DeMarco TV ad:*** *Here's what Gary Palmer wrote about the billion-dollar tax increase called Amendment One: 'To the surprise of many of my conservative friends and colleagues, I am of the opinion that the state needs more revenue. I would be willing to support a tax increase*'" ("Editing Out the Facts," 2014). In a not uncommon practice in political advertising, a portion of the statement was omitted in the ad. What Palmer said was the following: "***Palmer, Sept. 6, 2003:*** *To the surprise of many of my conservative friends and colleagues, I am of the opinion that the state needs more revenue. I would be willing to support a tax increase* ***but only on the condition that we first set in place some meaningful accountability measures. Unfortunately, the proposal before the people of Alabama falls well short of the mark***" (Nacht and Kiely, 2014). The omission of the essence of Palmer's full statement falls short of the practice of integrity in political campaigns. For potential voters, the complete assessment and opinion of Palmer is not only missing but also deceptive. Voters are thus unable to decide if they agree with Palmer's position or not. The deception knows no partisan party lines; many campaigners are guilty of this kind of dissimulation. All citizens should be deeply concerned about the implications for our democracy by such dishonest practice. DeMarco could have kept silent on Palmer's statement, which would not have been deceptive, but his campaign's actions constitute an informational failure that could have been omitted.

There is a premise that underlies the work of these organizations (and other individuals and organizations engaging in similar activities): There are people and institutions who choose not to do the right thing. The individuals and the institutions are sometimes overtaken by urges to act according to narrow (sometimes venal) self-interest or according to ideologies that run counter to the public good. The politician who accepts favors from businesses—vacations, gifts, even money—does not act with integrity. Actions and choices that eschew practical wisdom are frequently selfish and are based on perverse ends. The end of the work of the politician is *not* to enrich himself or herself; the end for the student athlete is *not* to receive a new car from a corrupt alumnus. These actions are mistaken at best and illegal at worst. Korsgaard (2009) again helps us understand the state of affairs: "The reason for an action is not something outside of or behind or separate from the action at all, for explicating the action, and explicating the reason, are the same thing. Rather, an action is an essentially intelligible object that *embodies* a reason, the way a sentence is an essentially intelligible object that embodies a thought" (p. 14). Her description assists in comprehending precisely what action is. It is embedded in choice itself and cannot be separated from the choices we make and the reasons for the choices. The politician *chooses* corruption and self-interest. In doing so, the politician *chooses* to place that self-interest *above* the public good. The politician abandons integrity, honesty, and the other hallmarks of the public good. In short, the politician *chooses* to replace the putative purpose of public office with selfish choices. When these choices and actions are made known to the citizenry, informational potential is realized.

## Defining the Potential

Understanding what informing is can be the first step toward determining what informational potential can be. The understanding comes about, in part, by reaching a philosophical knowledge of information and informing, achieved through analytical action. This action is reached, in the first instance, by returning to, and elaborating on, practical wisdom. For Korsgaard (2009), "An action for Aristotle is like a work of art, with the parts working together to produce a beautiful and harmonious whole. It is *well formed.* A bad action by contrast is something misshapen and defective" (p. 17). Schwartz and Sharpe (2010) likewise turn to Aristotle and say that he "emphasized two capacities that were particularly important for . . . practical skill—the ability to *deliberate* about . . . choices and the ability to *perceive* what was morally relevant in a particular circumstance. Good deliberation and discernment were at the heart of practical wisdom." (p. 19).

Even with the foregoing advice, there remains the matter of translating maxims into a working means of incorporating *phronesis* into life. Miščević (2012) has the following suggestion:

> When we combine first-level (reliability like) correctness of evaluation and the second-level coherent reflective picture, that can take control if needed, we obtain the following . . . two-level picture of full reflective wisdom:
>
> *Wisdom is the reflective meta-level coherent endorsement of one's φ-generated* [*phronesis*-generated] *action-guiding desires-preferences, one's first level reliably generated factual beliefs about the causal structure in human matters and, knowledge of fact-value dependencies.* (emphasis in original; p. 67)

The statement seems complicated at first, but what is to be taken away is that practical wisdom requires reliable facts but also needs reflection that includes the value, or subjective, assessment of facts so that the conclusion can be applied to authentic situations. The human element must be a component of practical wisdom—applied by people to human action. As a process, the quest for, and application of, practical wisdom is analytical in some way (despite what Korsgaard says).

A bit more should be said about a fact-based approach to practical wisdom. As we examine what people say, write, or show, we have to take into account what is *real*, what actually *is*. The technical philosophical term for this is "ontology." Sokolowski (2000) describes this phenomenon: "A fact is where the ingredients of the fact are located: the fact that the grass is wet exists in the wet grass, not in my mind when I say the words" (p. 14). In the previous chapters, we have seen instances where something is passed off as fact but really is not a fact. Disingenuousness, dissimulation, and deceit exist, but they cannot be examined *as though* they were facts; they are other types of things (see Sokolowski, 2000, p. 15). To fulfill this kind of investigation completely—as a philosopher would—one would engage in phenomenology: "Phenomenology is the study of human experience and of the ways things present themselves to us in and through such experiences" (Sokolowski, 2000, p. 2). This sounds simple, but there are some complications to address. Lyotard (1991) takes care of some of those complications: "The term signifies a study of 'phenomena,' that is to say, of *that which* appears to consciousness, that which is 'given.' It seeks to explore this given—'the thing itself' which one perceives, of which one thinks and speaks—without constructing hypotheses concerning either the relationship which binds this phenomena to the being of which it is phenomena, or the relationship which unites it with the I for which is phenomena" (emphasis in original; pp. 32–33). Phenomenology is ineluctably related to consciousness and perception and that which we perceive is the thing in its purest form. Bakhtin (1993) elaborates as follows: "To experience an object is to have it as something actually unique or singular, but this singularity of object and of the world presupposes its being correlated with my own uniqueness or singularity" (p. 44).

For one thing, we must accept that the actions of people are conscious (following Korsgaard and others, the action is a matter of choice; it is not accidental). Furthermore, we humans are conscious beings, and that consciousness is *of* something. The consciousness we embody is not blank; it is always directed at things. One of the fathers of phenomenology, Edmund Husserl, maintains that consciousness must be examined from a first-person point of view; the structures of perception and action are, in this way, subjective (although they lead to objective outcomes). Also in keeping with Korsgaard, the actions people undertake are intentional. Smith and Smith (1995) explain as follows: "We grasp in phenomenological reflection that consciousness is *intentional* in the sense of *being directed towards an object*: consciousness is consciousness *of* something" (emphasis in original; p. 11). Within the context of this book, the preceding means that, for example, a perception of democracy entails consciousness of specific features of democracy that is constitutive and regulative of democracy. A consciousness of democracy necessitates defining what democracy is and how it is supposed to operate (what constitutes democracy as opposed to other forms of governance). It also necessitates determining *how* democracy works, what its essential structures are, and how the structures translate into action.

When a form of governance like democracy has an agreed-upon constitution (in the generic sense), there is then understanding of what sorts of actions fit within that constitution. Regulation should follow that constitution in that the ways democracy operates should be in sync with the ways democracy is defined. If democracy, for instance, entails representation determined by the free elections of voters from within a jurisdiction, then regulations must handle precisely how the elections are to be held, including the schedules of elections, terms of representatives, qualifications of voters, and so on. Regulations must not conflict with the qualitative aspects of democracy. From the personal perspective, each citizen has rights according the constitution of democracy and chooses to act according to the established regulations. The individual volition includes evaluating the candidates for a constituted office, perceiving the strengths and weaknesses of each candidate, and deciding for whom to vote. These actions are not capricious, though; they depend (ideally) on the application of such phenomenological operations as perception and intentionality. As Hintikka (1995) says, "It is not part of this position that what is so given to me are mere phenomena. On the contrary, the overall phenomenological project would make little sense unless the phenomenological reductions led us closer to actual realities" (p. 83).

Hintikka's assessment is extremely important for the project of enhancing informational potential. Does the action to which he refers always occur? No, and that is one of the foremost characteristics of informational failure. It is also, however, a path to the potential to rectify the problems that we experience. Our task is to discover what *is*. "Our task" must be emphasized here, for each of us has a responsibility to apply the kinds of phenomenological operations detailed here. In the course of much of our lives, we are caught up in what we can call the "natural attitude," which "is the focus we have when we are involved in our original world-directed stance, when we intend things, situations, facts, and any other kinds of objects" (Sokolowski, 2000, p. 42). There is an alternative—the "phenomenological attitude"—that "is the focus we have when we reflect upon the natural attitude and all the intentionalities that occur within it. It is within the phenomenological attitude that we carry out philosophical analyses" (Sokolowski, 2000, p. 42). The potential for combatting the informational failures rests within the difference between these two attitudes. With the first, we may have a tendency to accept what is presented to us; with the second, we are critical of what we see and hear, and we assess it all according to the standpoint of consciousness *of* what is spoken and written and the intentionality that lies behind those phenomena. As we will see, the task ahead of us is not so much directed at grousing about the rhetoric and images that affect us, but directed at adopting that critical stance so that we can tease out those things that violate the constitution of the ideal political system, economic and financial structure, and the public good. With that beginning, we will be able to discern what may cross the regulatory lines as well. In short, each of us assumes the ability to dispute the failures, such as those that have been depicted so far.

## What about Democracy?

In Chapter 1, various elements of democracy, and politics in general, were mentioned. What is the potential that can be realized to bring about the most just and free society, within a political structure that offers both organization and protection? Some of Philip Pettit's ideas have been mentioned, but a few more should be offered here as a preamble to informational potential that can give meaning to our discussion. As an expression of an ideal, he (2014) writes, "My own view is that nothing less than full democracy can be normatively satisfactory, grounding the obligation of citizens to oppose the laws, if they oppose them, only within the system" (p. 156). It is by means of the system that laws are propounded, so dissent should be systemically expressed. The government, though, has a responsibility to its citizens—not merely to affirm freedom rhetorically but to ensure that people can act freely. On this matter, Pettit (2014) says, "The Republication [not the lower-case 'r'] tradition remains distinctive in emphasizing that freedom requires power against interference, *not just the absence of interference*" (emphasis added; p. 195). It is necessary to provide the absence, but it is not sufficient; there must be mechanisms that are active in preventing interference (just as there must be mechanisms that are active in preventing coercion).

There has been much said and done that has endangered democratic thought and action in recent years, and some of that was reported in Chapter 1. At this time, the political world is less than civil; the party differences are tending to manifest themselves in vituperative terms. With the disputes come claims that push the envelope of not just civility but also veracity. Given the challenges to the citizenry, the question arises about how to evaluate what is said and how to discern facts from empty or disingenuous claims. It should be noted that both major parties in the United States articulate claims that cry for examination. Journalists also bear responsibility for behavior that warrants analysis. One instance can serve as an example of what is said and what kind of analysis can be undertaken. In 2005, columnist Robert Novak wrote the following:

> [Joseph C.] Wilson's report that an Iraqi purchase of uranium yellowcake from Niger was highly unlikely was regarded by the CIA as less than definitive, and it is doubtful Tenet ever saw it. Certainly President Bush did not, before his 2003 State of the Union address, when he attributed reports of attempted Iraqi uranium purchases to the British government. That the British relied on forged documents made Wilson's mission, nearly a year earlier, the basis of furious Democratic accusations of burying intelligence, though the report was forgotten by the time the president spoke.

It turned out that Wilson's report was accurate, and no reporter could be certain that either the CIA director or the president had seen it or at least heard of it (that would require internal knowledge that would be almost impossible to verify). Novak was dismissive of Wilson and his report, but the problematic column did not end with Novak's dismissal. Further in the column, Novak wrote, "Wilson never worked for the CIA, but his wife, Valerie Plame, is an agency operative on weapons of mass destruction" (Novak, 2003). Plame was working undercover, and Novak outed her as a CIA agent.

As it happens, Valerie Plame encountered no material harm as a result of Novak's reportage, but in the interests of integrity and honesty, that is irrelevant. It is always and everywhere wrong to compromise the safety and security of a covert CIA agent. It does not require a serious or deleterious consequence to render an action morally suspect (or worse). The obligation to obey laws and regulations is separate from the outcome of disobedience. In an interview after the fact, Novak offered his view of the predicament:

> If you read my book, you find a certain ambivalence there. Journalistically, I thought it was an important story because it explained why the CIA would send Joe Wilson—a former Clinton White House aide with no track record in intelligence and no experience in Niger—on a fact-finding mission to Africa. From a personal point of view, I said in the book I probably should have ignored what I'd been told about Mrs. Wilson.
>
> Now I'm much less ambivalent. I'd go full speed ahead because of the hateful and beastly way in which my left-wing critics in the press and Congress tried to make a political affair out of it and tried to ruin me. My response now is this: The hell with you. They didn't ruin me. I have my faith, my family, and a good life. A lot of people love me—or like me. So they

> failed. I would do the same thing over again because I don't think I hurt Valerie Plame whatsoever (Matusow, 2008).

His response displays a vindictiveness and whining that passes as an excuse for his being caught doing something wrong. Again, that Plame was not hurt misses the point. He acted irresponsibly, as did the officials who gave him the information about Plame. In retrospect, no reporter should have published Plame's name and position; no federal official should have given her name to any reporter. Lewis Libby, chief of staff to then-vice president Cheney, was indicted on related matters (not the leak itself) and was convicted on several counts; he was sentenced to serve thirty months in prison. That result points to the seriousness of this action. Although no legal action was taken against Novak, he was culpable as well in releasing the name of a covert CIA agent. Analysis of the informational state of affairs should reveal the culpability, and trust in any reporter who would engage in the action would be destroyed. The analysis would also find that the complete investigation of all those associated with the events cost the government more than $2.5 million.

What is required of journalists is more than obeying laws; they are bound to follow the ethics of their profession. The Society of Professional Journalists has articulated a code of ethics, which holds in part the following:

> **SEEK TRUTH AND REPORT IT**
>
> Journalists should be honest, fair and courageous in gathering, reporting and interpreting information.
>
> **MINIMIZE HARM**
>
> Ethical journalists treat sources, subjects and colleagues as human beings deserving of respect.
>
> **ACT INDEPENDENTLY**
>
> Journalists should be free of obligation to any interest other than the public's right to know.
>
> **BE ACCOUNTABLE**
>
> Journalists are accountable to their readers, listeners, viewers and each other. (Society of Professional Journalists, 1998)

This code (which is, in spirit, similar to many other professional codes of ethics) provides guidance for responsible reporting. One thing that is missing is that journalists must follow the law; that is an essential component of acting responsibly. There are certainly times when the law is ambiguous and professional judgment should come into play, but Robert Novak did not act to minimize harm to Valerie Plame.

Stephens (2014) takes a different view of what journalism should be and what journalists should be doing in the twenty-first century. He even comes up with a new moniker for this different age of journalism: "*Wisdom journalism* is a term for journalism that is more than workmanlike, for journalism that aspires to do more than just tell the news, more than just report what happened. I am proposing it as a new standard—a different and, in my view, higher standard—for quality in journalism. It is a standard that can help guide journalists as they grapple with the field's current crisis and take on the future" (emphasis in original; p. 11). Stephens does invoke Aristotle's name but does not delve deeply into practical wisdom for his new model. That said, his description does resemble *phronesis* closely. For example, he (2014) adds that "familiarity with history and a propensity toward research . . . are almost de rigueur for the wisdom journalist. Considerable skill in making an argument—interpretation usually being involved, opinion often being involved—is also important" (pp. 12–13). Argumentation also has an Aristotelian foundation; logic should be a feature of wisdom journalism as well.

There are times of ambiguity, though, and journalists—and others—have to make decisions about what to make public, in the interests of the political good of the nation. The most recent incident that has tested the lines of ambiguity and power is that of Edward Snowden. This instance has received so much press that it may not be necessary to offer more than a brief summary here (although readers who are unfamiliar with Snowden should read further). Snowden had experience as a technical analyst with the CIA, the Defense Intelligence Agency, and the National Security Agency (NSA). In 2013, he deliberately leaked many classified documents while working as an NSA contractor. Most of the documents were about a number of surveillance programs that the US government was conducting nationally and globally. At this time, he is living in exile and is wanted by the federal government. Snowden's actions, as do those of Bradley/Chelsea Manning, push the envelope when it comes to freedom of information. In both cases, many of the documents indicated that the US government was engaged in questionable espionage that, at the very least, was hovering on the edge of legal action. Was it right for Snowden and Manning to leak the documents? Is it the responsibility of any American who has access to questionable—or outright illegal—activities to make the information public?

A balance must be struck. There are undoubtedly national security matters that must be considered. That said, there have been actions that have crossed the security line to border on serious instances of potentially terrorizing citizens of America and other sovereign nations. There is an unfortunate element in cases such as those of Snowden, Manning, and WikiLeaks. For the most part, we in the United States are left with responding to individual cases of leaks. The press has certainly provided a great amount of coverage on these cases (although there may still be many people who are unaware of them). What has been largely absent in the public discourse (and, in particular, the kind of ethical discourse for which Habermas argues) is a serious and profound discussion of what is legitimate when it comes to the actions of our country. Is extraordinary rendition a reasonable and ethical response to terrorist activities? Is sequestration at Guantanamo Bay prison a legitimate way to treat "enemy combatants"? Are drone strikes within the territories of not only sovereign nations but also putative allies OK, even if innocent victims may also be killed or wounded? How far should the federal government be allowed to go? There is a question that is not asked here, and it has to do with intelligence gathering by covert agents in the name of national security. It is not that this question does not constitute a reasonable concern, but most people would likely say that intelligence is vital to national security. All the previous concerns are important to democracy and to the freedom of the American people. Too often rhetoric holds that some freedoms must be sacrificed in the name of national security. Is it sufficient for citizens to trust government officials to make decisions about specific actions? What is the responsibility of the press in ensuring that dialogue occurs and that dissent be permitted? The position here is that the press has an essential role in creating the dialogue, and the potential for an informed public is at stake.

The previous questions, if unasked, open a pathway to coercion. Citizens are compelled, usually by rhetoric, to act in certain ways or to permit actions by others (for instance, the government itself). The matter of coercion, while mentioned earlier, is not a new concern, and it is discussed by some of the foremost theorists of the twentieth century as well as contemporary commentators. F. A. Hayek (2011 [1960]) made the point more than half a century ago:

> Coercion occurs when one man's actions are made to serve another man's will, not for his own sake but for the other's purpose. It is not that the coerced does not choose at all; if that were the case, we should not speak of his "acting" . . . Coercion implies, however, that I still choose but that my mind is made someone else's tool, because the alternatives before me have been so manipulated that the conduct that the coercer wants me to choose becomes for me the least painful one. (pp. 199, 200)

Hayek's analysis does not depart from Korsgaard's, but it augments it to include those instances where there are pressures upon the agent. These pressures are real, and, frequently, they are political in nature. For example, acceptance of the rhetorical necessity for security at the cost of freedom is a kind of not-so-subtle coercion based primarily on fear. The coercion runs counter to liberty regardless of the specific definition of, and conditions for, liberty.

Ideally, the possibility of coercion should be eliminated entirely from people's lives. One way to consider the ideal is to recall Bourdieu's (1998) conception of "habitus" and what it means for life in a democracy: "Habitus are generative principles of distinct and distinctive practices—what the worker eats, and especially the way he eats it, the sport he practices and the way he practices it, his political opinions and the way he expresses them are systematically different from the industrial owner's corresponding activities. But habitus are also classificatory schemes, principles of classification, principles of vision and division, different tastes. They make distinctions between what is good and what is bad, between what is right and what is wrong" (p. 8). According to Bourdieu (1998), the state itself is a combination of forms of capital. This includes not just economic capital but also informational and symbolic capital. Those forms, those classifications, are present in habitus.

Again, the matter of liberty and coercion is one that should be placed before the public. As is the case for the questions stated previously, the press should raise the issue. The responsibility does not belong solely to the press, though. Educational institutions must also broach the subject. Colleges and universities, for instance, should be fora where these conversations occur. General education should cover the politics of the United States and should allow for discussions of what democracy and politics can and should be. Education for citizenship should do no less. In actuality, secondary school civics and government courses should raise the fundamental issues that are brought up here. At the risk of offending, many of the matters surrounding democracy and citizenship are normative ones. While opinion is a powerful, and frequently necessary, force, there are facts (in keeping with the spirit and practice of phenomenology) that can be found normative. Those are the issues that should be rooted in education. They should also be assured as being part of the contents of libraries. Hayek's *Constitution of Liberty* is, without question, a complex work, but it should be in all sizable public library collections (as well as, of course, in all college and university libraries). Not every reader will agree with every claim, but the arguments put forth by a serious thinker (certainly not limited to Hayek, but including the likes of Habermas, Keynes, Marx, Dahl, etc.) should be considered.

## Economics and Finance

These subjects present particular challenges, since they have been technologized over the past few decades. One can, for instance, read the works of Adam Smith and glean the thinking that underlies his analysis. It is more difficult to read the technical works by late twentieth- and twenty-first-century economists. What exacerbates the challenge to the average person is that a substantial amount of economics reporting is also rather opaque. The fact that present financial instruments are very complex and render the task more difficult for reporters is not really an excuse for obscurantism. A criticism that arose during the recession was that many people did not fully comprehend the mortgage documents they signed. There was a lack of awareness that rates could, and very probably would, rise shortly after the signing. Financial reporters may well have read typical mortgage forms, but little was said about the red flags that were embedded in the texts. Why was more not said about the difficulty for prospective homeowners? Why was Rick Santelli's rant left fundamentally unchallenged? Why were new mortgage holders vilified? Could active bloggers have alerted people to the challenges of getting a mortgage for the first time? What was the responsibility of gospel of prosperity preachers?

To be fair, there were some sources that provided some information about the complicated instruments that were contributors to the dire economic problems. One factor that was such a contributor was mortgage-backed securities; one's original mortgage backer might trade the mortgage to investors. In 2009, though, PIMCO's website stated,

> If you financed your home, there's a good chance that your mortgage is backing up a publicly traded security. A high percentage of individual mortgages originated by banks and other lenders are ultimately pooled and used as collateral to issue mortgage-backed securities (MBS), which are then sold to investors.
>
> With $8.9 trillion in mortgage-related debt outstanding as of September 30, 2008, mortgages are the largest segment of the U.S. bond market, accounting for 26% of all bond market debt outstanding. For comparison, corporate bonds account for 18% of the market, and Treasury debt accounts for 17%. ("Mortgage-Backed Securities," 2014)

Granted, PIMCO's site does not tell prospective home buyers not to borrow, but it does provide some simply stated background that people can use as they consider borrowing. In short, there was some information available, but that information was not widespread or clearly reported in mainstream sources. Given that many mortgage companies (some now defunct) were guilty of obscuring the facts of the mortgages, there should have been some resources for consumers whose knowledge was not sufficient to discern the arcane language of the instruments.

One of the problems of pointing out bad news is that people tend not to like it nor to follow the warnings attached to it. PIMCO's website includes implicit warnings, and the company is a large and respected one. Paul Krugman (2006) issued a prediction well before the tide turned. He (2006) observed that, even with data pointing in the other direction, there were still optimists (Alan Greenspan among them) who were touting good times. Krugman (2006) himself took a very different view:

> Since last summer, when the housing bust became unmistakable, interest rates on long-term bonds have fallen sharply. They're now yielding much less than short-term bonds. The fact that investors are willing to buy those long-term bonds anyway tells us that these investors expect interest rates to fall. And that will happen only if the economy weakens, forcing the Federal Reserve to cut rates. So bond buyers are, in effect, betting on a future economic slowdown.
>
> How serious a slump is the bond market predicting? Pretty serious. Right now, statistical models based on the historical correlation between interest rates and recessions give roughly even odds that we're about to experience a formal recession. And since even a slowdown that doesn't formally qualify as a recession can lead to a sharp rise in unemployment, the odds are very good—maybe 2 to 1—that 2007 will be a very tough year. (Krugman, 2006)

The year 2007 was a very tough year indeed; it was the year that Bear Sterns failed and the optimists changed their opinions. If someone as respected as Paul Krugman, someone with a very solid track record of predictions, was not heeded, we are left with serious questions. Of importance is the fact he was not issuing merely a personal opinion but was adding analysis to his position. Krugman was embodying precisely the kind of journalism for which Stephens calls.

Krugman was not the only big-time economist to issue early warnings of recession. Joseph Stiglitz analyzed the economic landscape and said,

> "I'm very pessimistic," Stiglitz said in an interview in London today. "Alan Greenspan really made a mess of all this. He pushed out too much liquidity at the wrong time. He supported the tax cut in 2001, which is the beginning of these problems. He encouraged people to take out variable-rate mortgages."
>
> Stiglitz said there is a 50 percent chance of a recession in the U.S. and that growth will certainly slow to less than half its 3 percent potential. A worldwide jump in credit costs following the collapse of the subprime

> mortgage market is choking off finance to American consumers. (Landberg and George, 2007)

Among other things, Stiglitz cites the 2001 tax cuts and economic mismanagement as contributing causes of the looming economic problems. Again, accurate warnings were trumped by hope that the fundamental flaws would somehow disappear.

One thing must be noted regarding the Krugman and Stiglitz predictions. Their assessments were stated in plain, easy-to-comprehend language; they were not couched in highly technical jargon. In short, both Krugman and Stiglitz, and the publications that published their warnings, engaged in precisely the kind of potential that is the focus of this chapter. They all exercised responsibility, but somehow they were not heeded. Stephens's words should be reexamined; other business and financial journalists did not embrace wisdom journalism, even when some research and inquiry would have suggested that there were dark clouds on the horizon. To speculate, what would have been the outcome if many journalists and other informational outlets had inquired deeply? If the sources to which people could turn, including such outlets as blogs, had the public good in mind and had sought the truth of the matter, there might have been a different state of affairs a few years ago.

The reporting about the coming recession was one matter of concern in the mid-2000s, but another concern that affected people directly was the housing bubble. This problem is mentioned previously, but specific aspects of the bubble were, perhaps, insufficiently known by home buyers. For one thing, the rise in home prices, particularly in certain parts of the country, was thought to be a long-term phenomenon by many buyers. The seeming attractiveness of home ownership in the early 2000s was fueled, in part, by the low interest rates for conventional loans. The problem was that fewer and fewer of the loans were conventional. As Tanneeru (2009) says,

> Some banks and other institutions were even eager to lend money to prospective homebuyers with poor credit and a spotty financial history who would not typically qualify for loans.
>
> These transactions are known as "subprime" mortgage loans. They generally have interest rates that are above "prime" interest rates available to borrowers with good credit.
>
> On its face, there is nothing devious or illegal about a high interest "subprime" loan. It's simply a case of lender taking on a higher risk and receiving a higher interest rate in return.
>
> However, nearly half of the loans made in 2006 were of the subprime variety, which increased the risk of borrowers defaulting on many banks' balance sheets.

> "Prime mortgages dropped to 64 percent of the total in 2004, 56 percent in 2005 and 52 percent in 2006," the Brookings study notes. (Tanneeru, 2009)

The risk of the subprime loans was extremely high for two basic reasons: the interest rates could rise very quickly and rise higher than prime rates, and if the value of houses fell, the mortgage holders would be left owing more than the houses were worth. As a result, many homeowners could not afford the monthly payments as the rates rose, and selling the home could still leave the individuals in debt. As a result, there were many thousands of mortgage defaults and bank foreclosures.

The need that was manifest at that time—and now and in the future—was (and is) for ethical business practices. Realtors, to mention one group, should have been fully informing potential home buyers about the nature of subprime mortgages. Could a prediction of the bursting bubble have been made? Perhaps, but perhaps not. Realtors, however, were and are fully aware of the risks inherent in subprime mortgages. Did some realtors make the sales so that they could receive commissions? Possibly. What about the lending companies, though? Many of them, now defunct, used mortgage-backed security instruments, as is mentioned previously. These are also inherently risky, and mortgage holders would bear some of that risk. There is more to the picture, though. Skidelsky and Skidelsky (2012) articulate the challenge with admirable clarity:

> Capitalism is a two-edged sword. On the one hand, it has made possible vast improvements in material conditions. On the other, it has exalted some of the most reviled human characteristics, such as green, envy and avarice . . . The banking crisis has shown yet again that the present system relies on motives of greed and acquisitiveness, which are morally repugnant. It also divides societies into rich and poor, latterly very rich and very poor, justified by some version of the "trickle down" idea. (pp. 3, 5)

Wood (2005) offers an even broader analysis: "Capitalism is driven by competition, yet capital must always work to thwart competition. It must constantly expand its markets and constantly seek profit in new places, yet it typically subverts the expansion of markets by blocking the development of potential competitors" (p. 22).

The raising of moral issues in connection with economic and political ones is not new. For one thing, and Haidt (2012) points this out, the previous are all emotional matters, and rationality may not come directly into play when emotions take over. This phenomenon is natural in human beings, but there can be a mixture of emotion and reason. None of us is perfectly rational, and it is a good thing; otherwise we may not have the capacity for altruism, philanthropy, and other qualities we value individually and societally. As Haidt (2012) says, public policy needs the mix that will combine attributes of liberty, fairness, loyalty, and authority. Haidt warns that at this time, we are bound by adherence to a kind of Manichaeism, or an absolute belief that there are nothing more than forces of good and evil; what is not deemed good is by definition evil. Haidt (2012) warns,

> Once the two [political] parties became ideologically pure—a liberal party and a conservative party—there was bound to be a rise in Manichaeism . . . Before 1995, congressmen from both parties attended many of the same social events on weekends; their spouses became friends; their children played on the same sports teams. But nowadays most congressmen fly to Washington on Monday night, huddle with their teammates and do battle for three days, and then fly home on Thursday night. Cross-party friendships are disappearing; Manichaeism and scorched Earth politics are increasing. (pp. 363–64)

There is no shared informing in the root definition of the word; the same things do not give shape to the politicians from the different parties. Some politicians become bullies for the same reasons that adolescents do; there are only cliques, and there is no collective to build upon. The us-them mentality rules, and anyone speaking with the "enemy" is chided or even shunned. The body politic is ill, and the only hope is sharing concerns so as to understand the differences (not merely to be vaguely aware that they are on different sides). Politicians could once find common ground (or at least disagree in a civil and respectful manner) because they actually shared a common ground. Unfortunately, when Barry Goldwater said, "I would remind you that extremism in defense of liberty is no vice. And let me remind you also that moderation in the pursuit of justice is no virtue," the seeds of Manichaeism were planted. When members of one party begin to believe in their hearts that their position is absolutely superior, the possibility for compromise quickly fades. Such an attitude is something that actually has trickled down.

With respect to the financial fiasco of the recession, there has at least been one positive move. Within very recent years, there has been debate about the establishment of a consumer protection agency by the federal government, but no official body existed when the risk was highest and the lending and borrowing activities were greatest. Legislation for the Consumer Financial Protection Bureau was passed in 2010, well after the bursting of the housing bubble. If the bureau operates as it should, there should be informing mechanisms in place to prevent large-scale events like the housing bubble. The bureau will have to be active and should do more than maintain a passive website that may supply data. This is an opportunity for social media to be employed to reach as many people as possible with language that is plain and straightforward. The bureau can set up a Facebook presence and create Twitter feeds that can reach, potentially, millions of people.

## Is There Potential for Education?

As we have seen, education is a particular whipping boy; people do enjoy complaining about it. With regard to P–12 education, the Common Core is the set of standards garnering the most attention. Whether one believes in the efficacy of standards (in general) or in the Common Core (in particular), there are efforts made to assure those who consult the site that the Common Core has been carefully created and vetted. For example, in addressing one issue, it notes the following:

> **Myth:** Adopting common standards means bringing all states' standards down to the lowest common denominator. This means that states with high standards are actually taking a step backwards by adopting the Common Core.
>
> **Fact:** The standards are designed to build upon the most advanced current thinking about preparing all students for success in college, career, and life. This will result in moving even the best state standards to the next level. In fact, since this work began, there has been an explicit agreement that no state would lower its standards. The standards were informed by the best in the country, the highest international standards, and evidence and expertise about educational outcomes. We need college-and career-ready standards because even in high-performing states, students are graduating and passing all the required tests but still need remediation in their postsecondary work. ("Myths vs. Facts," 2014)

It is unknown if the Common Core will solve any of education's problems at this time. If application results in less concentration on frequent testing and offers guidance for teaching and learning, there is promise. Another criticism of P–12 education is that teachers are not sufficiently prepared for the classroom. Many maintain that substantial and substantive student teaching experience is necessary to ready those who will teach America's pupils. The University of Missouri offers a multitiered set of experiences that begin quite early in the student's academic program; it could serve as something of a model that could allay criticism. With each successive year, students gain increasing amounts of classroom experience, preparing them to be proficient not only in the subject matters being taught but also in things such as classroom management. The University of Missouri College of Education website details the experiences students will be engaged in as part of their programs ("Getting Real World Experience," 2014). Every prospective student, every school administrator, and every parent can easily retrieve the information.

A more pressing matter afflicts education, and it has to do with the present and future of schooling and just what it is we hope to accomplish in schools. Touraine (2009) puts his finger on the problem: "Many people are more concerned with public security than with giving every child the chance to construct his or her own identity. If we cannot resolve that problem, schools will become factors that produce greater inequality because they refuse to take into account the psychological, social, and cultural particularity of every individual, and that refusal will harm the weakest and the most oppressed" (pp. 8–9). Schooling exists for something more than ensuring that aggregates of pupils meet sets of standards, regardless of the legitimacy of the standards. It is the place and time for the growth of individual pupils in every way. The growth must be epistemological, psychological, and cultural. The attention that bullying is receiving is necessary, but bullying will never end if teachers, administrators, and parents do not realize that there is an effect on the bully *and* the bullied. Teacher preparation programs represent the place to stress Touraine's analysis and the reasons for its importance; that is the only means by which potential can be fulfilled.

## Higher Education

The challenges with respect to colleges and universities may be more daunting than those for elementary and secondary education. One difficulty is that higher education has fallen victim to neoliberalism in ways that the rest of education has not. As an example, here is a statement by two respected academics, including the former president of the University of Michigan:

> Although it is perhaps impolitic to be so blunt, the simple fact is that the contemporary university is a public corporation that must be governed, led, and managed with competence and accountability in order to benefit its stakeholders. The academic tradition of extensive consultation, debate, and consensus building before any substantive decision can be made or action taken poses a particular challenge, since this process is simply incapable of keeping pace with the profound changes facing effective governance of the

> public university. *Not everything is improved by making it more democratic.* (emphasis added; Duderstadt and Womack, 2003, p. 173)

Duderstadt and Womack are mistaken on several fronts. For one thing, a university is not a corporation in the sense that it does not completely control pricing, receives public money (in the form of direct appropriations for public institutions and in the form of grants and contracts for all universities), does not have a salable product, and does not have paying consumers. In many instances, tuition and fees are set by a higher body (a governing board or even the state). Public universities receive direct state appropriations even though, as is shown in an earlier chapter, that amount has been shrinking. While some observers will claim that students are the university's product, they are not; the institution in no way "produces" them, even as it may graduate them. Some also claim that students are consumers, but students do not consume knowledge, and students are not always in a position to know everything that can be gained from courses or programs. Duderstadt and Womack reduce education to a set of transactions, but they misstate what those transactions are even as they err in maintaining that there *are any* transactions to begin with. Finally, colleges and universities will be strengthened if they become more democratic. A hallmark of higher education is shared governance, with faculty and administrators working closely together in advise and consent capacities so that the primary work of teaching, learning, and inquiry can thrive.

The neoliberal push is something that should be combatted with accurate and complete information about the totality of the state of higher education. We have seen what Harvey, Giroux, and others have to say about neoliberalism in general. In spite of some critique of the discourse on neoliberalism, the economics of colleges and universities (public institutions in particular) clearly represents a corporatized model. Enrollment at the University of Missouri has climbed to more than 35,000 students. The tuition dollars collected obviously depend on enrollment—the more paying students, the greater the revenue. That increase in revenue has been necessary to offset the decline in public funding. Students and those related to them (especially their parents) are painfully aware of the amount that must be paid and the almost certainty of annual increases. That amount strikes home, but most people are probably unaware of the decline in state appropriations. Accountability has, in many ways, shifted from the public to individuals who seek higher learning. To be fair, some commentators question the need for a higher education degree to succeed in all aspects of life, but, for the most part, the financial data are irrefutable.

There are at least two ways to examine the predicament of higher education funding. One rests on the assumption that education is a private good, benefiting only those who can avail themselves of a degree. The other, to which I subscribe, assumes that the education of the citizenry is a public good primarily because one measure of success should be the preparedness to participate as part of the body politic. If this second examination holds sway, the education of the populace is something to which the public should be committed. That conclusion means that public funding for higher education (and education writ large) should be a very high priority for society. It also means that individuals should not be deprived of higher education because of cost. In fact, social conditions may improve if those from the lower socioeconomic levels are presented with better educational opportunities at all levels. Students and their parents must be informed about the differences that having a degree can make. That informing, however, will mean little without the accompanying affordability of all higher education. The matter of educating the populace is (1) necessary, (2) expensive, and (3) invaluable for individuals and society. Media outlets alone are not equipped to realize this informational imperative. Schools, social agencies, libraries, and other resources that are available to the public must be involved in getting the essential message across to everyone. Businesses should be active lobbyists of state legislators to ensure that they will have an unending source of well-prepared workers who are able to analyze and solve problems, be creative, and contribute to the organizations' missions. If there is genuine concern about the low rankings of American students when it comes to skills and knowledge, everyone can and should engage in the urgent informing process.

To stay with financing of education for a moment, it must be noted that there is concern regarding the debt incurred by college and university students. Those data require some investigation, though. While debt is a large dilemma, it is not spread evenly among the population:

> The graduation likelihoods of students from modest economic backgrounds attending public universities are significantly contingent on the debt loads that they carry. Access to at least some debt increases the graduation probabilities of these students. However, starting at about $10,000, debt effects on graduation level out and do not increase further. Beyond $10,000 increasing debt actually undercuts graduation probabilities for these students. The pattern of first positive, then flattening, then negative effects of taking on additional debt indicates mixed support for the ability of debt-financed education to facilitate the goals of outreach and inclusion underlying the model of college for all. (Dwyer, McCloud, and Hodson, 2012, p. 1150)

When it comes to affordability and costs, the words of Deresiewicz (2014) ring true:

> The truth is, there are powerful forces at work in our society that are actively hostile to the college ideal. That distrust critical thinking and deny the proposition that democracy necessitates an educated citizenry. That have no use for larger social purposes. That decline to recognize the worth of that which can't be bought or sold. Above all, that reject the view that higher education is a basic human right . . . Free, high-quality higher education . . . : That is what we used to believe in; that's what many other countries still believe in; that is what we must believe in again. (p. B9)

He is most articulate, and his message should be spread as widely as possible.

The mistake of neoliberalism with respect to education has to do with corporatizing something that should not be considered a component of a market. Since education should everywhere and always be thought of as a public good available to all people, rendering it as a marketplace necessarily leads to the exclusion of some to this public good. As Sandel (2012) writes, "The great missing debate in contemporary politics is about the role and reach of markets. Do we want a market economy, or a market society? What role should markets play in public life and personal relations?" (p. 11). Of course, all this applies to public education. Imagine education to be (somewhat) akin to food. Those who can afford gourmet items may purchase them, and those who cannot afford them are excluded. Those who can afford private colleges and universities may avail themselves of them, while those who have no money will not be able to attend (except under extraordinary circumstances). No one thinking democratically, though, would say that the poor in society should not eat. Likewise, no one should claim that poor people should not be able to gain a degree. Satz (2010) refers to "public bads": "To be uneducated is not simply to be missing out on potential earnings for oneself or for one's society; education is also important for things we cannot buy: the ability to value and to know, to make informed choices about ourselves and our path in life, to experience the world in a difference way than an uneducated person . . . There is no reason to think that markets will supply the appropriate level of education for all" (pp. 48–49).

The only corrective to the previously stated kind of challenge is widespread discourse on the limitations of markets and the costs to society of attempting to turn everything—perhaps especially education—into a commodity. The result, as Jonathan Cole (2009) rightly observes, is that "over the past decade, many of [the] states, which have refused to increase taxes because of the political fallout—or have been unable to increase taxes because of measures constraining them—have been expecting their universities to do more with a lot less" (pp. 470–71). Those who argue for "free markets" should comprehend that there are some things that cannot be squeezed into narrow conceptions of commodities and markets. What needs to be communicated is what colleges and universities *cannot* do because of the fiscal straitjacket and what the absence of public funding does to the health of society as a whole.

## Inequality of Income and Wealth

The matters of inequalities in wealth distribution have been reported in Chapter 2. We know that about 72 percent of financial wealth is controlled by the top 5 percent of the population (Smith, 2013). This kind of distribution can be reported widely and can be spread effectively via social media to reach the maximum audience. As seemingly clear as data show, they still begs for some interpretation and analysis. For example, inquiry could be conducted to see how easy or difficult it is for people in the bottom 80 percent to make it into the top 20 percent. If it is, as one might guess, extremely difficult to make that kind of socioeconomic move, people should be informed about the fact. That reality needs to be communicated widely, and it is the responsibility of reportage in all forms and media to inform in the interests of the public good. That means that integrity and truthfulness must guide communication.

Anecdotal stories can help tell people what the predicaments really look like. For example, suppose there is a family of four and both household heads work at least forty hours per week, but at minimum wage. At the present time, the minimum wage in the state of Missouri is $7.50 an hour. The aforementioned family will have an approximate gross income of $600 per week. With no vacation time and continuous employment, the annual family income is $31,200. The family lives about 35 percent above the poverty level. The average rental price for a three-bedroom apartment outside Kansas City is roughly $940 per month. Adding in about $140 a month in utilities, almost $1,100 of the family's after-tax income is taken up by absolute essentials. When food, clothing, and other necessities are added, the vast majority of the take-home income is spent. Saving is almost impossible, and the hope of high-paying jobs is rather dim. Suppose the minimum wage were increased to $15 an hour; what would be the material difference for this hypothetical family? Simply calculated, the gross income level doubles to $1,200 per week. The annual income of $62,400 affords the family many more options (including the possibility of saving), even without a substantive change in their working conditions. What would be the impact if millions of people were informed of this kind of hypothetical circumstance? What might be the effects of a concomitant rise in pay in keeping with the relative difference between the lowest paid workers and those earning somewhat more? For instance, suppose someone is earning about 20 percent more than the minimum wage and would continue to earn that margin above the minimum. An outcome of the increase in minimum wage, which is seldom mentioned, is an increase in state and federal income tax revenues (even if nothing is changed for the wealthiest individuals and families). One thing that would probably be required in the event of a substantial rise in the minimum wage is a widespread educational program to enable the individuals and families to make the most of the difference. There is certainly informational potential in this arena.

## Argument

Perhaps the most important and overarching matter when it comes to informational potential is the responsibility of argument (which is used here in the more technical, and not the pejorative, sense). Those who intend to inform and/or persuade others should do so honestly; this certainly does not always occur, so there are some strictures that should be followed regarding this argument. The first guideline is that anyone who would speak on behalf of something should believe it. That is a mark of the integrity that is part and parcel of the public good. There are self-evident reasons why people argue, notable among them is the desire to create agreement with one's position on a topic. For example, someone who believes that democracy in present-day America should be of the Federalist version would probably refer to the Federalist Papers and other documents by particular Founding Fathers for support for the stance. That person might also mention the thoughts and writings of anti-Federalists so as to refute those positions. In short, one would seek evidence—factual, documentary, or other—to provide a foundation for a position. An argument made with full integrity would acknowledge all possible evidence and would weigh the efficacy of it all in an effort to find the soundest, most consistent, and most coherent evidence. Argument, as described here, is not entirely separate from epistemology; what can *count* as knowledge can count as the logic of an argument.

What separates argument from knowledge is a measure of certitude. For something to count as knowledge, there usually has to be a kind of indefeasible character about it. Argument does not necessarily include indefeasibility but does attempt to include reasonable support and eliminate that which is not reasonable to the points made. A tactic for seeking reason is interpretation leading to understanding. This interpretation might be said to treat the world as a text to be comprehended. The understanding, of necessity, analyzes ideological speech to determine if it is genuinely the expression of ideas or if it is the inclusion of falsity so as to assume the trappings of legitimacy (see, for example, Ricoeur, 1991, pp. 35–36). According to Ricoeur, all language has discursive qualities and can be understood as multiparticipant discourses. The discourse has a discernible structure that must first be comprehended; moreover, discourse constitutes a projection, or picture, of the world (either as it is or as the speaker *says* it is). Gaining a full understanding of what is said is a product of critical apprehension of the discursive practice, which includes understanding of the *who* is speaking and the *context* of the speech. Toulmin emphasizes the role of logic in argumentation; logic's "primary business is a retrospective, justificatory one—with the arguments we can put forward afterwards to make good our claim that the conclusions arrived at are acceptable, because justifiable, conclusions" (p. 6). Justification is an essential component of logic and, so, argument. As for warrant, it "is, in a sense, incidental and explanatory, its task being simply to register explicitly the legitimacy of the step involved and to refer it back to the larger class of steps whose legitimacy is being presupposed" (p. 100). The explanatory character is quite important since the legitimacy of the argument must be established.

In making an argument via the standard media that has legitimacy, a certain definition of "objectivity" must be adhered to. This objectivity is not the type that avoids judgment or evaluation; indeed, the contrary is true. Objective analysis that enters argument is that which begins without bias but which seeks accuracy and truth. An objective reporter would, then, point out lies when they are apparent and inaccuracies when they are apparent (see Stephens, 2014). Objective examination does not simply accept what is said as legitimate (there should be warrant to support what is said or written). Stephens quotes Ezra Klein (2010), who writes, "It's trite to say it, but the news business is biased toward, well, news. There are plenty of outlets that tell you what happened yesterday, but virtually no organizations that simply tell you what's going on. Keeping up on the news is easy, but getting a handle on an ongoing situation that you've not really been following is hard." In other words, argument (in the sense that the word is used here) is missing. There is an absence of analysis, which means that there tends to be a blind acceptance of whatever it is, including the false, that people say. As Toulmin (1958) says, "A man who makes an assertion puts forward a claim—a claim on our attention and to our belief" (p. 11). For the claim to be worthy of our belief, there must be truth conditions to which the claim can be subjected (see Searle, 1999). Nothing short of genuine argumentation and truth claims can count as informational potential.

## Discussion

One purpose of all that has come before this is to point out that there are imminently practical reasons for correcting informational failures; the failures have the potential to do material damage to society. We have seen some of the damage that can be wrought when it comes to democracy and economics, for example. The damage violates Dworkin's (2006) first principle regarding human dignity: every human life has a kind of objective value (p. 9). He means that the weighing of the value is not subjective; its determination is not dependent upon the whim or caprice of any individuals or groups. Dworkin uses the language employed here; every life has potentiality that should not, under any circumstances, be denied simply because a person is a member of, say, a particular socioeconomic group. Prejudice that denies the objective value obviates that potential before it has any chance of being realized. Potential success in material (and other) elements of life is removed from the volition and from the responsibility of the individual, where it should reside. How close are we to this ideal? At this point in time, we are some distance from it, and Dworkin agrees. He (2006) says that "our politics are now so debased that they threaten our standing as a true democracy—that they have begun to undermine, that is, the legitimacy of our political order" (p. 130). As long as some people can be systematically marginalized, the threat exists. And as long as there are what we can call truth claims that support marginalization, society will remain at risk of failing to be democratic (not in the majoritarian sense but in the partnership sense that Dworkin advocates).

It is necessary for there to be an ethical foundation for the examination and reality of politics, economics, and the public good. Without that, society is lost and founders. As Eagleton (2009) puts it, "Without the ethical to challenge, disrupt and renew it, political society can engender no profound value in itself" (p. 245). This message is not substantively different from Adam Smith's. We must remember that Smith maintained that economics is a *social* system and that a moral foundation has to underpin it. Eagleton (2009) reminds us that "the necessary corollary of treating others as oneself is to treat oneself as another" (p. 14). That is Paul Ricoeur's message. He (1992) emphasizes that our ethical lives are bound to the institutions within which we live, for example: "What fundamentally characterizes the idea of institution is the bond of common mores and not that of constraining rules. In this, we are carried back to the *ethos* from which ethics takes its name" (Ricoeur, 1992, p. 194). Eagleton revives the importance of phenomenology as a strategy for realizing the potential spoken of here. Husserl (1970) articulates the aim: "True being is everywhere an ideal goal, a task of *episteme*, or 'reason,' as opposed to being which through *doxa* is merely thought to be, unquestioned and 'obvious'" (p. 13). The phenomenological attitude, which is characterized by reason, is richer than the natural attitude, which is limited to opinion. Smith (2004) makes a similar point: "The ontological foundation of intentionality includes not only the neural activity in the subject's brain but also his background ideas about the world, ideas extant in his culture, not in his brain" (p. 166).

As is noted previously, truth is a vital component of the potential resolution to the failures mentioned earlier. In examining truth, we do not need a hard-core absolutist position; we can follow Lynch (2004), who says, "A belief in fundamental rights does not require that one believe in Natural, God-given Rights or other bizarre metaphysical entities. It requires only an objective notion of truth in the minimal sense of 'objective'" (p. 171). Michel Foucault (2011), though, has a unique take on truth. He advocates for what he calls *parrhēsia*, or the modality of truth telling and speaking freely (p. 2). He claims that *parrhēsia* is the antithesis of rhetoric (defined very specifically as the following): "Basically a technique concerning the way that things are said, but does not in any way determine the relations between the person who speaks and what he says. Rhetoric is an art, a technique, a set of processes which enable the person speaking to say something which may not be what he thinks at all, but whose effect will be to produce convictions, induce certain conducts, or instill certain beliefs in the person [to whom he speaks]" (p. 13). This definition of rhetoric lies at the heart of many of the informational failures detailed in the previous chapters. What is said may not be what speakers believe, but it is said to persuade and convince, sometimes to convince others of something that is not true. Foucault (2011) provides the opposite: "*Parrhēsia*, on the other hand, involves a strong and constitutive bond between the person speaking and what he says, and, through the effect of the truth, of the injuries of truth, it opens up the possibility of the bond between the person speaking and the person to whom he has spoken being broken . . . It is a stance, a way of being which is akin to a virtue, a mode of action" (p. 14). Prado (2006) clarifies where Foucault stands: "His genealogical aim has nothing to do with reducing reality to constructs, and little to do with simply showing constructs to be constructs. Foucault's genealogical aim is to reveal how certain constructs, in being deployed as discerned essences, generate norms that dictate how we think and live" (p. 168). The demands of informational potential are indeed as strong as Foucault maintains.

# References


2013 world hunger and poverty facts and statistics. (2014). Worldhunger.org. Retrieved from http://www.worldhunger.org/articles/Learn/world%20hunger%20facts%202002.htm

Abizadeh, A. (2005). In defense of the universalization principle in discourse ethics. *Philosophical Forum, 36*, 193–211.

About ALEC. (2014). American Legislative Exchange Council. Retrieved from http://www.alec.org/about-alec

Academic Bill of Rights. (n.d.). Students for Academic Freedom. Retrieved from http://www.studentsforacademicfreedom.org/documents/1925/abor.html

Akers, B. (2011). Taking the road less traveled. *New American, 27*(9), 33–34.

Akerlof, G. A., & Shiller, R. J. (2010). *Animal spirits: How human psychology drives the economy, and why it matters for global capitalism*. Princeton: Princeton University Press.

Albritton, R. (2007). *Economics transformed: Discovering the brilliance of Marx*. London: Pluto Press.

Alden, W. (2014, March 12). Average Wall St. bonus increased by 15% in 2013. *The New York Times*. Retrieved from http://dealbook.nytimes.com/2014/03/12/wall-street-bonuses-go-up-as-the-number-of-jobs-goes-down/?_php=true&_type=blogs&_r=0

Alperovitz, G. (2005). *America beyond capitalism*. Hoboken, NJ: John Wiley.

American Association of University Professors. (2013). Here's the news: The annual report on the economic status of the profession, 2012–13. Retrieved from http://www.aaup.org/report/heres-news-annual-report-economic-status-profession-2012-13

Appleby, J. (2010). *The relentless revolution: A history of capitalism*. New York: Norton.

Aristotle. (2007). *The basic works of Aristotle*. R. McKeon (Ed.). New York: Modern Library.

Armey, D., & Kibbe, M. (2010). *Give us liberty: The tea party manifesto*. New York: William Morrow.

Arrigo, B. A., & Bullock, J. L. (2008). The psychological effects on solitary confinement prisoners in supermax units. *International Journal of Offender Theory and Comparative Criminology, 52*, 622–40.

Ashbee, E. (2011). Bewitched—the tea party movement: Ideas, interests, and institutions. *Political Quarterly, 82*, 157–64.

Average starting + current salaries by major. (2014). Students Review. Retrieved from http://www.studentsreview.com/salary_by_major.php3

Bacevich, A. (2009). *The limits of power: The end of American exceptionalism*. New York: Henry Holt.

Baker, B. D., Sciarra, D. G., & Farrie, D. (2014, January). *Is school funding fair? A national report card* (3rd ed.). New Brunswick, NJ: Education Law Center.

Baker, D. (2014, July 23). Stress test: The indictment of Timothy Geithner. *Huffington Post*. Retrieved from http://www.huffingtonpost.com/dean-baker/stress-test-the-indictmen_b_5385423.html

Bakhtin, M. M. (1993). *Toward a philosophy of the act*. V. Liapunov (Trans.). Austin: University of Texas Press.

Barnes, J. E. (2008, April 18). 1 in 5 veterans found with mental disorder. *The Boston Globe*. Retrieved from http://www.boston.com/news/nation/articles/2008/04/18/1_in_5_veterans_found_with_mental_disorder

Barr, C. (2011, February 18). Jamie Dimon, bonus king. *Fortune*. Retrieved from http://fortune.com/2011/02/18/jamie-dimon-bonus-king

Basu, K. (2011). *Beyond the invisible hand: Groundwork for a new economics*. Princeton, NJ: Princeton University Press.

Bauerlein, M. (2008). *The dumbest generation: How the digital age stupefies young Americans and jeopardizes our future*. New York: Tarcher/Penguin.

Becker, G. S. (1993). *Human capital* (3rd ed.). Chicago: University of Chicago Press.

Bennett, W. J., & Wilezol, D. (2013). *Is college worth it?* New York: Thomas Nelson.

Berfield, S. (2013, July 11). Raising the minimum wage to keep D.C. Walmart-free? BusinessWeek.com. Retrieved from http://www.businessweek.com/articles/2013-07-10/raising-the-minimum-wage-to-keep-d-dot-c-dot-walmart-free

Berlin, I. (2002). *Liberty*. Oxford: Oxford University Press.

Black, G. (2011, June 2). Workers who pick produce in Georgia's fields make $12 to $18 an hour. Politifact.com. Retrieved from http://www.politifact.com/georgia/statements/2011/jun/14/gary-black/some-farm-workers-do-earn-high-wages-not-all-do

Blinder, A. S. (2014). *After the music stopped*. New York: Penguin.

Blix: Iraq unlikely to use chemical, germ weapons. (2003, March 19). CNN.com. Retrieved from http://www.cnn.com/2003/WORLD/meast/03/19/sprj.irq.blix.saddam/index.html?iref=allsearch

Bloom, A. (1987). *The closing of the American mind*. New York: Simon & Schuster.

Boaz, D. (1997). *Libertarianism: A primer*. New York: Free Press.

Boczkowski, P. J., & Mitchelstein, E. (2013). *The news gap: When the information preferences of the media and the public diverge*. Cambridge, MA: MIT Press.

Boggs, C. (2000). *The end of politics: Corporate power and the decline of the public sphere*. New York: Guilford Press.

Bok, D. (2003). *Universities in the marketplace: The commercialization of higher education*. Princeton, NJ: Princeton University Press.

BondGraham, D. (2013, June 26). Public research for private gain. *East Bay Express*. Retrieved from http://www.eastbayexpress.com/oakland/public-research-for-private-gain/Content?oid=3619535

Borg, M. J. (1989). *Speaking Christian*. New York: HarperOne.

Bourdieu, P. (1998). *Practical reason: On the theory of action*. Stanford, CA: Stanford University Press.

Bozell, L. B., III, & Graham, T. (2013). *Collusion: How the media stole the 2012 election and how to stop them from doing it in 2016*. New York: HarperCollins.

Bramwell, J. (2013, May 1). $53,300: The average starting salary for new accounting grads. *Accounting Web*. Retrieved from http://www.accountingweb.com/article/53300-average-starting-salary-new-accounting-grads/221716

Britt, R. R. (2009, January 10). 14 percent of U.S. adults can't read. Livescience.com. Retrieved from http://www.livescience.com/3211-14-percent-adults-read.html

Broder, J. M. (2010, October 20). Climate change doubt is Tea Party article of faith. *The New York Times*. Retrieved from http://www.nytimes.com/2010/10/21/us/politics/21climate.html

Brooks, D. (2011, July 5). The mother of all no-brainers. *The New York Times*. Retrieved from http://www.nytimes.com/2011/07/05/opinion/05brooks.html?_r=0

Buchheit, P. (2014, February 19). 4 ways privatization is ruining our education system. Salon.com. Retrieved from http://www.salon.com/2014/02/19/4_ways_privatization_is_ruining_our_education_system_partner

Budd, J. M. (2007). Information, analysis, and ideology: A case study of science and the public interest. *Journal of the American Society for Information Science & Technology, 58*, 2366–71.

———. (2009). *Higher education's purpose: Intellectual and social progress*. Lanham, MD: University Press of America.

———. (2011). Meaning, truth, and information: Prolegomena to a theory. *Journal of Documentation, 67*, 56–74.

The Buffett rule. (2012, April). Whitehouse.gov. Retrieved from http://www.whitehouse.gov/economy/buffett-rule

Bumiller, E., & Kopicki, A. (2012, March 26). Support in U.S. for Afghan war drops sharply, poll finds. *The New York Times*. Retrieved from http://www.nytimes.com/2012/03/27/world/asia/support-for-afghan-war-falls-in-us-poll-finds.html?pagewanted=all

Burke, E. (1960). Letter to a noble lord. In L. I. Bredvold & R. G. Ross (Eds.), *The philosophy of Edmund Burke* (pp. 141–45). Ann Arbor: University of Michigan Press.

Burnett, J. (2014, April 1). Can a television network be a church? The IRS says yes. *NPR*. Retrieved from http://www.npr.org/2014/04/01/282496855/can-a-television-network-be-a-church-the-irs-says-yes

Burns, A. (2011, August 9). Barack Obama's 2012 plan: "Kill Romney." Politico.com. Retrieved from http://www.politico.com/news/stories/0811/60929.html

Bush, G. W. (2003, January 28). State of the Union address. Johnstonarchive.net. Retrieved from http://www.johnstonsarchive.net/policy/bushstun2003.html

Carlson, S. (2014, February 5). Administrator hiring drove 28% boom in higher-ed work force, report shows. *Chronicle of Higher Education*. Retrieved from http://chronicle.com/article/Administrator-Hiring-Drove-28-/144519

Carr, D. (2014). The human and educational significance of honesty as an epistemic and moral virtue. *Educational Theory, 64*, 1–14.

Carter, Z. (2012, September 21). Mitt Romney tax returns for 2011 released. *Huffington Post*. Retrieved from http://www.huffingtonpost.com/2012/09/21/mitt-romney-taxes-released_n_1904262.html

Cassidy, J. (2002). *Dot.con: The greatest story ever told*. New York: HarperCollins.

———. (2014, June 10). Cantor loses, and Washington goes ape. *The New Yorker*. Retrieved from http://www.newyorker.com/news/john-cassidy/cantor-loses-and-washington-goes-ape

Cauchon, D. (2008, April 15). From O. J. to Dick Morris: Taxes go unpaid. *USA Today*. Retrieved from http://abcnews.go.com/Business/PersonalFinance/story?id=4650368

Census: U.S. poverty rate spikes, nearly 50 million Americans affected. (2012, November 15). *CBS*. Retrieved from http://washington.cbslocal.com/2012/11/15/census-u-s-poverty-rate-spikes-nearly-50-million-americans-affected

Chait, J. (2011). No such thing as equal opportunity. *New York, 44*(36), 14–16.

Chatterjee, J. (2014). Falling through the cracks and bridging the gap—India and USA showing similar trends. *Current Science, 106*, 691–97.

Chilcote, R., King, J., & Starr, B. (2003, March 20). U.S. launches cruise missiles at Saddam. CNN.com. Retrieved from http://www.cnn.com/2003/WORLD/meast/03/19/sprj.irq.main

Choma, R. (2013, January 29). Lobbying again on downward slide in 2012. Opensecrets.org. Retrieved from https://www.opensecrets.org/news/2013/01/lobbying-spending-down-in-2012

*Citizens United v. Federal Election Commission*, 558 U.S. ___ (2010).

Clement, S. (2013, September 3). Most in U.S. oppose Syria Strike, Post-ABC poll finds. *The Washington Post*. Retrieved from http://www.washingtonpost.com/blogs/the-fix/wp/2013/09/03/most-in-u-s-oppose-syria-strike-post-abc-poll-finds

Cockrell, J. F. (2013). Solitary confinement: The law today and the way forward. *Law & Psychology Review, 37*, 211–27.

Codevilla, A. M. (2010). America's ruling class—And the perils of revolution. *The American Spectator, 43*(6), 18–36.

Cohen, A. (2014, April 29). Oklahoma just neutered its state Supreme Court. *The Week*. Retrieved from http://theweek.com/article/index/260632/oklahoma-just-neutered-its-state-supreme-court

Cole, J. R. (2009). *The great American university*. New York: PublicAffairs.

Conniff, R. (2013). A police chief's sage advice. *The Progressive, 77*(6), 14–16.

Cosgrove-Mather, B. (2003, January 23). Poll: Talk first, fight later. CBS.com. Retrieved from http://www.cbsnews.com/news/poll-talk-first-fight-later

Crawford, S. (2014). First amendment common sense. *Harvard Law Review, 127*, 2343–91.

Crichton, K., Lamb, G., & Jacquette, R. F. (2011, October 21). Timeline of major events in the Iraq war. *The New York Times*. Retrieved from http://www.nytimes.com/interactive/2010/08/31/world/middleeast/20100831-Iraq-Timeline.html

Denson, B. (2014, May 3). Oregon prisoner locked in solitary confinement for 27 months loses appeal to punish prison system. *The Oregonian*. Retrieved from http://www.oregonlive.com/politics/index.ssf/2014/05/oregon_prisoner_locked_in_soli.html

Deresiewicz, W. (2014). The miseducation of America. *Chronicle of Higher Education, 60*(40), B6–B9.

DeSilver, D. (2013, December 5). U.S. income inequality, on rise for decades, is now highest since 1928. Pewresearch.org. Retrieved from http://www.pewresearch.org/fact-tank/2013/12/05/u-s-income-inequality-on-rise-for-decades-is-now-highest-since-1928

DesRosiers, D. (2013, May 14). [Review of the book *Is college worth it? A former United States secretary of education and a liberal arts graduate expose the broken promise of higher education*, by W. J. Bennett & D. Wilezol]. *The Washington Times*. Retrieved from http://www.washingtontimes.com/news/2013/may/14/book-review-is-college-worth-it/?page=all

Dewey, J. (1916). *Democracy and education*. New York: Macmillan.

———. (1954 [1927]). *The public and its problems*. Athens, OH: Ohio University Press.

*Digest of Education Statistics, 2011*. (2012). Washington, DC: National Center for Education Statistics.

Dilanian, K. (2013, July 31). Concerns about NSA surveillance persist despite release of files. *Los Angeles Times*. Retrieved from http://articles.latimes.com/2013/jul/31/nation/la-na-nsa-surveillance-20130801/2

Doherty, B. (2011). Ron Paul's radical vision. *Reason, 43*, 84–87.

Domhoff, G. W. (2013). *Wealth, income, and power*. Santa Cruz: University of California at Santa Cruz.

Duderstadt, J. J., & Womack, F. W. (2003). *Beyond the crossroads: The future of the public university in America*. Baltimore: Johns Hopkins University Press.

Duncan, C., & Machan, T. R. (2005). *Libertarianism for and against*. Lanham, MD: Rowman & Littlefield.

Dworkin, R. (1997). Comment. In G. S. Wood (Ed.), *A matter of interpretation* (pp. 115–27). Princeton, NJ: Princeton University Press.

———. (2006). *Is democracy possible here? Principles for a new political debate*. Princeton, NJ: Princeton University Press.

Dwyer, R. E., McCloud, L., & Hodson, R. (2012). Debt and graduation from American universities. *Social Forces, 90*, 1133–55.

Eagleton, T. (1991). *Ideology: An introduction*. London: Verso.

———. (2004). *After theory*. New York: Basic Books.

———. (2009). *Trouble with strangers: A study of ethics*. Malden, MA: Wiley-Blackwell.

Editing out the facts. (2014, June 25). Factcheck.org. Retrieved from http://www.factcheck.org/2014/06/editing-out-the-facts-in-alabama

Edmondson, J., & D'Urso, A. (2009). Considering alternatives for federal education policy in the United States: A critical perspective of No Child Left Behind. *Critical Studies in Education, 50*, 79–91.

Edwards, L. (1999). *The conservative revolution: The movement that remade America*. New York: Free Press.

Eisenstein, E. (1979). *The printing press as an agent of change*. Cambridge: Cambridge University Press.

Ellwanger, A. (2009). Bloom and his detractors. *Pedagogy, 9*, 475–86.

Evolution, creationism, intelligent design. (2012, July 24). Gallup.com. Retrieved from http://www.gallup.com/poll/21814/evolution-creationism-intelligent-design.aspx

Fact Booklet, 2013–2014. (2014). Lexington: University of Kentucky.

Ferguson, C. H. (2012). *Predator nation*. New York: Crown Business.

Fields, G. (2013). Parallel problems: Applying institutional corruption analysis of Congress to big PHARMA. *Journal of Law, Medicine & Ethics, 41*, 556–60.

Fives, A. (2009). Reasonable, agonistic, or good?: The character of a democrat. *Philosophy & Social Criticism, 35*, 961–83.

Fletcher, M. A. (2013, January 16). More workers raiding 401(k) plans long before retirement. *The Boston Globe*. Retrieved from http://www.bostonglobe.com/business/2013/01/16/more-workers-raiding-retirement-accounts-pay-bills/5iK9IJygU1TLR3cnw2n9EP/story.html

Flynn, D. J. (2013). There's something about Cambridge. *The American Spectator, 46*(5), 32–34.

Fodor, J., & Piattelli-Palmarini, M. (2010). *What Darwin got wrong*. New York: Farrar, Straus, and Giroux.

Foucault, M. (2011). *The courage of truth: The government of self and others II; Lectures at the Collège de France, 1983–1984*. New York: Palgrave Macmillan.

Frank, R. H. (2011). *The Darwin economy: Liberty, competition, and the common good*. Princeton, NJ: Princeton University Press.

Frederick, M. (2010). Rags to riches: Religion, media, and the performance of wealth in a neoliberal age. In C. J. Greenhouse (Ed.), *Ethnographies of neoliberalism* (pp. 221–37). Philadelphia: University of Pennsylvania Press.

Freeden, M. (1996). *Ideologies and political theory: A conceptual approach*. Oxford: Oxford University Press.

Friedman, M. (1962). *Capitalism and freedom*. Chicago: University of Chicago Press.

Fritzberg, G. J. (2004). No child left behind? Assessing President Bush's assessment law. *Educational Foundations, 18*, 7–24.

Frumin, A. (2013, September 13). 10 years later: Mission accomplished? MSNBC.com. Retrieved from http://www.msnbc.com/hardball/10-years-later-mission-accomplished

Gardner, H. (2005). Beyond markets and individuals: A focus on educational goals. In R. H. Hersh & J. Merrow (Eds.), *Declining by degrees: Higher education at risk* (pp. 97–112). New York: Palgrave Macmillan.

Garnham, N. (1992). The media and the public sphere. In C. Calhoun (Ed.), *Habermas and the public sphere* (pp. 359–76). Cambridge, MA: MIT Press.

Gathegi, J. N. (2005). The public library as a public forum: The (de)evolution of a legal doctrine. *Library Quarterly, 75*, 1–19.

Geithner, T. (2014). *Stress test: Reflections on financial crises.* New York: Crown.

Get the facts on voter fraud in the United States. (2014). Voterfraudfacts.com. Retrieved from http://voterfraudfacts.com

Getting real world experience as a student. (2014). University of Missouri. Retrieved from http://education.missouri.edu/undergraduate/field_experience_new.php

Geuss, R. (2001). *History and illusion in politics.* Cambridge: Cambridge University Press.

———. (2010). *Politics and the imagination.* Princeton, NJ: Princeton University Press.

Giroux, H. A. (2004). *The terror of neoliberalism: Authoritarianism and the eclipse of democracy.* Boulder, CO: Paradigm.

Glantz, A. (2014, June 28). GI bill funds flow to for-profit colleges that fail state aid standards. *Center for Investigative Reporting.* Retrieved from http://cironline.org/reports/gi-bill-funds-flow-profit-colleges-fail-state-aid-standards-6477

Goldman, A. I. (2004). *Pathways to knowledge: Public and private.* Oxford: Oxford University Press.

Gonzalez, A. R. (2002, January 25). Memorandum for the president. GWU.edu. Retrieved from http://www2.gwu.edu/~nsarchiv/NSAEBB/NSAEBB127/02.01.25.pdf

Goode, L. (2005). *Jürgen Habermas: Democracy and the public sphere.* London: Pluto Press.

Goodin, R. E. (2003). *Reflective democracy.* Oxford: Oxford University Press.

Graves, L., & Fischer, B. (2014). Show me the money: Meet the multimillionaire squeezing Missouri's schools. *The Progressive, 78*(5), 16–21.

Green, J. (2013, June 6). Jumbo severance packages for top CEOs are growing. BusinessWeek.com. Retrieved from http://www.businessweek.com/articles/2013-06-06/jumbo-severance-packages-for-top-ceos-are-growing

Greenhouse, S. (2011, September 7). The challenge of creating good jobs. *The New York Times.* Retrieved from http://economix.blogs.nytimes.com/2011/09/07/the-challenge-of-creating-good-jobs

Greenspan, A. (2013). *The map and the territory.* New York: Penguin Press.

Greenwald, G. (2011). *With liberty and justice for some.* New York: Picador.

Gregorian, V. (2005). Six challenges to the American university. In R. H. Hersh & J. Merrow (Eds.), *Declining by degrees: Higher education at risk* (pp. 77–96). New York: Palgrave Macmillan.

Gulati, G. J. (2012). Super PACs and financing the 2012 presidential election. *Society, 49*(5), 409–17.

Gulf war to Iraq war: 2 August 1990–19 March 2003. (n.d.). Warchronicle.com. Retrieved from http://www.warchronicle.com/iraq/news/timeline_two_wars.htm

Gutmann, A. (1999). *Democratic education.* Princeton, NJ: Princeton University Press.

Gutmann, A., & Thompson, D. (2004). *Why deliberative democracy?* Princeton, NJ: Princeton University Press.

Habermas, J. (1989). *The structural transformation of the public sphere*. T. Burger (Trans.). Cambridge, MA: MIT Press.

———. (1990). *Moral consciousness and communicative action*. C. Lenhardt & S. W. Nicholsen (Trans.). Cambridge, MA: MIT Press.

———. (1994). *Justification and application: Remarks on discourse ethics*. C. P. Cronin (Trans.). Cambridge, MA: MIT Press.

———. (1998). *The inclusion of the other: Studies in political theory*. C. Cronin & P. De Grieff (Trans.). Cambridge, MA: MIT Press.

Haidt, J. (2012). *The righteous mind: Why good people are divided by politics and religion*. London: Penguin Books.

Haiken, M. (2013, February 5). Suicide rate among vets and active duty military jumps—now 22 a day. *Forbes*. Retrieved from http://www.forbes.com/sites/melaniehaiken/2013/02/05/22-the-number-of-veterans-who-now-commit-suicide-every-day

Harvey, D. (2005). *A brief history of neoliberalism*. Oxford: Oxford University Press.

———. (2010a). *A companion to Marx's "Capital."* London: Verso.

———. (2010b). *The enigma of capital and the crises of capitalism*. Oxford: Oxford University Press.

———. (2014). *Seventeen contradictions and the end of capitalism*. Oxford: Oxford University Press.

Hastings, M. (2010, June 22). The runaway general. *Rolling Stone*. Retrieved from http://www.rollingstone.com/politics/news/the-runaway-general-20100622

Hayek, F. A. (2011 [1960]). *The constitution of liberty*. Chicago: University of Chicago Press.

Here's why the dot com bubble began and why it popped. (2010, December 15). *Business Insider*. Retrieved from http://www.businessinsider.com/heres-why-the-dot-com-bubble-began-and-why-it-popped-2010-12

Hintikka, J. (1995). The phenomenological dimension. In B. Smith & D. W. Smith (Eds.), *The Cambridge companion to Husserl* (pp. 78–105). Cambridge: Cambridge University Press.

Hobhouse, L. T. (1964). *Liberalism*. New York: Oxford University Press.

Hodai, B. (2013, May 20). Dissent or terror: How Arizona's counter terrorism apparatus, in partnership with corporate interests, turned on Occupy Phoenix. PRWatch.org. Retrieved from http://www.prwatch.org/news/2013/05/12112/dissent-or-terror-how-arizonas-counter-terrorism-apparatus-partnership-corporate-

Hodge, R., & Kress, G. (1993). *Language as ideology* (2nd ed.). London: Routledge.

Hollifield, G. (2011). Does God want you to be rich? A practical theologian's response to the gospel of prosperity. *Journal of Ministry and Theology, 15*(2), 25–53.

Honderich, T. (2005). *Conservatism: Burke, Nozick, Bush, Blair?* (rev. ed.). London: Pluto Press.

Horowitz, J., & Cammarano, S. (2013, February 5). 20 extraordinary facts about CIA extraordinary rendition and secret detention. *Open Society Foundations*. Retrieved from http://www.opensocietyfoundations.org/voices/20-extraordinary-facts-about-cia-extraordinary-rendition-and-secret-detention

Hundley, K. (2011, May 9). Billionaire's role in hiring decisions at Florida State University raises questions. *Tampa Bay Times*. Retrieved from http://www.tampabay.com/news/business/billionaires-role-in-hiring-decisions-at-florida-state-university-raises/1168680

Hunt, P., & Kennedy, J. (2004). *Financial derivatives in theory and practice*. New York: Wiley.

Husserl, E. (1970). *The crisis of European sciences and transcendental phenomenology: An introduction to phenomenological philosophy*. D. Carr (Trans.). Evanston, IL: Northwestern University Press.

In the grips of a delayed mid-life crisis. (2003, July 17). *Economist*. Retrieved from http://www.economist.com/node/1927195

Jensen, E. M., & Entin, J. L. (1998). Commandeering, the Tenth Amendment, and the federal requisition power: *New York v. United States* revisited. *Constitutional Commentary, 15*(2), 355–81.

Justice Rehnquist's dissent in *First National Bank of Boston v. Bellotti*. (2014). *Reclaim Democracy!* Retrieved from http://reclaimdemocracy.org/rehnquist_dissent_bellotti/#wrap

Kahn, N., & Carson, C. (2012, August 11). New database of U.S. voter fraud finds no evidence that photo ID laws are needed. NBCNEWS.com. Retrieved from http://investigations.nbcnews.com/_news/2012/08/11/13236464-new-database-of-us-voter-fraud-finds-no-evidence-that-photo-id-laws-are-needed

Kaiser health care tracking poll: August 2013. (2013, August 28). *The Henry J. Kaiser Family Foundation*. Retrieved from http://kff.org/health-reform/poll-finding/kaiser-health-tracking-poll-august-2013

Kekes, J. (1998). *A case for conservatism*. Ithaca, NY: Cornell University Press.

Kellner, D. (2000). Habermas, the public sphere, and democracy: A critical intervention. In L. E. Hahn (Ed.), *Perspectives on Habermas* (pp. 259–87). Chicago: Open Court.

Kirk, R. (2002). *The American cause*. Wilmington, DE: ISI Books.

Kirsch, I. S., Jungeblut, A., Jenkins, L., & Kolstad, A. (2002). *Adult literacy in America* (3rd ed.). Washington, DC: U.S. Department of Education, Office of Educational Research and Improvement.

Klein, E. (2010, June 22). Do the news media spend too much time on news? *The Washington Post*. Retrieved from http://voices.washingtonpost.com/ezra-klein/2010/06/does_the_news_media_spend_too.html

Klein, N. (2007). *Shock doctrine*. New York: Metropolitan Books.

Klinger, S. (2013, April 4). American taxpayers increasingly picking up the tab for unpaid corporate taxes. *The Contributor*. Retrieved from http://thecontributor.com/economy/american-taxpayers-increasingly-picking-tab-unpaid-corporate-taxes

Konrad, W. (2012, September 11). As Medicare fraud evolves, vigilance is required. *The New York Times*. Retrieved from http://www.nytimes.com/2012/09/12/business/retirementspecial/medicare-fraud-victimizes-patients-and-taxpayers.html

Kornhaber, M. L., & Griffith, K. (2014). It's not education by zip code anymore—but what is it? Conceptions of equity under the Common Core. *Education Policy Analysis Archive, 22*(4), 2–20.

Korsgaard, C. M. (2009). *Self-constitution: Agency, identity, and integrity.* Oxford: Oxford University Press.

Krugman, P. (2006, December 1). Economic storm signals. *The New York Times.* Retrieved from http://www.nytimes.com/2006/12/01/opinion/01krugman.html?_r=0

Kurdish officials say 150 killed by U.S. bombing, scores of Iraqi civilian casualties elsewhere. (2003, March 25). *Democracy Now.* Retrieved from http://www.democracynow.org/2003/3/25/kurdish_officials_say_150_killed_by

Kymlicka, W. (1989). *Liberalism, community and culture.* Oxford: Clarendon Press.

Landberg, R. V., & George, P. (2007, November 16). Greenspan "mess" risks U.S. recession, Stiglitz says. Bloomberg.com. Retrieved from http://www.bloomberg.com/apps/news?pid=newsarchive&sid=abh8h7M3uKBA

Lazere, D. (2009). Thumbs up on Hirsch, thumbs down on Bloom. *Pedagogy, 9,* 501–8.

Lessig, L. (2011). *Republic lost: How money corrupts Congress—and a plan to stop it.* New York: Twelve.

Lewin, T. (2012). Record number complete high school and college. *The New York Times.* Retrieved from http://www.nytimes.com/2012/11/06/education/record-numbers-of-young-americans-earn-bachelors-degree.html?_r=0

Light, D. W., Lexehin, J., & Darrow, J. J. (2013). Institutional corruption of pharmaceuticals and the myth of safe and effective drugs. *Journal of Law, Medicine & Ethics, 41,* 590–600.

Lipton, E., & Labaton, S. (2008, November 17). Deregulator looks back, unswayed. *The New York Times.* Retrieved from http://www.nytimes.com/2008/11/17/business/economy/17gramm.html?pagewanted=all

Lor, P. J., & Britz, J. J. (2007). Is a knowledge society possible without freedom of access to information? *Journal of Information Science, 33,* 387–97.

Lukács, G. (1971). *History and class consciousness: Studies in Marxist Dialectics.* R. Livingstone (Trans.). Cambridge, MA: MIT Press.

Lukacs, J. (2005). *Democracy and populism: Fear and hatred.* New Haven: Yale University Press.

Lukes, S. (2008). *Moral relativism.* New York: Picador.

Lynch, M. P. (2004). *True to life: Why truth matters.* Cambridge, MA: MIT Press.

Lyotard, J-F. (1984). *The postmodern condition: A report on knowledge.* G. Bennington & B. Massumi (Trans.). Minneapolis: University of Minnesota Press.

———. (1991). *Phenomenology.* B. Beakley (Trans.). Albany: State University of New York Press.

Machado, D. (2010). Capitalism, immigration, and the prosperity gospel. *Anglican Theological Review, 92*(4), 723–30.

Machan, T. R. (2006). *Libertarianism defended.* New York: Ashgate.

MacIntyre, A. (2007). *After virtue: A study in moral theory* (3rd ed.). Notre Dame, IN: University of Notre Dame Press.

MacLean, S., Gayle, E., Tanton, E, & Greyson, O. (2013, October 2). Reader's panel—publish and be damned. *Nursing Standard, 28*(5), 24–26.

Marglin, S. A. (2008). *The dismal science: How thinking like an economist undermines community*. Cambridge, MA: Harvard University Press.

Marx, K. (1976). *Capital, volume 1*. B. Fowkes (Trans.). London: Penguin Books.

Matusow, B. (2008, December 1). An interview with Robert Novak. *National Ledger*. Retrieved from http://www.nationalledger.com/news-tech/an-interview-with-robert-novak-263876.shtml#.VAYIdmOOpBA

Maurer, B. (2002). Repressed futures: Financial derivatives' theological unconscious. *Economy and Society 31*(1), 15–36.

McChesney, R. W. (2013). *Digital disconnect*. New York: Free Press.

*McCutcheon v. FEC*, No. 12–536 (2013). Retrieved from http://www.supremecourt.gov/opinions/13pdf/12-536_e1pf.pdf

*McCutcheon v. FEC*: Supreme Court strikes down overall limits on campaign contributions. (2014, April 2). *Huffington Post*. Retrieved from http://www.huffingtonpost.com/2014/04/02/mccutcheon-v-fec_n_5076518.html

McLellan, D. (1995). *Ideology* (2nd ed.). Minneapolis: University of Minnesota Press.

Merrill, R. E. (2013). *Ayn Rand explained: From tyranny to Tea Party*. Chicago: Open Court.

Mill, J. S. (2007 [1869]). *On liberty* (4th ed.). M. B. Mathias (Ed.). New York: Pearson Longman.

Miron, J. A. (2010). *Libertarianism from a to z*. New York: Basic Books.

Miščević, N. (2012). Learning about wisdom from Lehrer. *Philosophical Studies, 161*, 59–68.

Mishel, L. (2013, February 21). Declining value of the federal minimum wage is a major factor driving inequality. *Economic Policy Institute* (Issue Brief No. 351). Retrieved from http://www.epi.org/publication/declining-federal-minimum-wage-inequality

Misztal, B. A. (2007). *Intellectuals and the public good: Creativity and civil courage*. Cambridge: Cambridge University Press.

Morgenson, G. (2013, June 29). An unstoppable climb in C.E.O. pay. *The New York Times*. Retrieved from http://www.nytimes.com/2013/06/30/business/an-unstoppable-climb-in-ceo-pay.html?pagewanted=all

Mortgage-backed securities. (2014). PIMCO.com. Retrieved from http://www.pimco.com/en/solutions/pages/mortgage-backedsecurities.aspx

Mottor, A. L. (2007). *Morales* and *Taylor*: The future of lethal injection. *Appalachian Journal of Law 6*, 287–311.

Mouffe, C. (2000). *The democratic paradox*. London: Verso.

Murphy, B. A. (2014). *Scalia: A court of one*. New York: Simon & Schuster.

Murphy, T. F., III. (1994). Discourse ethics: Moral theory or political ethic? *Political Theory, 62*, 111–35.

Murray, D. (2009). *Neoconservatism: Why we need it*. New York: Encounter Books.

Myths vs. facts. (2014). *Common Core State Standards Initiative*. Retrieved from http://www.corestandards.org/about-the-standards/myths-vs-facts

Nacht, A., & Kiely, E. (2014, June 25). Editing out the facts in Alabama. FactCheck.org. Retrieved from http://www.factcheck.org/2014/06/editing-out-the-facts-in-alabama

Nagel, T. (2013). *Mind and cosmos: Why the materialist neo-Darwinian conception of nature is almost certainly false*. Oxford: Oxford University Press.

National Education Association. (2014). *Rankings of the states 2013 and estimates of school statistics*. Retrieved from http://www.nea.org/home/rankings-and-estimates-2013-2014.html

Nichols, J., & McChesney, R. W. (2012). The assault of the super PACs. *Nation, 294*(6), 11–17.

———. (2013). *Dollarocracy: How the money and media election complex is destroying America*. New York: Nation Books.

Noam, E. M. (2009). *Media ownership and concentration in America*. Oxford: Oxford University Press.

Norton, A. (2004). *Leo Strauss and the politics of American empire*. New Haven: Yale University Press.

Novak, R. D. (2003, July 14). Mission to Niger. *The Washington Post*. Retrieved from http://www.washingtonpost.com/wp-dyn/content/article/2005/10/20/AR2005102000874.html

Nozick, R. (1974). *Anarchy, state, and utopia*. New York: Basic Books.

Oakeshott, M. (1991). On being conservative. In T. Fuller (Ed.), *Rationalism in politics* (pp. 129–78). Indianapolis: Liberty Press.

O'Harrow, R. (2010, April 21). A primer on financial derivatives. *The Washington Post*. Retrieved from http://www.washingtonpost.com/wp-dyn/content/article/2010/04/20/AR2010042004666.html

The open internet. (2014, April 25). *Federal Communications Commission*. Retrieved from http://www.fcc.gov/openinternet

Osteen, J. (2013). *Break out!* New York: Faith Words.

Other than honorable: Army strips benefits of wounded veterans by kicking them out for misconduct. (2013, May 22). *Democracy Now*. Retrieved from http://www.democracynow.org/2013/5/22/other_than_honorable_army_strips_benefits

Paul, R. (2011). *Liberty defined*. New York: Grand Central.

Pearson, M. (2012, November 12). The Petraeus affair: A lot more than sex. CNN.com. Retrieved from http://www.cnn.com/2012/11/12/us/petraeus-cia-resignation

Peck, J. (2010). *Constructions of neoliberal reason*. Oxford: Oxford University Press.

Peikoff, L. (2012). *The DIM hypothesis: Why the lights of the West are going out*. New York: New American Library.

Pettit, P. (2014). *Just freedom: A moral compass for a complex world*. New York: Norton.

Phillips, D. (2013, May 22). Lawmakers react to Gazette investigation on wounded soldiers. *Colorado Springs Gazette*. Retrieved from http://gazette.com/lawmakers-react-to-gazette-investigation-on-wounded-soldiers/article/1501069

Pigliucci, M. (2013). [Review of the book *What Darwin got wrong*, by J. Fodor & M. Piattelli-Palmarino]. *Philosophy Now* (81).

Piketty, T. (2014). *Capital in the twenty-first century*. Cambridge, MA: Harvard University Press.

Piketty, T., & Saez, E. (2003). Income inequality in the United States, 1913–1998. *Quarterly Journal of Economics, 118*, 1–39.

Pinker, S. (2007). *The stuff of thought: Language as a mirror into human nature*. New York: Viking.

Plait, P. (2013, July 24). The price of defame. Slate.com. Retrieved from http://www.slate.com/blogs/bad_astronomy/2013/07/24/antiscience_defamation_climate_scientist_michael_mann_lawsuit_to_move_forward.html

Plass, J. L., Moreno, R., & Brünken, R. (2010). *Cognitive load theory*. Cambridge: Cambridge University Press.

Plumer, B. (2013, January 29). We're running out of farm workers: Immigration reform won't help. *The Washington Post*. Retrieved from http://www.washingtonpost.com/blogs/wonkblog/wp/2013/01/29/the-u-s-is-running-out-of-farm-workers-immigration-reform-may-not-help

Poll: Vast majority believes Iraq mission not accomplished. (2006, May 1). CNN.com. Retrieved from http://www.cnn.com/2006/POLITICS/05/01/iraq.poll/index.html?eref=sitesearch

Pope Francis. (2014). *The church of mercy*. Chicago: Loyola Press.

Posner, R. A. (2010). *The crisis of capitalist democracy*. Cambridge, MA: Harvard University Press.

Powers, R. (2005). Deployment rates: Iraq and Afghanistan from September 11, 2001 to 31 October 2004. About.com. Retrieved from http://usmilitary.about.com/od/terrorism/a/deploymentrates.htm

Prado, C. G. (2006). *Searle and Foucault on truth*. Cambridge: Cambridge University Press.

Putterman, T. L. (2006). Berlin's two concepts of liberty: A reassessment and revision. *Polity, 38*, 416–46.

Radice, H. (2013). How we got here: UK higher education under neoliberalism. *ACME: An International E-Journal for Critical Geographies, 12*, 401–18.

Rand, A. (1967). *Capitalism: The unknown ideal*. New York: Signet.

———. (1974). *The virtue of selfishness*. New York: New American Library.

———. (1990). *Introduction to objectivist epistemology* (2nd ed.). New York: Meridian.

Raskin, M. G. (2004). *Liberalism: The genius of American ideals*. Lanham, MD: Rowman & Littlefield.

Ravitch, D. (2013). *Reign of error*. New York: Alfred A. Knopf.

Rawls, J. (1996). *Political liberalism*. New York: Columbia University Press.

———. (1999). *A theory of justice* (rev. ed.). Cambridge, MA: Harvard University Press.

Raz, J. (1986). *The morality of freedom*. Oxford: Oxford University Press.

Read, M. (2012, November 13). A flowchart of the Petraeus Affair's love pentagon, from the shirtless FBI agent to Chuck Klosterman. Gawker.com. Retrieved from http://gawker.com/5960202/a-flowchart-of-the-petraeus-affairs-love-pentagon-from-the-shirtless-fbi-agent-to-chuck-klosterman

Reeve, E. (2012, December 31). Earth to fiscal-cliff pundits: $250K does make you rich. *The Wire*. Retrieved from http://www.thewire.com/politics/2012/12/fiscal-cliff-pundits-250k-makes-you-rich/60453

Rein, L. (2012, January 11). IRS' tight budget is hurting taxpayers, watchdog says. *The Washington Post*. Retrieved from http://www.washingtonpost.com/politics/irs-tight-budget-hurting-taxpayers-watchdog-says/2012/01/10/gIQAXVXwqP_story.html

Reyes, G. M. (2006). The Swift Boat Veterans for Truth, the politics of realism, and the manipulation of Vietnam remembrance in the 2004 presidential election. *Rhetoric & Public Affairs, 9*, 571–600.

Ricardo, D. (2004). *The principles of political economy and taxation*. Mineola, NY: Dover.

Ricoeur, P. (1991). *From text to action*. K. Blamey & J. B. Thompson (Trans.). Evanston, IL: Northwestern University Press.

———. (1992). *Oneself as another*. K. Blamey (Trans.). Chicago: University of Chicago Press.

———. (2000). *The just*. D. Pellauer (Trans.). Chicago: University of Chicago Press.

Risen, J., & Lichtblau, E. (2005, December 16). Bush lets U.S. spy on citizens without courts. *The New York Times*. Retrieved from http://www.nytimes.com/2005/12/16/politics/16program.html?pagewanted=all

Roberge, J. (2011). The aesthetic public sphere and the transformation of criticism. *Social Semiotics, 21*, 435–53.

Rogers, A. (2014, May 16). GM to pay record $35 million fine over ignition switch recalls. *Time*. Retrieved from http://time.com/102906/gm-fine-ignition-recalls

Rosin, H. (2009). Did Christianity cause the crash? *Atlantic Monthly, 304*, 38–48.

Rothschild, M. (2013). Spying on Occupy activists: How cops and Homeland Security help Wall Street. *The Progressive, 77*(6), 20–24.

Rowbottom, J. (2013). Politicians, the press, and lobbying. *Journal of Media Law, 5*, 253–75.

Saad, L. (2013, April 8). Americans' concerns about global warming on the rise. Gallup.com. Retrieved from http://www.gallup.com/poll/161645/americans-concerns-global-warming-rise.aspx

Sandel, M. J. (2009). *Justice: What's the right thing to do?* New York: Farrar, Straus & Giroux.

———. (2012). *What money can't buy: The moral limits of markets*. New York: Farrar, Straus & Giroux.

Santoro, D. A. (2013). "I was becoming increasingly uneasy about the profession and what was being asked of me": Preserving integrity in teaching. *Curriculum Inquiry, 43*, 563–87.

Satz, D. (2010). *Why some things should not be for sale: The moral limits of markets*. Oxford: Oxford University Press.

Scalia, A. (1997). *A matter of interpretation: Federal courts and the law*. Princeton, NJ: Princeton University Press.

Scheffler, S. (1994). *The rejection of consequentialism*. Oxford: Oxford University Press.

Schieman, S., & Jung, J. H. (2012). "Practical divine influence": Socioeconomic status and belief in the prosperity gospel. *Journal for the Scientific Study of Religion, 51*(4), 738–56.

Schlefer, J. (2012). *Assumptions economists make*. Cambridge, MA: Belknap Press of Harvard University Press.

Schrag, F. (2009). [Review of the book *Real education: Four simple truths for bringing America's schools back to reality*, by C. Murray]. *Studies in Philosophy & Education, 28*, 369–74.

Schwartz, B., & Sharpe, K. (2010). *Practical wisdom: The right way to do the right thing*. New York: Riverhead Books.

Schweizer, P. (2013). *Extortion: How politicians extract your money, buy votes, and line their own pockets*. Boston: Houghton Mifflin Harcourt.

Searle, J. R. (1999). *Mind, language, and society*. New York: Basic Books.

Sen, A. (2009). *The idea of justice*. Cambridge, MA: Harvard University Press.

Shapiro, I. (2003). *The state of democratic theory*. Princeton, NJ: Princeton University Press.

Shapiro, I., & Green, D. (1996). *Pathologies of rational choice theory*. New Haven: Yale University Press.

Skidelsky, R., & Skidelsky, E. (2012). *How much is enough? Money and the good life*. New York: Other Press.

Skocpol, T., & Williamson, V. (2012). *The Tea Party and the remaking of Republican conservatism*. Oxford: Oxford University Press.

Skorupski, J. (2006). *Why read Mill today?* London: Routledge.

Skousen, C. (2009 [1981]). *The 5000 year loop*. Washington, DC: National Center for Constitutional Studies.

Smith, A. (1991 [1776]). *Wealth of nations*. Amherst, NY: Prometheus Books.

———. (2000 [1759]). *The theory of moral sentiments*. Amherst, NY: Prometheus Books.

Smith, B., & Smith, D. W. (1995). Introduction. In B. Smith & D. W. Smith (Eds.), *The Cambridge companion to Husserl* (pp. 1–44). Cambridge: Cambridge University Press.

Smith, C. H. (2013, May 30). How cheap credit fuels income/wealth inequality. *Financial Sense*. Retrieved from http://www.financialsense.com/contributors/charles-hugh-smith/how-cheap-credit-fuels-income-wealth

Smith, D. W. (2004). *Mind world: Essays in phenomenology and ontology*. Cambridge: Cambridge University Press.

Smith, S. B. (1989). *Hegel's critique of liberalism: Rights in context*. Chicago: University of Chicago Press.

———. (2006). *Reading Leo Strauss: Politics, philosophy, Judaism*. Chicago: University of Chicago Press.

Society of Professional Journalists. (1998). *Code of ethics*. Retrieved from http://www.spj.org/ethicscode.asp

Sokolowski, R. (2000). *Introduction to phenomenology*. Cambridge: Cambridge University Press.

Solow, R. M. (2013, December 16). Alan Greenspan is still trying to justify his bad decisions: What the maestro doesn't understand. *New Republic*. Retrieved from http://www.newrepublic.com/article/115956/alan-greenspans-map-and-territory-reviewed-robert-solow

Sorkin, A. R. (2009). *Too big to fail*. New York: Viking.

Sorman, G. (2009). *Economics does not lie: A defense of the free market in a time of crisis*. New York: Encounter Books.

Stephens, M. (2014). *Beyond news: The future of journalism*. New York: Columbia University Press.

Stiglitz, R. (2012). *Inequality: How today's divided society endangers our future*. New York: Norton.

Stockman, D. (2013). *The great deformation: The corruption of capitalism in America*. New York: PublicAffairs.

Stone, G. R. (2012, September 10). Why did the Republicans win the House? *Huffington Post*. Retrieved from http://www.huffingtonpost.com/geoffrey-r-stone/why-did-the-republicans-w_b_2110673.html

Strauss, L. (1953). *Natural right and history*. Chicago: University of Chicago Press.

Sullivan, A. (2006). *The conservative soul: Fundamentalism, freedom, and the future of the right*. New York: Harper Perennial.

Sullivan, S. (2014, November 8). Everything you need to know about *McCutcheon v. FEC*. *The Washington Post*. Retrieved from http://www.washingtonpost.com/blogs/the-fix/wp/2013/10/08/supreme-court-takes-up-the-sequel-to-citizens-united

Sullivan, T. (2009). Rick Santelli and the "rant of the year" [Video file]. Retrieved from https://www.youtube.com/watch?v=bEZB4taSEoA

Survey results detail what top entry level employers want. (2014). Collegegrad.com. Retrieved from https://collegegrad.com/press/what-employers-want

Tanneeru, M. (2009, January 29). How a "perfect storm" led to the economic crisis. CNN.com. Retrieved from http://www.cnn.com/2009/US/01/29/economic.crisis.explainer/index.html?iref=newssearch

Taylor, C. (2011). Why we need a radical redefinition of secularism. In E. Medieta & J. Vanantwerpen (Eds.), *The power of religion in the public sphere* (pp. 34–59). New York: Columbia University Press.

Taylor, J., & Van Doren, P. (2011, May 3). Eliminating oil subsidies: Two cheers for President Obama. *Forbes*. Retrieved from http://www.forbes.com/2011/05/02/eliminate-oil-subsidies.html

Taylor, R. (2002). *Virtue ethics: An introduction*. Amherst, NY: Prometheus Books.

The TBN story. (2014, September 1). *Trinity Broadcasting Network*. Retrieved from http://www.tbn.org/about-us/the-tbn-story

Telecommunications Law—Internet Regulation—D.C. Circuit Holds that Federal Communications Commission Violated Communications Act in Adopting Open Internet Rules.—*Verizon v. FCC*, 740 F.3d 623 (D.C. Cir. 2014). (2014). *Harvard Law Review, 127*, 2565–84.

Thompson, J. B. (1990). *Ideology and modern culture.* Stanford: Stanford University Press.

Tienken, C. H. (2011). Common Core standards: The emperor has no clothes, or evidence. *Kappa Delta Pi Record, 47,* 58–62.

Tolson, F. (2014). The constitutional structure of voting rights enforcement. *Washington Law Review, 89,* 379–439.

Tomasi, J. (2012). *Free market fairness.* Princeton, NJ: Princeton University Press.

Toulmin, S. E. (1958). *The uses of argument.* Cambridge: Cambridge University Press.

Touraine, A. (2001). *Beyond neoliberalism.* Cambridge: Polity.

———. (2009). *Thinking differently.* D. Macey (Trans.). London: Polity.

Transcript of Blix's remarks. (2003, January 27). CNN.com. Retrieved from http://www.cnn.com/2003/US/01/27/sprj.irq.transcript.blix

Tribe, L. (1997). Comment. In G.S. Wood (Ed.), *A matter of interpretation* (pp. 65–94). Princeton, NJ: Princeton University Press.

Tyler, G. R. (2013). *What went wrong: How the 1% hijacked the American middle class and what other countries got right.* Dallas, TX: Benbella Books.

Tyreman, S. (2011). Integrity: Is it still relevant to modern healthcare? *Nursing Philosophy, 12,* 107–18.

Tyrrell, R. E., Jr. (2013). The continuing crisis. *The American Spectator, 46*(5), 10–11.van Overtveldt, J. (2007). *The Chicago school.* Chicago: B2 Books.

Vogel, K. P. (2014). *Big money.* New York: PublicAffairs.

von Mises, L. (2005). *Liberalism: The classical tradition.* Indianapolis: Liberty Fund.

Waldron, J. (2012). *The harm in hate speech.* Cambridge, MA: Harvard University Press.

Walzer, M. (1983). *Spheres of justice: A defense of pluralism and equality.* New York: Basic Books.

———. (2004). *Politics and passion: Toward a more egalitarian liberalism.* New Haven: Yale University Press.

Warner, M. (1992). The mass public and the mass subject. In C. Calhoun (Ed.), *Habermas and the public sphere* (pp. 377–401). Cambridge, MA: MIT Press.

Warren, E. (2014). *A fighting chance.* New York: Metropolitan Books.

Weidhorn, M. (2013). The dark side of democracy. *Midwest Quarterly, 54,* 226–43.

Weisman, S. R. (2005, September 9). Powell calls his U.N. speech a lasting blot on his record. *The New York Times.* Retrieved from http://www.nytimes.com/2005/09/09/politics/09powell.html

Why do Americans mistrust for-profit universities? (2013, July 2). *The Economist.* Retrieved from http://www.economist.com/blogs/economist-explains/2013/07/economist-explains-0

Wiles, R. (2011, October 19). Chase's CEO backs a bright outlook. *Arizona Republic.* Retrieved from http://www.azcentral.com/business/articles/2011/10/19/20111019chases-ceo-dimon-backs-bright-outlook.html

Williams, B. (1995). *Making sense of humanity.* Cambridge: Cambridge University Press.

Williams, T. (2012, June 8). Suicides outpacing war deaths for troops. *The New York Times*. Retrieved from http://www.nytimes.com/2012/06/09/us/suicides-eclipse-war-deaths-for-us-troops.html

Willoughby, J (2000, March 26). Burning up. *Barron's*. Retrieved from http://online.barrons.com/news/articles/SB953335580704470544?tesla=y

Wilson, D. C., & Brewer, P. R. (2013). The foundations of public opinion on voter ID laws: Political predispositions, racial resentment, and information effects. *Public Opinion Quarterly, 77*, 962–84.

Wilson, Joseph C. (2003, July 6). What I didn't find in Africa. *The New York Times*. Retrieved from http://www.nytimes.com/2003/07/06/opinion/what-i-didn-t-find-in-africa.html

Witte, J. F. (2004). Is it privatization or educational choice that matters? Comments on market- or mission-oriented charter schools. *Social Science Quarterly, 85*, 1052–56.

Wong, V. (2014, April 18). Top CEOs make 331 times the average worker. Does anyone care? BusinessWeek.com. Retrieved from http://www.businessweek.com/articles/2014-04-18/top-ceos-make-331-times-the-average-worker-dot-does-anyone-care

Wood, E. M. (2005). *Empire of capital*. London: Verso.

Woodard, D. (2013, June 6). The corporate takeover of public education. *Huffington Post*. Retrieved from http://www.huffingtonpost.com/diann-woodard/the-corporate-takeover_b_3397091.html

Yoo, J. (2002, February 1). Memorandum for William J. Haynes, II, General Counsel of the Department of Defense. Retrieved from http://www.lawfareblog.com/wp-content/uploads/2013/10/Memorandum-from-John-C-Yoo-Sept-25-2001.pdf

Zakaria, F. (2011, November 9). Downward path of upward mobility. *The Washington Post*. Retrieved from http://www.washingtonpost.com/opinions/the-downward-path-of-upward-mobility/2011/11/09/gIQAegpS6M_story.html

Zhang, L. (2009). Does state funding affect graduation rates at public 4-year colleges and universities? *Educational Policy, 23*, 714–31.

Žižek, S. (1989). *The sublime object of ideology*. London: Verso.

# Index

CPSIA information can be obtained at www.ICGtesting.com
Printed in the USA
LVOW09*1622160115

423106LV00010B/28/P

9 781137 448156